# Is it me?

# TERRY WOGAN

## AN AUTOBIOGRAPHY

**BBC**

*Illustrations*
Family photographs courtesy of the author.
Other photographs © BBC

Published by BBC Worldwide Limited,
Woodlands, 80 Wood Lane, London W12 0TT

First published in 2000
Copyright © Terry Wogan 2000
The moral right of the author has been asserted

ISBN 0 563 55139 6

Commissioning editor: Sally Potter
Project editor: Martha Caute
Text editor: Barbara Nash
Designer: Linda Blakemore

Set in Berling by BBC Worldwide
Printed and Bound in Great Britain by Butler and Tanner Limited,
Frome and London
Colour separations by Radstock Reproduction, Midsomer Norton
Jacket printed by Lawrence Allen Limited, Weston-super-Mare

# CONTENTS

# ACKNOWLEDGEMENTS

First and always, Helen and my children for their support, encouragement, love and unquestioning faith. Particularly Katherine, relentlessly typing in between *Aristocrats* and *Grafters*. Jo Gurnett, loyalty incarnate, Bill O'Donovan, the sage of Henry Street. The friends who lighten my life, Paul Walters, the TOGs and TYGs who brighten the darkest morning. BBC Worldwide, who thought that this might be a good idea, Anna Ottewill and Sally Potter, who ran with it, Martha Caute and Barbara Nash who had to put the jigsaw together. I hope you all think it was worth it …

*To Helen,*
*Alan, Mark and Katherine –*
*my life*

# ONE

# GROWING UP IN LIMERICK

Michael Thomas Wogan – the 'Da' – was born in Enniskerry, Co. Wicklow, in 1900. Enniskerry was widely regarded as Ireland's prettiest village, and Wicklow the garden of Ireland. Unfortunately, you cannot eat the scenery, and times were hard for young Michael Thomas and his family of an elder brother, two older sisters, a mother whom he adored and a father he never talked about.

The Da's father was a builder with a tidy little business that he drank away in the time-honoured Irish paternal manner. There may have been more or less to it than that, but my father avoided the topic all his life, just as he avoided Enniskerry, lovely an' all as it was.

For an intelligent, sensitive young man, the place left a lot to be desired. Apart from a boorish, drunken bully of a father, there was the parochial nature of the little town. The bank manager, police sergeant, schoolteacher and parish priest were the ruling junta. You tipped your hat to them, and crossed them at your peril.

There was one bigger fish in the pond: the local lord of the manor. Powerscourt was one of the largest, lushest, most beautiful estates in all of Ireland, not to mind Co. Wicklow. It still is. You go there to admire the beautiful Italianate gardens, and the ruin of a once-imposing great house – the Anglo-Irish ascendancy, at the peak of their form. I doubt if my father ever bothered to go there to gasp in admiration. He probably would not have been allowed past the gate. As it was, he was not too thrilled at having to step off the pavement in deference to Lord Powerscourt's passing, whenever His Lordship deigned to grace Enniskerry with his august presence.

According to himself, the Da walked barefoot to school, at least twenty-five miles a day, and uphill both ways. The teacher was no more a favourite of his than his father or Lord Powerscourt. The lack of books, writing materials and, indeed, paper, meant that lessons on the blackboard were transferred by the pupils on to their slates, with bits of chalk – not the best way of accumulating knowledge. One day, Michael Thomas Wogan let fly the slate at the teacher's head, and that was the end of that.

My father always left me with the impression that all this happened when he was about five years of age, but since he could read, write in a fine hand, and add up with the best of them, I suppose we must take all that with a pinch of salt. Where he learned to read music, sing in a manly baritone and play the violin, he never vouchsafed to me. Probably by osmosis, the way *I've* learned the little I know…

## TYING UP TALENTS

It was more a bag of sugar than a pinch of salt, when himself was packed off to learn the arcane art of the grocer and victualler in the town of Bray, about ten miles away from his home, on the coast. I have no idea how old he was, probably no more than fourteen, when he became a grocer's curate. He quickly mastered the difficult skills entailed, and it was his proud boast that when it came to tying up a bag of sugar, he had no equal.

I obviously inherited the tying-up talent, because, years later, while clerking in the Royal Bank of Ireland, Phibsborough, Dublin, it was my task to tie up old lodgement documents and seal them. What happened to them after that I cannot tell you, not being senior enough to be told more than was good for me. Anyway, my knotting and sealing reached such heights that the bank manager, Dudley Robertson, called me into his office to compliment me:

'Wogan!' he barked in his gravelly voice. 'Good work!'

I blushed prettily.

'Always remember,' he continued, his little feet in their children's sandals, peeping out from beneath his desk, 'always remember: there's no business like show-business. And there's no people like show-people. They laugh when other people cry …'

This cameo of heartless, hard-as-nails show-people is one I shall carry to the grave. What it had to do with tying up lodgement dockets remains a mystery. Perhaps if I had continued to pursue my career with the Royal Bank of Ireland, my confusion might have been lifted. Indeed, my foolishness in not continuing with the bank-clerking was brought home forcefully to me, some years ago. I had left the service of the dear old bank some fifteen years previously, and, in the intervening years, had enjoyed success, fame and all that other stuff, firstly on television and radio in Ireland, and then extraordinarily enough in Britain.

On a visit to Dublin, I called in at a branch of the Royal Bank, or, as it had become, Allied Irish Banks, to get some cash. Lo and behold, there, behind the cashier's grille, was a face I recognized from the quondam days. Perhaps we had played in the same rugby team, or drank a Saturday night away together in the Bankers' Club.

'There y'are,' he greeted me, as if we had never been apart. 'How's it goin'?'

'Not bad,' says I, modestly, 'you know, I've been lucky.'

'Oh, yeah?' says your man. 'Y'know, you left the bank at the wrong time. D'you remember Mick Murtagh?'

'Yes,' I answered, hesitantly, 'I think he joined the bank at the same time as me.'

'He did, right enough. And now look at him: deputy manager in Timoleague! Snug as a bug in a rug ...'

I left, chastened. What a fool I had been, to throw over the permanent, pensionable position. To be snug in Timoleague ... Perhaps even courting a well-set-up farmer's daughter ... Made for life ... Ah, well ...

It reminds me of two of our best friends, Kits and Hacker Browning. He is the only, much-loved son of the late, great Dame Daphne du Maurier, of *Rebecca*, *Frenchman's Creek*, 'The Birds' (in *Kiss Me Again, Stranger*), 'Don't Look Now', and many another literary triumph. His father was hardly less distinguished: General 'Boy' Browning, Commander of the Paras at Arnhem (a bridge too far, sir), the handsomest man in the British Army, and, at the time of Kits' marriage to Hacker, Treasurer to HRH Prince Philip.

Hacker, or Olive White, to give her her maiden name, was of humbler circumstances. Her father was a carpenter, and she had been a shop-girl, before her beauty brought her to the attention of photographers and model agencies. She worked with my wife Helen as a model in London, and won the Miss Ireland title.

Radio Telefís Éireann (RTÉ) gave her the onerous task of hostess on its most popular quiz-show, *Jackpot*, which was hosted by yours truly: the bank clerk who left too soon. It was a none-too-taxing game for cheap and cheerful prizes – in many ways it prepared me for the depths and degradation of *Blankety Blank* – and it involved a wheel of fortune, from which the unfortunate contestants could select their chosen subject.

It was the task of the hostess to turn this wheel. 'Spin the Wheel, Olive!' became the nation's catchphrase: not much to write home about, I will grant you, but those were the early days of Irish television, and it was the first chance the Irish public had to grow their own media heroes and heroines.

Olive White was one of the first, and on the day that she married Kits Browning, in a church on the Dublin Quays, the church itself and the surrounding streets were jammed with an excited throng. Dame Daphne and the good General were bemused, ignored, and delighted with it all. The streets rang to shouts of 'God bless you, Olive!', 'Isn't she gorgeous?' and 'The image of her mother!' But the comment that tickled the good Dame's fancy, and the one she loved to recount, was from an old biddy who she saw turn to a friend, and with a shake of her shawlie head, say: 'Ah, she'll never want for nothin', no more.'

## FAMILY MATTERS

We left Michael Thomas Wogan tying up bags of sugar and sleeping above the shop in Bray, Co. Wicklow. Bray was another place that if my father never saw again he would think it too soon, so I take it that his memories of the old spot were not too hot. In the way that we all get wrapped up in ourselves from an early age, I never taxed him too closely about his early years, his steady climb from grocer's assistant, to his quantum leap to work in the select emporium of Leverette & Frye, Grafton Street, Dublin, where he met and courted Rose Byrne, who was working upstairs on the books.

Would that I could tell you more of the courtship, engagement and eventual marriage of Michael and Rose, but I never probed – don't ask me why. We needed a sister, my brother Brian and I. She would have found out the details, in all their romantic glory. It's a girl thing – at least if my daughter Katherine is anything to go by. She left no stone unturned in her relentless pursuit of what she saw as the timeless grand passion that was the love-story of her mother and me.

From the time she was old enough to talk, Katherine conducted a relentless third-degree inquisition on her parents' romance. How did we meet? When? Where? Why? How did we feel? Was it love at first sight? This last question was a particular favourite of my daughter's, and would come up at virtually every family meal-time. She loved to hear her mother say: 'Yes! Across a crowded room ...' and then go into details with which I will not trouble you, in case you are trying to digest something.

Michael Wogan was well into his thirties, and a good ten years older than Rose Byrne, when they married, with George, a friend of his, as best man, and Auntie May, my mother's favourite sister, as bridesmaid. It was a quietly cheerful family affair, with the reception held in Granny Byrne's front parlour, on Cloniffe Road, Drumcondra, Dublin. It can't have been a big affair: the room, as I remember it, was about 12 feet by 15 feet and housed a piano, a three-piece suite and the obligatory china cabinet. Cats were swung at your peril.

Rose Byrne was born to Frank and 'Muds' Byrne, the third of five daughters, in an army barracks in Belfast. The bold Frank was a sergeant, possibly a sergeant-major, in the British Army. There is a picture of him wearing an MP's (Military Policeman's) armband, and the rest is a closed book.

Was he young enough to fight in the trenches of World War One? Was he old enough for the Boer War? Why did I never ask? Why did nobody ever tell me? Why can't I remember my grandmother's real first name? 'Muds', that's what they called her. Frank is a hazy, happy memory, with a waxed moustache. I can't have been more than three, when he died. Muds lived longer, long enough to see me married if she had been strong enough to come to the wedding.

After the wedding, we stopped at Cloniffe Road to see her. She was weak, spent and frail, but she sat up, held our hands and smiled. Nobody has ever smiled like Muds, except, perhaps, my daughter. It was a smile that lit up Drumcondra, not to mind 207 Cloniffe Road. It was not a huge Mary Tyler Moore-like American number to make a horse whinny in envy, but an Irish granny's smile, one that took over her whole face, lighting up the eyes with a twinkling delight – the kindest thing I have ever seen.

I have been very lucky – I have been surrounded by kind, gentle, good-humoured women all my life. 'Muds' – short for mother – was possessed of such a gentle, beautiful soul that you couldn't but love her, and her five daughters did, deeply, abidingly. Maybe it's a loving grandson's rose-tinted contact lenses, but I never heard Muds raise her voice in anger, nor anyone ever raise theirs to her.

Maybe it is because of the loving kindness with which she surrounded them, that only two of the Byrne sisters ever married: my mother and her younger sister, Dinah. What names! Nellie, May, Rose, Kitty and Dinah – like whispers from another century. And not forgetting Auntie Maggie – she was Muds's elder sister, a formidable maiden lady, the very antithesis of her sister: tall, erect, unbending, unsmiling and not at all keen on human contact.

She dressed entirely in black from hat to shoes, and I am sure that bombazine came into it a good deal. She always seemed hundreds of years old to me, but she can't have been. She was a career woman – a French-polisher – and, like my Aunties' names, there are not many of *them* left, these days. As a matter of fact, Auntie Kitty followed Great-Aunt Mag into the French-polishing, and became a dab hand. Auntie Dinah followed my mother into the cash-books of Leverette & Frye. Auntie May, my godmother, worked in Veritas, the Catholic Truth Society bookshop.

Censorship was the Roman Catholic order of the day, and Auntie May was part of the vetting procedure. As I grew into adolescence, many's the racy novel I discovered, after rigorous searching in Auntie May's bedroom. Not that you had to be all that outrageous to fall foul of the Irish censor. James Joyce had not been seen for years and D.H. Lawrence could only be guessed at. The way things were, *Tom Brown's Schooldays* was lucky to get in under the razor wire.

If I owe my literacy to anybody, apart from the sainted Michael and Rose, I owe it to Auntie May. Throughout my childhood and early adolescence, she kept me supplied with books, comics and magazines, that opened a new, different and wider world for a boy living in a parochial, narrow-minded town in the south-west of Ireland.

Her parcels would arrive every Friday without fail: *Beano*, *Dandy*, *Wizard* and *Champion*, *Film and Radio Fun*, and, later on, the miracle of shiny colour that was the *Eagle*. Every couple of weeks, a new book: progressing from *Doctor Dolittle* to *The Wind in the Willows*, on to *Just William* and *Billy Bunter*, to *Bulldog Drummond* and *The Thirty-Nine Steps*, my dear Auntie May inculcated in me a love of books and reading that has never left me, and has given me a breadth of vocabulary and general knowledge that I could never have otherwise reached.

Auntie Nellie was in curtains in Clery's, Dublin's premier department store, in O'Connell Street. Nellie was the eldest of the Byrne girls and utterly unlike the others. She got the Great-Aunt Mag genes, I'm afraid. Humourless, unsmiling, she had a deep distrust of anything in trousers, including little boys. 'Men!' she said to my mother once. 'They're only after the one thing!' 'And how would you know?' riposted the Ma, who always had the sharpest tongue and the keenest wit in 207 Cloniffe Road, Drumcondra.

I don't think Auntie Nellie had ever been kissed, much less put in a position to defend her honour. She had a friend, Nellie Nolan, as formidable as herself – tall, severe, given to hats.

As I remember, there were a lot of hats around then, on men as well as women. There is a remarkable picture of Michael Collins addressing a huge crowd outside the General Post Office, Dublin, in 1921, and there is not a bare head in sight. Twenty-five years on, in the 1940s, and the hat still held sway in Dublin. 'Here's your hat and what's your hurry?' was a well-worn method of moving an unwelcome guest right along.

I don't remember a surfeit of liquor lapping around the

place whenever I visited my granny in Dublin. The cup of tea, that was the favoured libation. Indeed, I am sure I am right in saying that there was more tea drunk in Ireland per head of population than anywhere else in the world at that time, including England, traditional heartland of Mazawattee, orange pekoe and Earl Grey.

It was a comfort to a nation that hadn't much else. The old Irish countrywoman's saying: 'Ah, sure, what is there left to us, except the cup o' tea, and itself ...' ('itself' being the 'one thing' that my Auntie Nellie was convinced all men were after) had a ring of truth about it.

Nellie Nolan liked a cup of tea as well as the next woman, but, occasionally, she would ask for a glass of water. 'And let the tap run, Nell!' she would admonish. It became a catchphrase between my mother and me. 'Let the tap run, Nell!' Mind, there was method in Nell's admonition. The taps were lead, and it wasn't a bad idea to let a little lead poisoning run off, before you filled your glass with 'Adam's Ale'.

Nellie Byrne and Nellie Nolan holidayed together, in Britain and Europe, and in the year I was born, 1938, visited Germany. My father, no great fan of Auntie Nellie, any more than school-teachers, Bray, Enniskerry and Lord Powerscourt, was of the firm opinion that this visit, if not the direct cause of the Second World War, was certainly a contributory factor. He always called Auntie Nellie the 'Magpie', believing her to be a harbinger of ill fate, if not doom itself.

Frank Byrne, Nellie's dad, was against the visit of the two Nellies to Hitler's Reich, largely on the basis of my good Auntie's appearance. She was small and dark, with circles under her eyes, and Frank was convinced she would be arrested on arrival by the Waffen S.S. as a Jew. Luckily, it didn't happen, but the two Nellies did attend a Nazi Rally, where the mass audience was addressed by Martin Bormann. Someone took a pot-shot at the bold Martin, apparently, and the meeting broke up in disorder, at least according to my Auntie Nellie. Perhaps if she could have hung around Germany a bit longer, she might have had the necessary disruptive influence, and nipped the Third Reich in the bud, before it really got going.

# CULINARY 'DELIGHTS'

I spent almost as much of my childhood in Muds's house in Dublin, as I did at home in Limerick. Summer holidays in Irish schools were always three months long, with almost a month at Christmas and a couple of weeks at Easter. Oft my mother and I would pop on the train, up to the Big City, leaving the tireless, dutiful Michael to labour alone among the hams, jams and other comestibles of Limerick's finest victualler.

I loved these visits. Who wouldn't? For six years, until, against all expectations, my brother Brian turned up, I had the individual attention and affection of a granny, three maiden aunts and a mother. I have left out Great-Aunt Mag and Auntie Nellie, because I never felt that their admiration for me was quite as unstinting as the others.

What a life for a little chap – more comics, magazines and books than even Mr Voracious could read. And the pictures, at least once a week. Afterwards it was Cafollas Café for a Knickerbocker Glory, a huge ice-cream soda with every known variety of tinned fruit and syrup, topped with cream, and eaten with a long spoon. Oh, and it had jelly in it, as well.

And the Granny, dear old Muds, was a good cook. For some reason – and, of course, you could never tell from looking at me – food has always been important to me. 'A racing snake', is the most frequent comparison made by the thinking listener. I am quick to demur. I will point to a millimetre of superfluous sub-cutaneous at belt level, a suggestion of slack around the pecs, the six-pack stomach a mite less than perfect, but they won't have it. 'How do you stay so trim?' they query, enviously. I have no answer. It's a gift!

I love my food, the savour, the flavour. I don't know why – Rosie Wogan (Byrne that was) was Ireland's worst cook. And that's saying something, in a nation that traditionally burnt the finest of meat to a frazzle, and reduced its vegetables to mush. Auntie May always maintained that when she got married, her sister Rose 'couldn't boil water'. I believed her because my mother never improved. She never learned a *thing* at Muds's knee: she never knew that you put butter in mashed potatoes;

I never saw a mushroom until I was seventeen; all meat was cooked to the consistency of an old boot, and the only egg she ever really mastered was a fried one.

Strangely enough, she *could* do tripe and onions. Luckily, we only got that when Uncle Charlie Foster (no relation, just a commercial traveller befriended by my father) arrived for tea. And it *was* tea – *tea* with tea, and bread and butter. The other meals were breakfast and lunch. Even for the middle classes, 'dinner', not to mind 'supper', didn't catch on in Ireland until the 1960s.

Uncle Charlie was from Dublin; tall, florid, handsome, ebullient and full of charm. My mother said he looked like Preston Foster, a Hollywood star of the 1930s. She must have liked him a lot because not many got past our front door in Limerick … She would dole out the tripe and onions, and Uncle Charlie Foster would exclaim, 'Lovely grub!' It's only now that I wonder what sort of a cook *his* wife was.

Rose was not bad on the old pastry; her steak-and-kidney pie was okay, but, once she got hold of an idea, it was very hard to shake her off. For years, every Sunday, we had round steak (topside, to you), cooked in silver paper. I don't know who passed on this culinary gem, but it was a good job they never came knocking on our front door on a Sunday.

Michael, the Da, never complained. Mind you, Rose could never do any wrong in his eyes, anyway. She was his life, his light, his lodestar. In any relationship, there is always a lover, and a loved. He was the lover. Tactile, sentimental, gentle, caring – and not a bad cook. I wish he had done more of this when I was a child.

Later in life, when my mother's arthritis became very bad, and her hands were more useless, the Da would do the cooking. But, no less than my mother, he was a man of fixed culinary ambitions. For tea, he liked toast, buttered, then topped with tomato and cheese. Watching him prepare this could not have been much dissimilar to watching Escoffier do his stuff.

The bread carefully buttered, tomatoes peeled, then sliced, cheese thinly pared – the whole was then slipped under a pre-heated grill. 'The loveliest meal you ever ate,' was how Michael described it. 'What about tea?' he would say, around about six o'clock every evening. 'What do you fancy, Rose? What about the old reliable?' – meaning the cheese and tomatoes on toast. My mother would look at me and cast her eyes to heaven. She always fancied a rasher and egg.

The Granny could cook a bit: I mind well the wondrously succulent fresh mackerel, caught that very day off Howth pier by the Da, when he would join us in Dublin for his two-week summer holiday. He loved fishing. It was his only release from the hard grind of grocering. He liked to watch Limerick Football Club as well, and go to the dogs on a Wednesday night, but fishing was his passion.

In Limerick he would fly-fish for trout on the Maigue River, a tributary of the Shannon. Occasionally, if he got a lift from a friendly fisherman, he would hurl a line into the surf at Quilty, Co. Clare, in search of sea-bass. 'The chicken of the sea,' he called it. The French call it 'loup' – the wolf – but what do they know?

We didn't have a car in Limerick – just the Da's bike. And up on the cross-bar would pop little Michael Terence on a Sunday after Mass, and off we would go a-fishing, just the Da and I, with a flask and some Limerick ham sandwiches. There was not much Rose could do to these, although they *could* have done with a little more mustard.

Out past the docks we would go, past the flour mills, the steel works, the cement factory, and then the muddy banks of the Maigue. We didn't fish immediately. We hardly fished at all. For my father the getting ready was all, just as it was with the cheese and tomato on toast. Meticulous preparation: rod, line, flies tied and carefully affixed, then, as the sun was going down behind the cement factory, the first cast of the day.

I do not, unsurprisingly, remember any great creels of fish being landed: just the rare trout and the odd flounder, and plenty of eels, which we threw back. I know, *I know*, but it was just as well. What my mother could have made out of cooking an eel does not bear thinking about. Those days by the riverbank are misty memories now, but I saw the curlew and heard the corn-crake, something my children never have …

I never took to fishing, myself. A boy rebelling against his father? Not me. I never rebelled against anything in my life.

Conventional, bourgeois, middle-class, that's me. Do what you are told; follow orders; listen to your betters; don't show off; who do you think you are?; do your homework; go to bed; get a job. That's me … How I ever stumbled into the racy world of radio, television and showbiz is a mystery, not least to myself. Later on in this mighty tome, we will delve deeper, if you haven't lost interest by then.

I think it was Howth put me off the fishing. Howth Harbour was where my father, Uncle Charlie Foster and me would go to hurl a line off the pier into the Irish Sea, in the usually forlorn hope of chancing upon a mackerel, a pollock or e'en a pinkeen with suicidal tendencies.

Uncle Charlie and the Da would swing their lines, hooked and weighted with lead, and let fly into what a fellow Dublin schoolboy, James Joyce, referred to lovingly, as the 'snotgreen sea'. Not little Terence – that was too easy. I watched other fishermen just pick up the lead weight, and hurl that into the sea. Seemed a lot more straightforward to me. But that is the way I have been all my life: the line of least resistance: the easy way out. I can't be bothered …

I got my just deserts that day: as the lead weight flew out of my hand, the fish-hook flew into a finger, caught and buried itself. Although I have always fancied my philosophy to be Corinthian, with Stoical tendencies, there was little of the latter about me that day. Marcus Aurelius would have turned his nose up at my yelling and screaming, particularly when they took me, in Uncle Charlie's car, to the emergency ward of a Dublin hospital. There, an apprentice butcher removed the hook, without local anaesthetic, as if he had spent his formative years at Torquemada's knee. I have never picked up a line with a hook at the end of it since.

## A PROPER JOB?

If you have come this far, it will not have escaped your notice that I am not a great man for detail. As is the fashion nowadays, I blame my father. It is the new philosophy: nobody is responsible for their mistakes, their flaws, their failings. It is all the fault of the genes, the peer group, the teacher or the parent. So, it is the Da's fault. He was so hard-working, diligent and meticulous, that his elder son's subconscious must have taken flight: I could never work as hard as that! I haven't a painstaking bone in my body. Anything that doesn't come freely and easily to me is something from which I will stride away, with a spring in my step and a light laugh.

When I tell people I have never done a hard day's work in my life, they assume that I am joking. 'What about getting up at all hours of the morning to do your radio show?' they petulantly query. 'What about all those years of live television on *Wogan*?' 'What about *Children in Need*?' Pshaw! And when I say that, I mean it, whatever it means …

What I have done for nearly forty years has not been 'work'. It is not a proper 'job'. Even my four years spent in the employ of the Royal Bank of Ireland didn't seem like work. It was a piece of cake. Work? Toiling down a mine, that's work. Digging up a road, that's work. Snagging turnips and footing turf, that's what I call work …

Maybe it is the Jesuit training, but I have always felt the shadow of guilt about how easily things have come to me; I played games without too much effort, and even less training. Apart from maths, schoolwork came easily. A pretty undistinguished scholar, unless driven to it, I only excelled at Latin because the teacher frightened me to death. I seem to have floated on the sea of life, eschewing effort, avoiding conflict. An optimist – you know, someone who does not realize the seriousness of the situation.

## GROWING UP IN LIMERICK

So, without knowing too much of the details, Michael Terence Wogan was born to Rose and Michael Wogan, in Mother Cleary's Nursing Home, Elm Park, Limerick, on the 3 August 1938. It was a dark and stormy night. Or maybe it was the morning? Or the middle of the day? I never asked.

My mother used to make great play of the thunder and lightning that lit up Limerick upon my birth, but if Apollo was trying to tell me something, it has never been made clear. Rose used to claim that on the first day she took her beloved first-born out in his pram, a great gust of wind tried to pull it from her grasp. Perhaps I should have been a weather forecaster. I wonder if the same thing happened to Michael Fish? He missed a Great Wind, too, remember?

Born in the town of Limerick, then, Ireland's third biggest town. Not a city. No cathedral, you see. But more churches than Nashville, Tennessee. But, unlike Nashville, Tennessee, all of the same denomination: Roman Catholic.

Limerick was more Roman Catholic than the Vatican. Not a lot of Christianity, if by that you mean love and tolerance of your fellow man, but *plenty* of religion. They had something called the 'Arch-Confraternity', a sort of Catholic Freemasonry, except that there was no secrecy. If you got into the Arch-Confraternity, you let the whole of Limerick know about it. You had arrived: a pillar of the Church, a pillar of the community, people bought you drinks, paid your fare on the bus. 'Ah, don't stir, Seán. I have it here.'

The Da never joined. Maybe he was never asked, but he wasn't exactly big on religion. Neither was my mother. I think she had too much of a sense of humour for it. Oh, they went to Mass, ate fish on Fridays, kept the Lenten Regulations, and made sure their two sons had a good Catholic education and kept the Faith, but I never felt, at least in retrospect, that their hearts and souls were entirely in it. Maybe I am trying to make my own agnosticism easier to understand.

In his great Pulitzer Prize-winning book, Frank McCourt makes Limerick childhood seem like growing up in the Black Hole of Calcutta, and in the poverty-stricken slums behind St John's Castle, with a ne'er-do-well for a father, it surely was. In the lower-middle-class environs of Elm Park, Ennis Road, it was okay. It was not the lap of luxury – we didn't have a car or a tele-phone. We *did* have a radio, though. Along with the books, it saved my life. No, it *made* my life.

There, in that provincial Irish town on the banks of the Shannon, many miles from London, and light years away from its culture and sophistication, I grew up in the BBC, with the Light

Programme. It became my window on the world, my magic carpet to another place. It influenced my thoughts, my speech, my attitudes, my sense of humour. Everyone else of my contemporaries seemed to be listening to Irish Radio, but I struggled towards puberty with the help of *Workers' Playtime, Mrs Dale's Diary, Dick Barton: Special Agent, Much Binding in the Marsh* and then, *Take it from Here, Educating Archie, The Goons* and *Hancock's Half Hour.* I was a right little West Brit ...

As a young, and for six glorious years, *only* son and heir, I must have had a high old time of it, hopping between Limerick and Dublin, and enjoying the undivided attention, not to say devotion, of Michael, Rose, all those aunties and a granny. Youth is wasted on the young, as some other Irish seer once mumbled through his beard, and I don't remember a thing.

There are pictures extant of our boy as a babe, and of a manly little chap in a bathing suit. The latter would have been snapped on Sandymount Strand, a huge expanse of beach on Dublin Bay, about ten minutes by bus from the city centre, or Nelson's Pillar, as we used to call it. That was because, in the centre of O'Connell Street, Dublin, directly opposite the General Post Office, scene of the momentous and historic Rising of 1916, stood this memorial to one of *Britain's* greatest heroes, Horatio Nelson. You could climb up several hundred steps, and get a view over Dublin's Fair City from Nelson's balcony. No more: some eejit struck a proud blow for Irish independence by dynamiting poor old Nelson, mighty pedestal and all, in the mid-1960s. There has been a gap there ever since.

Of late, plans are afoot to fill that gap with some class of plinth or suitable sculpture. Modern, of course, this *is* the capital city of the Tiger Economy of Europe! They have even asked the citizenry what they should call it. They will never learn. There is a picturesque, statuesque fountain in O'Connell Street of a reclining woman, a representation of the River Liffey – 'Anna Livia Plurabelle', is how the City Fathers would have it. To the great unwashed of Dublin, it is 'The Floozy in the Jacuzzi'. Every statue in O'Connell Street has a nickname; that is about the only one suitable for your delicate ears. I have no high hopes for poor old Nelson's replacement.

Sandymount Strand, where you see yours truly so winsomely pictured, does have a couple of memories for me: I will never forget the panic of being lost there. I wandered into the sea, dug about a bit with my little spade, and when I turned around, everyone had gone. The beach was heaving with half the population of Dublin, but there was nobody I recognized. It was probably only about ten minutes before I was found, but the screaming fear of being lost, abandoned, seemed to me to last for hours. It must have been traumatic – it is one of very few memories of pre-school years that remain.

One other thing about Sandymount Strand, although this may well have struck me forcibly a little later: you could walk for miles out into the Irish Sea, without the water ever getting above your ankles. Some people claimed that they had strolled over to the Isle of Man and back, without ever getting their togs wet … Perhaps it was just as well that we never got immersed; one of the features of the Sandymount seashore was Dublin's raw sewage floating idly by.

According to my mother, I was a strange child. I would go out to play with the other toddlers of Elm Park, Limerick, but for no great length of time. Back I would come, shutting the gate firmly behind me, and into my own little world. It was ever thus. I love my wife and family, I have good and loyal friends, but I never tire of my own company. I need a little time to myself, every day. I have no difficulty meeting and socializing, but I like my own space. And I like things to finish when I am ready – back into my own cocoon, shutting the gate firmly behind me.

People often ask me whether in my declining years, I would go back to live in Ireland. Much as I love the Irish, their wit and warmth, I don't think so. You see, the Irish just won't go home. They arrive late and leave even later. I don't think I could bear it. I love long, lazy lunches, particularly French ones, but dinner party guests should remember they have homes to go to. Irish people do not. They will rise from the table at about one in the morning, pause for another hour at the dining room door, linger in the hall and exit through the front door a couple of hours later, still talking …

I admit it, I have become Anglicized. Years ago, when the

present Mrs Wogan and I first graced Blighty's shore, for our first dinner party at home, we invited people for eight o'clock. I was just getting out of the bath, when the guests arrived, right on time. I couldn't believe it. *Nobody* in Ireland arrives for a dinner party on time. Half an hour late is considered gauche. Those who *really* know the score, turn up an hour and a half late. You don't want to be standing around drinking for hours, do you?

## OFF TO SCHOOL

They piled me off to school at five, about a mile down the Ennis Road, to Ferrybank, a preparatory school run by the Salesian nuns. It was just up the road from Barrington's Pier, where the sallies grew, and Cleeve's Toffee Factory, which filled the air with the very scent of heaven.

Mother took me there with my little schoolbag, and left me in the care of the kindly nuns. She had barely returned home, before there was a knock on the front door. There I was again. Fresh-faced and fine-featured, I declared myself home, and enquired civilly on the prospects of lunch. That'll be enough of school, I had felt, after about ten minutes, and had walked out of the front gates and home …

I still like home best. Throughout the eight-year run of my thrice-weekly talk-show, *Wogan*, the high spot of the evening was dinner at home with my wife. I am sure that people imagined it to be an endless round of showbiz partying, and clubbing 'til the dawn, but after the show was over, at about 7.40 p.m., I would share a glass of the BBC's finest vintage, in what became known as 'Hostility', with my guests and the production team, and then I was outta there, heading for the comforts of home.

Mind you, when you love food as much as I do, and you are married to someone who cooks as well as my wife, then there is really no contest between the bright lights and home.

# TWO

# OCCASIONS OF SIN

After four gentle dream-like years at preparatory school, the Salesian nuns showed me the door and the nightmare began. They sent me off to the big boys' school, Crescent College, Limerick. It was not really nightmarish, but the end of innocence. It could have been worse, much worse. It could have been boarding school. It could have been the Christian Brothers, men whose legendary cruelty and brutality could only be compared to a particularly bad-tempered Mongol horde.

The Jesuit fathers who took charge of me were no Mary Poppinses, but glimmerings of humanity occasionally broke through their ascetic severity. The Jesuits dressed in black and had wings – panels to their black coats, that flew back as they walked. Black angels. Frightening – at least for a nine-year-old.

Over the years of growing up, fear was replaced by a certain amount of respect, and even a grudging affection – not for those who doled out the corporal punishment, though. You got beaten for everything: bad homework, wrong homework, inattention, misbehaviour – anything. Not that you got punished on the spot. No, they wanted you to think about it, before you got the works.

Corporal punishment was the way forward in education in those days, even for the highly educated and civilized Jesuits. And they had a most peculiarly sadistic way of dealing it out. A grammatical mistake in homework, or a moment of foolishness in class, and the good father would write out a little chit from his docket-book. Depending on the seriousness of the error or transgression, that chit would be good for three or six heavy welts across the hands with a reinforced leather strap, administered by a cheery, burly priest named Father Bates.

Here was a man who took real pleasure in his work, obviously deriving considerable spiritual benefit from offering your suffering up to God. The sadistic bit was that this was no instant, spur-of-the-moment leathering. No, you had to wait until lunchtime, to join a queue of other unfortunates, and watch them get their hands knocked off, until it came to your turn.

With no feeling in my swollen hands, I would cycle off home for lunch, then back an hour later, into class again, and a couple of hours after that, find myself queuing up *again* for more gratuitous violence, before the kindly Jesuits let me out for the day.

And in case you think you are dealing with a junior combination of Jack the Ripper and Joey the Eejit here, let me tell you that this ongoing torture was the lot of all but the brightest and most dutiful ... Extraordinary to think that men as sophisticated and supposedly intelligent as the Jesuits could use terror as their main tool in the education of young minds, even allowing for the fact that it was the norm in those days.

## SPORTING LIFE

At Crescent, I played rugby from the time I was about ten, and tennis. Strangely enough, it was when playing tennis rather than rugby that I received my most serious injury: missing a forehand, I knocked my own front tooth out. No great loss, although a more accurate shot would have knocked both of them out. Early pictures show a pair of front teeth more suited to a rabbit. These, combined with a pair of ears that would have given Mr Spock a run for his money, were the subject of many a cruel jibe from my peers, none of whom, incidentally, were oil paintings themselves.

The removal of one tooth pushed back the other one a bit, deflecting the slurs, and acting as a frightener for opposing prop-forwards, when I took the false tooth out for rugby.

We didn't play football, a game for hooligans and the lower orders; and cricket and hockey were regarded as Protestant activities. The Irish national games, Gaelic football and hurling, were for 'National' and Christian Brothers schools, that is non-fee-paying ones. Middle-class Irish schoolboys played middle-class British games. (There was no 'upper' class. If you were that high up the totem pole you went to a Catholic public school in England.) 'Garrison' games, they were called, by the true sons of the Gael: games played by the former army of occupation, the British soldiery.

Now that I think of it, given my maternal grandfather, I was entitled ... Golf, another game introduced by the British, got in under the wire somewhere and avoided stigma – perhaps because it was played by officers, and the Irish always had respect for anyone on a horse.

## CATHOLICS AND PRODS

The prejudices and hatreds generated by religion in Ireland are well documented over hundreds of years, and all too familiar over the last three decades, but, in my formative years, and well into the 1960s, there was a fair amount of fear and loathing attached not just to where you prayed, but what you played. The Gaelic Athletic Association (GAA) bestrode the island like a colossus, forming the third point of the triumvirate that ruled: Church, State and GAA.

Restrain the urge to laugh – it was not funny. Well, it was not meant to be. The GAA rule was simple: play rugby or football, and you were forbidden the joys of Gaelic football and hurling – and vice versa. We all *knew* it was ridiculous then, but, in retrospect, it is almost impossible to believe. The rugby and football fields of Ireland were crawling with pseudonyms. Woe betide anybody who was found out! Expulsion and disgrace – and if the local parish priest could have excommunicated you from the Holy Roman Catholic Church, he would have, and *laughed* at your chances of salvation.

There were a lot of ways of putting your immortal soul in peril in the Ireland of my youth: the non-observation of Lenten Regulations; the eating of meat on Fridays; non-attendance at Sunday Mass; impure thoughts ... The occasions of sin were all around us. Guilt – that's what kept you going.

## 'REMITTANCE MEN'

I think the reason my Da, Michael Thomas Wogan, was able to marry Rose Byrne was that he was promoted to the dizzy heights of Manager, Limerick Branch, Leverette & Frye, Grocers and Victuallers. It was an extraordinary place. I can smell it still:

cheeses, hams, dried fruit, herbs, spices, poppadoms, lychees, Bombay ducks, yams. But 'soft!', I hear you cry. 'Bombay ducks, lychees, yams? In a little grocer's shop in a town in the back of beyond of a country without a bob to its name? Get away with you!'

Calm yourselves, my children. Leverette & Frye, O'Connell Street, Limerick, was a haven for the gourmet – a Fortnum & Mason of the sticks. The Da, as shrewd a grocer as Margaret Thatcher's old man, quickly identified that his clientele was not made up of the wives of county councillors and the lubberly issue of farmers and policemen. Well, not entirely. There was the horsy set: trainers, owners, jockeys, dealers and knackers from the counties of Limerick and Tipperary, the 'Golden Vale' of Ireland, where the grass was lush, the cattle fat, and the horseflesh superb. They liked their fine wines, their crusted ports.

And then there were the 'Remittance Men' – the sons of the nobility and the wealthy of dear old Blighty, who had disgraced themselves on the home turf, and been despatched from their native shires by enraged fathers to a fine house and a couple of thousand acres of prime Irish farmland. They were never to darken their fathers' doors again, and, to make assurance doubly sure, they received a regular remittance, just so long as they stayed away.

My father's shop was a little bit of heaven for them: memories and scents of finer, more sophisticated days – Bombay duck for afters, mangoes for breakfast, bright lights for bright young things, before it all turned into damp grass, the rooks in the trees, boiled bacon and spuds.


## FORBIDDEN FRUITS

At the end of the Second World War, or, as it was known in Ireland, 'The Emergency', the Americans came to Limerick. ('The Emergency'? Don't ask! The Irish always have to use a euphemism – 'The Troubles' hardly sums up the tragedy and the bloodshed, does it?) Hallelujah, brothers and sisters! 'Got any gum, chum?' was the question. 'Not a lick, chick!' was the reply.

Shannon Airport, about fifteen miles up the road towards

Ennis, was a major staging post, as American forces flooded into Germany. Suddenly Limerick reverberated to an American nasal twang. Cheerios, Cornflakes and Grape Nuts brought an exotic flavour to the breakfast-table. Captain Marvel, Batman and Superman appeared out of the wide blue yonder.

For as long as it lasted, which can't have been more than a couple of years, the American Revolution transformed the dowdy old town by the river. It brought new sounds, new flavours, the almighty dollar, and a sinful touch of forbidden fruit to Holy Catholic Limerick. A black market thrived. Get your hands on a Limerick ham, bum a seat on an American transport to Hamburg or Frankfurt, and back you came loaded to the oxters with Leicas. If you could get hold of a few fully-fashioned nylons, of course, you might never see home and mother again, or, at the very worst, come back with a Valkyrie on each arm.

My father, grocer to toffs and gentry, was, of course, in a splendid position to oil the wheels and line the pocket. Who had better access to hams? They would kill you in Berlin for a tin of pineapple ... And did he line his pockets? Throughout a life, much of which he spent working his brains out for a pittance, old Michael Thomas never took a penny which did not belong to him ... So, the little Wogan family failed to benefit from the black-market opportunity. As the Da knew only too well, we could have done with it. Another little Wogan had appeared, as if by magic – or so it seemed to me who had had the world and the house to myself for six glorious years.

My little mother had such trouble with me, that it was thought the arrival of another behemoth might be dangerous. Plucky as ever, she threw caution to the winds, and here he was: the brother. Brian Wogan, for it was he, gave me no trouble. I was six years older, and a good deal bigger. I had been an only child long enough to be convinced of my own self-importance and major significance in the general scheme of things. Brian and I never had a falling out, not to mind a fight. We still haven't.

He was a troublesome rascal of a kid, quite unlike his elder goody-goody of a brother, but, as they say in Ireland, 'He hadn't a bad bone in his body.' He remains one of the warmest, kindest, and most gentle people I have ever met: he reminds me of my father and looks like my maternal grandfather. Stick a waxed handlebar moustache over his gob, dress him up as a British Army sergeant-major circa 1900, and Bob's your uncle: Frank Byrne to the life.

I don't know how we got so chunky, Brian and I. Rosie (Roughhouse Rosie, to give her her full name, because of her innate talent for smashing everything within an arm's reach. Her granddaughter, Katherine, has inherited the gift ... ), was a little woman, and Michael was of average height, and slim. It must have been the Limerick air, because it certainly was not my mother's cooking. Maybe tripe, lumpy mashed potatoes and steak like shoe-leather have body-building properties.

Maybe it was the exotic fruits because, even though loath to smuggle and play the black market, the Da occasionally brought home a breath of the warm south, under his raincoat. Fruits such as banana or a melon were forbidden indeed; unheard of during the war, and rarer than hen's teeth after 'The Emergency' had passed. The first banana turned out to be anti-climax enough, bland and tasteless to the unrefined palates of two little gobdaws such as the brother and myself, but the melon was an unmitigated disaster.

Proud as Punch, the old man sliced it into crescents: 'There y'are. Try that!'

I had never tasted anything like it – it was revolting. A foreign taste, a weird texture, alien. 'I don't like it.'

'You don't like it? It's a melon!'

'I know. But I don't like it.'

'You don't like it? There isn't a child in the country that has ever tasted anything like it! And you don't like it?'

'I don't like it.'

I was close to tears, and so was my father, in sheer frustration. A melon. His melon. The first tangible sign of a world returning to sanity from the madness of war, and his son would not eat it. Didn't even like it, if you don't mind.

'Here, put a bit of ginger on it.'

'That's worse.'

'A bit of sugar!'

'No, I don't like it.'

The gentlest of men became apoplectic. He threw the remains of the melon to the floor: 'It's a bloody good dose of starvation that you want!' he shouted, and stormed from the room.

My mother, who always had an eye like a hawk for the ridiculous, had a fit of laughter. Pretty soon, I saw the funny side, because I was my mother's son. Shortly after that, I heard my father laugh in the kitchen. Rose could always make him laugh. It was her greatest gift to him.

## MA AND DA

Rose Wogan was proud and shy, a fiercely loving wife and mother. Fearless, determined, indomitable – a cross between her mother, Muds, and her Auntie Mag. Loving, but never tactile, she had a witty but sometimes cruel tongue. Quick on the up-take, where Michael was slow and meticulous, she was impatient with his methodical ways, even as she loved him for his constancy, his uncritical love for her, his relentless commitment to working all the hours God sent for his little family.

He never got back home from work much before seven in the evening, and he was usually working on 'the books' – the ledgers – until past midnight. This suited the Ma, who never went to bed much before midnight anyway. I don't know what she found to do, but she was a night-bird, my mother. If she was a slip of a girl today, Tara Palmer-Tomkinson would only be in the ha'penny place …

Father and Mother retired late, but he liked to shave, earlier in the evening, after tea. He sang as he shaved, and I never understood why the bathroom wasn't blood-boltered, he must have had a steady hand. He certainly had a ringing baritone, the Da. As a young man, his singing voice had shown promise, and he had taken part in the competitive 'Feis Ceiol', the Dublin Music Festival, gaining high marks for his *lieder*, not to mention his come-all-ye's. The manly tones would reverberate not only around the bathroom, but shake every room of 18 Elm Park, Limerick.

Many of my friends said he could be heard in Ennis Road.

Since we were on the corner of a row of attached little houses, it must have been murder to live nearby, but the neighbours never complained. I suppose we were quiet and well behaved otherwise. My father did not hold back, he gave the bathroom's acoustics full rein, with Victorian crowd-pleasers such as 'Many Brave Hearts Lie Asleep in the Deep', and some of the more bravura arias, such as 'Valentine's Goodbye' from *Faust*.

A big favourite of his was 'Dead for Bread', which always convulsed my mother, listening downstairs in the kitchen. 'For God's sake Michael,' she would say, 'do you know no cheerful songs?' But he didn't. Singing was a serious business, particularly when you were trying not to cut your throat.

## AMATEUR DRAMATICS

Brian and I must have inherited some of the Da's vocal talent; we both took leading roles in Belvedere College productions of Gilbert and Sullivan, when we later attended school in Dublin. Brian went on to win many a prize in amateur drama festivals – indeed, he was invited to turn professional by a number of theatre companies, but he turned them down; he had a wife and family by then, and did not feel he could throw up the permanent and pensionable in favour of the fly-by-the-night hobbledehoy existence.

I sang leads in *The Gondoliers* and *Iolanthe* while at Belvedere, and I suppose it was a logical step for me to join the Rathmines and Rathgar Musical and Dramatic Society when I left school. We used to finish work at three o'clock in the afternoon in the bank, and time hung heavy on a young man's hands. In those innocent Dublin days, the place was heaving with musical and dramatic societies, with literally thousands of aspiring singers and actors ready and raring, with nowhere to go.

There were a couple of professional theatres and companies at the Abbey and the Gate, a couple of touring rep companies, and that was it. The young Irish person with a rage to perform joined an amateur company, and these companies kept the lesser theatres and the parish halls going.

The Rathmines and Rathgar were a step above. For two

seasons a year, a week in the spring and another in the autumn, they filled Dublin's premier music hall, the Gaiety; they papered the house with relatives and friends, for *Naughty Marietta*, *Bitter Sweet*, and 'Sir Harry', a stage Irishman in a Sigmund Romberg thing with a title that escapes me, probably because we have no memory of pain. Just you try playing a stage Irishman in front of an Irish audience ...

The present Mrs Wogan was a dab hand at the amateur dramatics and musicals as well, her long coltish legs and sweet coloratura making her an ideal choice for Principal Boy in the pantomimes of the Pioneer Society. It had got its own hall, a big one – I saw John Hanson play the *Red Shadow* there. It had to be big, that is where they had the meetings of the Pioneers – nothing to do with the Old West, getting the wagons in a circle, or John Wayne. The Pioneers were, and are, Irish people who take a pledge never to touch the demon drink, and every Irish person of my generation was one – some still are.

In my case, being a Pioneer lasted until I went on a school rugby tour to Scotland, and downed my first pint where neither my mother nor the parish priests could see me. Helen lasted a while longer; well, she had to: you could not be a member of the Musical and Dramatic Society if you were not still true to your pledge. When she was twenty, Helen took her first drink, and it was curtains for the Pioneers.

It has always been a regret that I never saw Helen as Prince Charming, but I did catch her in revue, a couple of years later. Revue was all the rage then, in Dublin's little theatres: Songs and Satire. I remember this tall, slim, stunning girl, looking like a cross between Maureen O'Hara and Arlene Dahl, singing a cheeky little parody called 'I'm a Model'.

I was smitten – but then, so was every other male within a hundred-mile radius. Helen *was* a model at the time, one of Ireland's most famous. It was to be a couple of years before our eyes met across a crowded room, but the memory of my first sighting of the present Mrs Wogan remains seared on what a Jesuit teacher of mine used to refer to as 'the fleshy tablets of my memory'.

While I am at the theatrical reminiscing, luvvy, I am not

unknown to the operatic stage either. My friend Ken, with whom I had made fast friends within ten minutes of arriving at Belvedere College, Dublin, was always keen on opera; and one day, about a year after we left school – he ensconced in insurance, while I separated the half-crowns from the two bobs in the bank – he suggested that we might go to the opera.

The Dublin Grand Opera Society staged a mighty season every year in the Gaiety, featuring some fine Italian solo talent. Not disposed to shelling out the hard-earned, Ken had divined how we might attend the feasts of fine singing for nothing. We would be extras – 'supers', as the Italian producer called us.

In less time than it takes to tell, I was hanging around an ill-painted backdrop of Venice, as a desultory Doge, in *Otello*. Ken and I featured as Ethiopian slaves in the Grand March in *Aida*: particularly anaemic-looking slaves we would have made as well, refusing point-blank to smear our pale bodies with disgusting brown cocoa-butter …

My appearance as a waiter in *La Traviata* brought me to the attention of the producer. It was not the flair with which I carried my tray, nor e'en the panache with which I dispensed the ginger ale masquerading as Champagne – no, it was my shoes. My brown suede shoes, which, picky, excitable Italian that he was, he felt might be just a tad anachronistic. It was a mercy that his shrieks were drowned by the bellowing on stage.

The producer did not have much of a leg to stand on – he did not have much of a pair of legs to stand on, if it came to that, being a little titch of a fellow. He could fulminate and fume, but we took that calmly; we were not being paid and he needed extras. You could come off stage as a consumptive Ethiopian slave, and then hare round the back to join the other end of the chain gang …

With all the coming and going, you needed that pint in the Green Room. And that is where we were, the half-dozen other extras and me, when we should have been at our devotions as altar-boys, bishops and priests, in the Easter Procession that is the affecting centrepiece of *Cavalleria Rusticana*. Fine-featured and in full fig, we missed the call. Enter the minuscule producer. This time, we had gone too far. 'So!' he shouted, little veins standing out on his forehead. 'So! You like to drink your beer? Drink it! The procession, she is over! You can go, at home!'

It did not leave you with much dignity, or indeed alternative. I often wonder what life would have been like in the great opera-houses of the world, had I but played my cards right ...

## HALF-MAN, HALF-BIKE

Most of my boyhood was spent on a bike – up and down the Ennis Road, back and forth over Sarsfield Bridge, Limerick, four times a day, between home and school. And every other place as well: out on the road to Bunratty, up the road to Ballinacurra, across the road to Barrington's Pier. It is no wonder I have the legs and arms of Arnold Schwarzenegger.

That marvellous writer, Flann O'Brien, has a wonderfully funny book called *The Third Policeman*, in which the Sergeant proposes the well-founded theory that he is half-man, half-bicycle; through many years of contact on the saddle there has been an exchange of atoms: he is his bicycle. His bicycle is him.

If this is true, then when I was a lad, half of Ireland must have been half-bicycle ... Everybody had a bike. Nobody had a car. Well, I tell a lie: both of my best friends' fathers had cars. James's da, because he was a solicitor, and Billy's because he was a commercial traveller. We didn't get a car until the Da rose to unheard-of heights in Dublin, but I don't feel I missed anything. There was nowhere much to go in Limerick, anyway – apart from the pictures every Wednesday with the lads, and sometimes with the Ma and Da on Saturday.

I hated it when they went to the pictures on their own. I would lie there in bed listening to my little brother's breathing, until I would hear their familiar steps, and the creaking of the front gate. I was always convinced something terrible was going to happen to them, as I lay there fretting about what the future held for two little orphaned lads ... I don't know where that anxiety came from, or where it went. Although, in common with everybody else, I will fret about the ones I love until the day I die, I have always been an optimist. I don't expect bad things to happen. I'm a useless patient, according to my doctor. If I wake up in the morning with a pain in my chest, I assume that it *is* indigestion.

Along with the books and the radio, the pictures were my lifeline to another world. It didn't matter all that much what kind of picture, although I probably favoured Roy Rogers more than Ginger. A little young for the sophistication of Astaire and Rogers, I was a Doris Day, Donald O'Connor kind of kid. Hopalong Cassidy, and all those B-movie cowboys were grist to my mill, and the Three Stooges, and Abbott and Costello. I preferred them to Laurel and Hardy, who were a little ancient, even for me, by then.

I could never understand Charlie Chaplin, Harold Lloyd or Buster Keaton – all too flickery, jumpy, silent. It was the fifties for heaven's sake! Gimme talkies, gimme Technicolor! You got value at the pictures in those days: ads, two B-features (one a cowboy, one a Scotland Yard drama with men in trench-coats and fedoras being introduced by Edgar Lustgarten), cartoons, and then the big picture.

If you went to Limerick's grandest cinema, the Savoy, you got cine-variety! This was all the above with a stage show thrown in! Comedian, 'spesh' act, crooner, band, dancing girls and an organist whose mighty Wurlitzer came out of the very bowels for fifteen minutes of excruciating sing-along. Why they persisted with this, year upon year, must remain a mystery. Nobody, but nobody, ever sang along. We were a self-conscious crowd. You might be at the pictures, lost in fantasy, but you could not lose face.

You did not get away with much in Limerick. The merest hint of a squint, and you were 'boss-eyed' for the rest of your life. Everybody in Limerick had a nickname, still has. Peter Clohessy, captain of Young Munster, and Irish international rugby prop-forward, is the 'Claw'. With gathering scorn, I recently read in a British paper, that this nickname had been given because of his great strength in the loose play, 'clawing' the ball from the grasp of opponents. No. He is called the 'Claw' because it is the first syllable of his surname as pronounced, correctly, in Limerick. Is it Occam's law – the simplest explanation is usually the most likely?

Limerick Football Club, whose every home game I attended with the Da for years, had a footballer whose nickname was 'Magua' after the character in the early movie version of *The Last of the Mohicans*. The decent man who kept the pub at which my father would rest his bicycle every so often, was known to all as 'Bokkles', because of a speech deficiency that gave him trouble with his 'Ts'. My friends were known as 'Mo', 'Bonk', 'Rogers' (after Roy the singing cowboy), 'Katy' (because he helped his mother in the kitchen) and worse, much worse. There did not seem to be any girls. Perhaps I was a late developer …

## AN OCCASION FOR SIN

Still, it was the fifties, and even the Catholic Church was making little genuflections towards the fact that we were in the second half of the twentieth century. Only *certain* elements of the Catholic Church, mind you. The Redemptorists were still holding hell-fire and brimstone 'missions' up and down the land. Usury, thievery, hypocrisy, cruelty and poverty bestrode the island, but the only sin that mattered to the Redemptorists was *sex*. Any hanky-panky outside the holy state of matrimony (and indeed quite a few things within it!) and you were doomed. Hell and damnation, into endless eternity.

The good fathers always spent a deal of time on the fires of Hell, the attendant pain and suffering, and their interminable nature. 'A hundred years – a millionth part of a second in eternity – and all that time, the searing fires of Hell wreaking your body, as you shriek in torment for just one drop of Holy Water, the second of release from the terrible pain and suffering …'

A Redemptorist missioner could go on like that for hours, striking fear and trembling into the hearts of even the most faithful and blameless. For in those days in Ireland, it was almost impossible not to commit a sin. Born with the stain of Original Sin (Adam and the apple, for goodness sake!), you and your immortal soul were on the road to Hell from Day One.

I do not know how such an essentially happy, kindly and good-natured people got lumbered with such an appalling, repressive religion – surely a more relaxed, Mediterranean-style

Roman Catholicism would have suited them better – but the priestly jack-boot remained on the neck of the Irish Catholics well into the sixties, and the dregs of it remain even yet.

A National Health Scheme was thrown out because of Church opposition in the fifties, divorce has only recently become legal in the Republic, and, right up until he died, a reactionary old git of an Archbishop of Dublin refused to allow Catholics to attend Ireland's oldest, most distinguished university, Trinity College, Dublin, on the grounds that it had been founded by Elizabeth I, and was full of Protestants. You *could* get in, of course. There are always ways, in Ireland: all you needed was money and an influential family. Then you got a dispensation. Rather like members of Roman Catholic royal families when they need a divorce ...

There *were* enlightened elements, even among the Jesuits. How they ever convinced the holy nuns of the Laurel Hill Convent – the girls' equivalent of Crescent College – to allow dances to take place in the new Crescent Hall, we will never know. How did they smuggle this radical concept past the Bishop of Limerick? Girls and boys, dancing together? Had the world gone mad?

The dances took place, among seething adolescent excitement that was somewhat vitiated by the fact that the hall was also seething with priests and nuns, supervising dress and decorum, and discreetly separating any boy or girl lucky enough to get within a foot of one another. The dances were held in broad daylight, and they consisted largely of foxtrots and waltzes. Anything lively was eschewed, deemed an occasion of sin. The priests and nuns were well pleased: sexual ignorance and adolescent frustration continued to thrive in Holy Catholic Ireland.

## IMPURE THOUGHTS

My friend Billy's family took a seafront house in Kilkee, Co. Clare, every summer. Kilkee was Limerick-on-Sea. Every summer, as soon as the school holidays began, the town by the Shannon River would empty of children and womenfolk, and the population of the little township in Co. Clare, with its beautiful, perfect crescent beach, would swell, tenfold.

Limerick would be deserted at the weekends, as the menfolk joined their families by the silvery Atlantic Sea. They brought with them the extraordinary rules, regulations and shibboleths that were such part and parcel of Limerick life. No undressing on the beach. You undressed in the privacy and chastity of your lodge, boarding house or hotel and made your way, discreetly be-towelled, to the beach – only divesting yourself of the modesty of your covering when you reached the shore. Out of the bounding main, back into the towelling, and off home at a smart trot, lest anyone caught a glimpse of anything that would encourage an impure thought.

As I remember it, there was not much sunbathing on that lovely beach, either. Modesty won again, I suppose. Or maybe there just was not much sun. We swam anyway, every day, twice. Billy's family used to invite their son's best friend down every summer for a couple of weeks, to keep the little toe-rag out of trouble.

As I have already said, I was a well-behaved, conventional little mother's boy, afraid of his own shadow. Billy's mother loved me. I kept him away from the rougher element: Limerick hooligans and local louts. I was a swimmer; I had been taught by Gordon Wood, a fine swimmer as well as an Irish international rugby player, and a British Lion. A great friend of my father's and the family, Gordon sadly passed away before he could see the heroic achievements of his Irish rugby international son, the splendid Keith Wood. Anyway, Billy and I swam twice a day. Up to Burns' Cove in the morning, down to the Pollock Holes in the afternoon, usually in the driving rain. It didn't seem to matter.

It usually rained in Limerick as well, winter and summer. The 'soft' day, that is such a feature of Irish life, reduced so many good Irish men and women to unspoken hysteria, or, at best, catarrh. There are worse things than catarrh, though not in the early morning if you are unlucky enough to be married to a sufferer. Ask the present Mrs Wogan …

I don't know if you have ever swum through jellyfish in any numbers, but it is a sensation not to be commended to the squeamish. Shoals of the strange creatures abounded in Burns' Cove, but that even stranger creature, a woman in a bathing costume, was a rare sight indeed.

Swimming in Burns' Cove was largely men's (and jellyfishes') work. Women, after all, could swim, in all due modesty and decorum, off the beach. They could also swim in the Pollock Holes, which we used to visit every afternoon. Well, when I say the Pollock Holes, I mean women could swim in the First and Second Pollock Holes.

Just a little past the Second Pollock Hole was a red line drawn on the rocks, and with it the legend: 'No Women Beyond This Point'. A hundred yards further on, and there, in all its glory, the Third Pollock Hole: and with it, and in it, in all *their* self-conscious, macho glory, the men of Limerick, naked as the day they were born.

How did these men, driven to the very limits of inhibition and repression by their upbringing and education and religion, ever get the nerve to take off all their clothes, in broad daylight and in front of strangers? Not in front of the womenfolk, of course. And there could certainly be no question of any woman taking all her clothes off. There is a limit.

## BORN TO DANCE

As the regular listener to my morning extravaganza on Radio 2 will know, I was born to dance. Anything lively at all, and to a hearty shout of 'Feet! Do your stuff!' I am up and at the old hard-shoe shuffle. Those in the Terpsichorean know are quick to acknowledge that Michael Flatley was a lucky man indeed to get his feet under the *Riverdance* door before my twinkling toes came to the producer's attention. 'He moves well, for such a big man ...' is the encomium, whenever I am observed tripping the light fantastic at a *thé dansant*.

Inexplicably, my children take the opposite view: from an early age, they have taken to the hills whenever their mother and father take to the floor. A sovereign method of clearing the hall of minor Wogans is for Mr and Mrs of that ilk to get down and boogie. Afterwards the post-mortem: 'You look like Des

O'Connor!' 'I should be so lucky!' is my lightning riposte, but I cannot help but feel a little wounded. The careless hurtfulness of the young ... They think they invented dancing, as well as pop music, dress-sense and sex ...

Come to think of it, we did not have much dress-sense in Kilkee when I was a youth. Or anywhere else, either. Sex was just a rumour; I didn't know anybody who had ever had any. I didn't know anybody who knew the first thing about it. There were a couple of girls' names that were bandied about; but I had seen them in their school uniforms and I could not believe it. There wasn't much pop music about in those pre-rock'n'roll days, either. An occasional rumbling of things to come with skiffle, but nothing to frighten the horses. Traditional or Dixieland jazz was the thinking teen's thing, but at the hop, it was waltz, foxtrot or quickstep.

And it was in Kilkee that I first learned to put one foot in front of the other. It was not like today, children, when you simply get out there and shake your thing. This was strict tempo stuff: one, two, three; one, two, three. I often think that if we had kept to the old strict tempo, and eschewed the free-form dervish style that became the vogue, the world might be a better, cleaner place today. I like to think that Victor Sylvester's *Book of Ballroom Dancing*, replete as it was, with incomprehensible arrows, dots and little footprints, helped to keep my young brain clean, and my body pure.

One unusually fine summer's day, I left Kilkee in a friend's car, having unaccountably picked up viral pneumonia, and was taken to the Mater Hospital, Dublin. I have not been back to Kilkee since. I am afraid that it will have been diminished, as all childhood memories are, and I want to keep mine untainted.

Kilkee was where I learned the foxtrot, waltz, tango and samba. Well, the rudiments. No flinging women around, that was for the oily Continentals. Kilkee was where I first held hands with a person of the opposite persuasion, and kissed her, clumsily ... And I don't want to go back to the Pollock Holes, particularly not the Third ... There might be women there ... And I bet they have wiped out the line, and erased the sign. Germaine Greer has a lot to answer for ...

# HOME-AND-AWAY GAMES

As an only child for six years, if I had a preference, it was for my own company. It was all books and tin soldiers. And then came Subbuteo – table soccer! A green baize football pitch, little goals, and little cardboard men with plastic bases that you flicked at the ball. It was as near to the real thing as you could get.

I could hardly wait to get home from school to lay out my pitch on the carpet of the front room, and away we went! Spurs against Arsenal, Manchester United v. Wolves – the greatest teams in the land were at my fingertips. I had a League Competition, a Cup, a League Cup, all of them fiercely contested, and all of them against myself. I was the only one with a Subbuteo set ... Things got more sophisticated as Subbuteo caught on. New goals, with netting instead of paper, plastic men instead of cardboard, and painted in your favourite team's colours!

I spent years on the good carpet, flicking little bits of plastic back and forward, and then, one fine day, James persuaded his parents to buy him a Subbuteo set. Within a week, Billy had got one. Then John and then another pal – and another. Suddenly, Subbuteo ruled! With our teams in little cardboard boxes, we would travel the roads and highways of Limerick to play one another, home and away. For a glorious couple of years, it took over our lives – and then, just as quickly, it was gone. Probably with the advent of the long trouser ...

A hundred years later, when I was flying back and forward between Dublin and London to present *Late Night Extra* on BBC Radio, I would stay with our friends Kits and Hacker in their lovely converted tithe barn, near Datchet, Berkshire. It was a good deal; I brought them a bottle of vodka and a bottle of whisky, and they fed, watered and bedded me down for the night before I flung myself back across the Irish Sea into the bosom of my family.

Kits is an Etonian, and therefore, a footer rather than a rugger man. We would talk football – occasionally, I would accompany Hacker and himself to Stamford Bridge to cheer on the boys in blue. I must have let it out about the great Subbuteo years in

Limerick, because the next week, Kits took me upstairs to his den, and there it was: pitch, goals, little plastic men with little plastic bases! My heart leapt, and the years rolled back ... From then on, whenever I arrived at the house, I had scarcely time to take off my coat before being rushed upstairs for a game of Subbuteo. No, several games.

I taught Kits everything I knew: how to line 'em up for a free kick – where to place your men for a corner – how to kick your men one way, while the ball went the other ... In no time, Kits' little plastic footballers were knocking seven bells out of mine. He had an unfair advantage: he could practise. His little men were trained to a hair. And I had left my Subbuteo behind in Limerick, eight years ago.

## THE DIARY FOR 1953

In the way that mothers do, Rosie Wogan kept an eclectic collection of memorabilia relating to her elder son, and, a couple of years ago, in some drawer or other, I came across a diary of mine that she had kept for posterity. Or maybe it just fell down the back of something. 'The Catholic Diary for 1953', obviously a present from Auntie May, from the ever-religious shelves of Veritas Ltd., Dublin.

Inside the flyleaf, I had written in Latin script: *Terentius Wogan, Limericense, Hibernia*. A couple of pages on: *Shoes: size eight. Height: five feet six inches*. In 1953, I was fourteen, my last year in Limerick, before probably the most momentous move of my life, the great Wogan exodus to Dublin. Yet, there is not a mention of it ... On reflection, we probably did not move until after the school year finished in June 1954, when I had completed my state exams.

There is not much of a mention of anything really. This small, black leather-bound diary is not a *Life of Johnson*. It is not even Adrian Mole ... There is no comment or reflection here, no indication of any real feelings about anything or anyone, just a record of a year in the life of a fourteen-year-old boy in an Irish country town in the early fifties. This boy seems very immature by today's standards: there is no mention of pop music, girls, parties, dances, illicit drinking, or even a quick Woodbine behind the bicycle sheds.

Some of my friends definitely smoked; one or two may well have groped about a bit with a particularly loose piece of stuff at the back of the one-shilling seats, but I must have been a late developer. Look at the very first entry, while a blush of shame mantles the writer's cheek:

**Friday January 2nd**: *We went to town in the afternoon with Mammy.* 'Mammy'! Fourteen years of age, and I'm still calling my mother 'Mammy'!]

**Saturday, January 3rd**: *Stayed in bed all morning, had my dinner in bed.* [That dinner was, of course, lunch but still a pretty pampered existence … ] *At about 3 o'clock in the afternoon, went to Dorset Street and bought stamps.* Stamps! Of course! I collected stamps. By fourteen, I had been a philatelist for about seven years, and a keen follower of Stanley Gibbons, repository of all stamp-collecting wisdom.

I don't know when I stopped being interested in postage stamps, ancient and modern from around the world, but one day it was there, and the next, zippo. Like little girls and ponies: for six or seven years her life revolves around the horse; mucking out, riding out, the endless fuss and loving care, and then, one day, suddenly it all stops – at least for most young women. The are lots of grown-up philatelists, too, I am sure, but not many without an anorak …

'Staying in bed all morning' seems to have been the norm for me in early January 1953, followed by a game of table-soccer in the afternoon. I had not realized the hold that Subbuteo had over me and my little coterie until I read the diary. I even went to watch other people playing.

**Wednesday, January 21st**: *Mr Marmion* [as I remember, a temperamental young man on the threshold of Jesuit priest-hood] *threw out six boys for six slaps this morning. The afternoon was uneventful* [!] *and after school I went to James's house to watch the match between John Sexton and Horgan. It was a terrific match. Horgan won 9-8. I got my postal order today so I will send away for the Vamping Chart and Ventrilo tomorrow …*

Don't hold me to it, but I think a Vamping Chart was something you put over the piano keys, enabling even the totally tuneless to accompany a vocalist or fellow-musician. Since we didn't have a piano I am foxed as to the utility of this particular item. The Ventrilo was a little contraption you put under your tongue, giving you the power to speak without opening your mouth, and, further, giving you the almost satanic power of throwing your voice to all four corners of the room. Think of the trouble you could get other people into in Latin class! It also did bird-songs. I have a clear recollection of the thing being absolutely useless.

**Wednesday, February 18th**: *Lent beginning! Hope I can keep my resolutions.* [What an unbelievable goody-goody this kid was!] *After school, I went up to Horgan's to play table-soccer. I played very badly, but won 10–4.* [And a cocky little swine ... ] And how come Horgan, whose name was John, was called Horgan when everybody else was Billy, Jack, James or some nickname like Snitch, or Bonk, or Mo?

I had forgotten that we had a debate with other schools until I read:

**Saturday, March 21st**: *We had a debate with St. Munchin's tonight. They were better than I thought they'd be. Sexton had his usual eejity speech. They won because they had half their school with them.* [And a lousy loser, too.] Apart from Subbuteo, my life appears to be taken up with school, football and going to the pictures.

**Thursday, April 30th**: *Went to 'Carson City' at the Lyric today. A very good western. Exercises were very hard and I wasn't finished until 9:30. Kids had a bonfire in the avenue and I couldn't drag Brian away from it. Top scorers for Limerick: Cusack, 9; Collery, 9; Bradley, 7. Limerick finished sixth in the league.*

Rugby was the game in Limerick, rugby was the game at Crescent College, Limerick, and I played in the school team. But there is not a single solitary mention of rugby *anywhere* in the Catholic Diary 1953. Did I imagine it? No, there is a picture to prove it. I fell over just before that picture was taken, which accounts for the stain at the right elbow of what should have been a spotless white shirt. Perhaps, if I had tied my bootlaces ... But then, I have never had any time for bootlace tying. Life is too short. It is the same reason why I can't abide winter sports holidays. They are all boots and laces. I have never attempted Everest either, for the same reason.

There are lacunae in the diary for long periods of May, June and July, due either to lack of interest or the hectic round of table-soccer, football and movies. Or perhaps I just left the thing behind when I went to Dublin on my holidays ...

Back in Limerick:

**Wednesday, August 5th**: *Went to the pictures with Billy today. 'Come On, George' with George Formby. Fair.* [Fourteen years old and a critic already.] *After tea, went for a drive to Killaloe with Uncle Charlie. I'm sleeping on the floor in the sitting-room ...* Well! What brought that on? At the bottom of every page of the Catholic Diary is an improving thought to carry throughout the day. Wednesday, August 5th's is: *'Suffering is the surest way, the nearest way, and the shortest way to Heaven.'* Appropriately enough for the silent sufferer on the sitting room floor. But it was ever thus. The loyal listener will attest only too readily that I am rarely without pain. But do you ever hear a whimper out of me?

It is August, and, suddenly, like philately and little girls and their ponies, table-soccer has disappeared. No more Subbuteo. Something that took up every spare moment, every waking thought, has just gone out of the window. Now I am an altar-boy and there is a new game in town:

**Tuesday, August 11th**: *Served mass this morning. After breakfast, played tennis with James: 9-7, 3-6, 4-4.* From then on it is tennis and pictures. And board games:

**Monday, August 31st**: *Played Monopoly in the afternoon with Billy and his cousin. After tea, went to the pictures. Limerick 2nd in table.*

Then, on **Sunday, November 1st**: *Hallelujah! Limerick have won their first F.A.I. Trophy! They beat Dundalk after being two goals down! Cronin scored the winning goal from a Lynam pass. There was tremendous exuberance when the result was heard ...* Exuberance, if you don't mind ... I wonder if your man was any relation of Des?

**Friday, December 18th**: *Got our holidays today. Mum told me that we were going to Dublin on Sunday, and that Uncle Charlie* *was bringing us up* … Good old Uncle Charlie, but have you noticed anything significant? Right. It is 'Mum' now. In a scant eleven months our boy has gone from Mammy to Mum. A rite of passage, if ever I saw one.

The rest of December is pictures [sometimes twice daily] and pantos, and the diary finishes on Christmas Day:

*Went to 11:30 Mass with Dad* [it is 'Dad' now, as well]. *Fed my face at dinner and tea, and read my books in between meals. Played Lotto and cards until 1:30 a.m.* What sort of year was *that*? For today's fourteen-year-old, soporifically, trance-inducingly BORING! I agree. It is just that I don't remember being bored. Every day seemed to be filled to bursting. And if it wasn't, I stayed in bed. Still do …

## ON THE MOVE

Leaving Limerick seemed to happen in a flash. One minute, there we are being rained on at 18 Elm Park, Ennis Road, and the next thing, snugly ensconced at 64 Ballymun Avenue, Dublin. By the way, in case you are thinking of going around to 64 Ballymun Avenue with a view to leaving flowers, or even placing a plaque on the wall, let me save you the time and trouble. It is not there any more. Not the house – Ballymun Avenue. The residents decided to change the name, because the word 'Ballymun' became inextricably linked with a development of Council flats a couple of miles up the road.

These flats – a monument to Council housing at its very worst – became, after a scant few years, a running sore on the face of Ireland, not to mind the suburbs of Dublin. If you saw the film of Roddy Doyle's book *The Commitments*, you have seen them. They say that they are going to raze them to the ground. To put it in Irish: they should have razed them to the ground before they built them.

We left nothing behind us in Limerick – some good friends, but no family, no possessions. It was years before I even went back for a visit. By then, I was one of the new stars of the infant Irish Television Service, Radio Telefís Éireann (RTÉ). In common with every village and small town in Ireland, Limerick had a 'festival'. There was a film festival in Cork, a theatre festival in Dublin, a music festival in Ennis, an oyster festival in Galway, a beer festival in Kilkenny. The idea, of course, was to drag in the Yankee dollar, the pound sterling, the German mark and whatever currencies could be dredged from passing foreigners.

But tourism was only in its infancy in the Ireland of the early sixties. Bord Fáilte Éireann, the Irish Tourist Board, had not quite got the hang of it. Over the last twenty years it has been a different story, but then tourists were pretty thin on the ground. There had been a pathetic attempt at a nationwide festival, 'An Tóstal', which I freely translate as 'The Welcome', that never got off the ground. Apathy was still prevalent in Ireland then, and a debilitating cynicism: 'Ah, sure, why bother? It'll never work ...' Which is why it is so nice to go back to Ireland now, with its optimistic drive, its fearlessness for the future.

In Dublin, the main feature of 'An Tóstal' was a horrific bowl with great plastic flames shooting upwards, that changed colour. They plonked it right in the middle of the O'Connell Bridge, across the Liffey, where no one could miss it. As I have pointed out earlier, Dubliners are pretty critical of statuary, even the good stuff. 'The Bowl of Light', as some misguided civil servant had named it, found little favour. It was cheap, and vulgar, and one evening some thinking Dubliners picked it up and threw it over the side of the bridge into the Liffey. Nobody bothered to retrieve it, and they allowed 'An Tóstal' to quietly pass away.

## THE BEST OF LIMERICK LIFE

I am not sure what the festival of Limerick was specifically designed to celebrate, but, as Ireland's third city, it was not going to be left out. As ever, a Queen of the Festival had to be chosen and, as one of the city's currently famous sons, I was invited to join the Lady Mayoress and a distinguished panel at a grand levee in Limerick's finest hotel to select Limerick's Loveliest. Except that, as in all beauty contests, it was not that simple.

Beauty was not the sole criterion. Poise, social skills, high intelligence, a ready grasp of national and world affairs, kindness to children and animals, purity of thought and action, and, if possible, a first-class degree, were all factors to be taken into account. This girl had to represent all that was best in Limerick life and carry Limerick's banner proudly in the salons of the world – or at least know how to behave herself at the Young Farmers' Annual Dinner Dance.

One after another, the contenders for the title sat before us, to be quizzed as to their suitability for such high office. All were pretty, dressed to their best, but only one remains in memory.

'Now, Mairead,' said the Lady Mayoress, all business, 'and tell me, are you interested in the news?'

'I am,' riposted the lovely Mairead stoutly.

'Do you read the papers?'

'Indeed I do, ma'am. Cover to cover, every morning.'

'Well, now, that's grand. Anybody got any questions?'

I thought I would keep it simple, give the girl a chance. 'What's the capital of France?' I asked.

She looked at me as if I had shot her. 'Oh, let me think, now … it's on the tip of my tongue …'

I didn't dare look at my fellow judges. After a couple of minutes of thoughtful frowning from the avid newspaper reader, I thought I would help: 'It begins with P,' I suggested.

She brightened. 'Is it Portugal?'

I don't remember which young lady we selected that night, but I am sure she was a credit to Limerick and herself. I became something of an expert in the selection of Irish Beauty Queens, being young, single and a media personality. Up and down the country I went, selecting a Queen here and a Princess there. I became familiar with the insides of small caravans, where I would interview the girls, once again looking for indications of general knowledge and high intelligence, which, even if they had any, they were too nervous to display. I grew to know all too well the musty aroma of fear, perspiration and heavy make-up. For me, it was a piece of cake. There was only one rule – if you wanted the readies and fancied getting out of town in one piece – pick the local girl.

One evening, in the driving rain of the midlands of Ireland, as I sought the location of a little place where I was engaged to select 'the Queen of the Carnival', I pulled into a rain-swept little town to seek directions. It was deserted, the lights shining on the wet main street. No way was I getting out of the car – you could drown in ten seconds in that downpour. Then, mercy me, the door of one of the pubs opened, out comes a man in a cap and coat, and reaches for his bicycle, shrewdly parked under the pub's window. Before he mounts and speeds away into the drenching gloom, I pull the car over.

'Excuse me,' I civilly enquire, 'can you tell me how to get to Claughan?'

'I'm a stranger here myself,' he answered wetly, bicycling off like a dervish.

I drove gloomily on down the main street, and there saw a sign: Claughan, 1 mile. Where had he come from then, this bicyclist of the night? Cycled down from Belfast for a reviving brew? A tourist, perhaps? Not in that coat and cap. How far could you go on a bicycle in that kind of weather? Perhaps he was the living embodiment of Flann O'Brien's *Third Policeman* principle – half-man, half-velocipede?

## THE ROSE OF TRALEE

The greatest beauty contest in all Ireland is 'The Rose of Tralee', based on the well-worn come-all-ye of the same name. It has been going great guns since God was a boy – or, at least, I was. Well, a boy broadcaster. It was a Big Thing – at least, in Tralee, Co. Kerry. Contestants came from all over the world: Europe, Britain, the States, South America.

I would like to have been there for the eliminating round in Asunción, Paraguay. The contestants had to be of Irish descent, but I think there was a bit of rule-bending – and why not? Jackie Charlton achieved considerable success with the Republic of Ireland football team, most of whom spoke broad Cockney, Scouse or Geordie. The current Irish rugby football team boasts at least four Gaels from the Southern Hemisphere. So, what if the Rose of Tralee cannot speak a word of English?

Tralee is the capital of Kerry, where men are men, and their Gaelic footballers are lured from their mountain fortresses by the promise of raw meat. Helen came with me to the Rose of

Tralee. We were married by then, and she needed a laugh. The local committee saw to our every need, and took us to the festival club, where the élite could converse like decent people over a pint of stout. There was a musician – Noel Healy and his Cordovox (a magical instrument, combining the best of the accordion and melodeon). I can hear it still.

As is the nature of things in Ireland, even in the best of company, the music led to the odd song and some spirited dancing. A young blade approached Helen:

'Excuse me, miss, would you care to dance?'

Now, in Ireland at that time, and in Kerry in particular, when a girl was asked to dance, she danced. It did not matter if the fellow was an eejit, a drunk or eighty years of age, nobody turned a man down; the loss of face was too grievous.

Mrs Wogan, never one to care much for the macho self-image of the Irish male, said: 'No thank you, I'm talking with my friends.'

Your man was astounded, affronted, but all that is best in a Kerryman bubbled to his lips: 'Ah, well, you're too old for me anyway ...'

Just about saved his face, I would say.

A couple of years ago, I was in Tralee again, filming for an epic documentary series called *Wogan's Ireland* (well, I liked it) and, lo and behold, the Rose of Tralee was in full swing. I watched it on the television in my hotel, compered by my good friend and Ireland's finest presenter, Gay Byrne. I switched it off when the young lady from Massachusetts produced a ukulele from behind her back, and went straight into 'The Star-Spangled Banner'. And I thought *I* had had it tough ...

# THREE

# FROM SHANNON'S SIDE
# TO LIFFEY'S SHORE

I suppose the Great Move to Dublin was in the air for at least six months, but I was up to my armpits in exams. State exams, the Intermediate Certificate. Not that I was ever a great student – application was never my strong suit. As I have said, unless motivated by fear and trembling, I did just enough to pass, relying on flair rather than graft. The child is father to the man … 'Too easily distracted' – that was the verdict of most of my school reports; if it wasn't *Dick Barton: Special Agent*, it was *Dan Dare*, in my pre-teens, and later if it wasn't *The Goon Show*, it was *Bulldog Drummond*.

The examiners were either drunk in my Intermediate Certificate year, or my mother's prayers had successfully stormed Heaven, because I passed six subjects out of eight, with honours. Indeed, I passed Latin with distinction, up there in the top ten per cent in the country, with nearly ninety per cent. It was the Latin teacher who frightened me to death … That man knew what he was doing.

Michael Thomas's endless hours at the ledgers and the bacon-slicer finally paid off in 1956, when he was offered the job of General Manager, Leverette & Frye, O'Connell Street, Dublin. I was too young then to realize how unusual it was for honesty, hard work and intelligence to get the reward they deserved, so I was not all that surprised.

My father took it modestly. Too modestly, according to my mother, particularly in the matter of remuneration. Michael was grateful, Rose was not. Humility and forelock-tugging were never her strong suits. She had seen her husband work all the hours God sent, for a pittance. Along with him, she had struggled, eked out every penny, to keep her little family warm, fed and well educated. She knew the Da's value, even if he was too reticent to put a figure on it. I could hear her in the kitchen, laying down the law. She nagged him to renegotiate, and when he had got most of what she wanted, she graciously agreed to move. Back to Dublin. To dear old dirty Dublin.

Rose Wogan had never really left Dublin, not in her heart. Limerick – 120 miles away from Dublin, three hours on the train – had never warmed her, never seemed like 'home'. She never stopped missing Muds and her sisters, and the Big City. I think she felt hemmed in, in Limerick. Although she had good neighbours and made friends, it was too narrow, too parochial. Dublin would allow her to go about her business, without everybody knowing it ... Rosie was a city girl; the four green fields of Erin failed to inspire her, she was never big on bogs. Donagh MacDonagh's poem, 'Dublin Made Me', sums up her attitude:

> *I disclaim all fertile meadows, all tilled land*
> *The evil that grows from it and the good,*
> *But the Dublin of old statutes, this arrogant city,*
> *Stirs proudly and secretly in my blood.*

Gordon Wood taught the Da to drive before he left Limerick, because a car came with the new, exalted position of General Manager. *A car!* The Wogans had *a car!* Not a gobdaw's car, either. A Ford Consul! Top of the range! And a phone! Can you beat it? I can still see that car: big, black and shiny. I sat in it for hours, behind the steering wheel, parked in front of the gates of 64 Ballymun Avenue that was.

We went out for a drive every Sunday after lunch. 'Will we go for a spin, lads?' he would say, and off we would pop to Portmarnock and take a stroll up the beach. Occasionally, we would even set off early – after Mass, of course – for a picnic in the Dublin Mountains. I loved it: the trees, the rocks and the heather, paddling in the freezing lakes, the lemonade and the sandwiches, and the ritual – the awful ritual of the lighting of the primus stove. Was there ever a primus stove made that lit at the first go? Was there ever a primus stove that was not a cause of bad language, dissension, and even occasional violence?

# HELEN'S DA

Long before we thought of each other, Helen, too, would go a-picnicking in the Dublin Mountains with her parents, Tim and Ellie, and whichever members of her family that had yet to take ship for the Antipodes.

Tim was a man who liked his comforts; in fact, he lived most of his life in the manner of a feudal chieftain: the kind of man who insisted that before his soup be served, it should be allowed to cool on the windowsill outside the kitchen door. Back rashers only, met his favour, and with the rind removed. Fillet steaks were not scorned, nor e'en the succulent ham.

The kind of man for whom a sandwich would never be enough, Tim required a full cooked lunch when a-picnicking *he* did go, and the saintly Ellie was required to cook a full three-course meal, including soup, boiled bacon, cabbage, potatoes and a hot pudding for six people, on a primus stove. I don't know how she was not assumed straight into Heaven.

Tim never drove a car; one of his sons gave him a couple of lessons, but it nearly killed them both. It was not his style, anyway: it suited him far better to be driven, whenever he deigned to move outside his purlieus – and he did not deign that often.

Tim was one of those rare people who never lost one of childhood's greatest gifts: utter self-absorption. For the first three or four years of his or her life, a child is convinced that life, the world, revolves around him or her. Constant parental and familial care convinces the baby that he or she is the very centre of the universe. Then comes nursery school, and the sharp realization that he or she is not alone in being the cynosure of all attention – there is at least a roomful of others with the same idea. And so, we learn that the world does not revolve around us alone.

Not Tim Joyce. Throughout a long and vigorous life, all he ever talked about was himself. All he ever cared or thought about was directly connected to himself: wife, family, business. He had no interests or relationships outside his trinity. He went to the pub or the golf club every evening, but only to talk to whoever would listen, of his own life and times. I don't think he ever heard a word that was said to him. If he did, he paid scant attention.

He, too, like my father, and indeed, most young Irishmen of his generation, grew up knowing hard times, and the desperate need to get out there and earn a crust. Like Michael Thomas Wogan of Enniskerry, Co. Wicklow, Timothy James Joyce of Ballylehaune, Co. Galway, became indentured to a grocer, in the ancient City of the Tribes, capital of the west of Ireland, Galway. He met and married the saintly Ellie from Sligo, and moved to Dublin, behind the counter at Findlater's.

Ellie bore him eight children, all reared on the salary of a grocer's assistant. Don't! You might as well ask how *most* Irish families of that era survived – well, some didn't. Tim and Ellie's family did, on self-help and the old Gaelic tradition of fosterage. One son went to live with a relation in Sligo, one left for Australia at sixteen, in the tender care of the Christian Brothers; Helen was boarded out to an aunt in Wicklow, the unhappiest time of her life. And the eldest son, Jim, took a degree in agricultural science, and, in his turn, helped to pay for Helen's schooling with the good Sisters of Mercy in Arklow. After her stay with her mad uncle and aunt in Wicklow, it seemed like Heaven.

Then, in the late fifties, Timothy Joyce hit pay-dirt. At the bottom of his garden in Leinster Road, Rathmines, he set up a little factory: a production line, wherein he packaged raisins, beans, lentils, dried fruits and anything else that could be stuck in a small brown bag, and sold them to the grocery stores.

It took off, and dear Ellie Joyce had to worry no more about where the next penny was coming from. Timothy was in his element: in Crombie coat and walking stick, he strode down the middle of the road. People listened when he spoke, cronyism flourished around him. His tales grew taller: he gave an interview to the local paper entitled 'An Old IRA Man Looks Back', in which our brave Tim hides in a cave for several days, a Republican hero on the run from the dreaded Black and Tans, exhausted and close to death, his hand shattered and bleeding from a stray bullet. By a strange coincidence, this was the very same hand that got caught in a bacon-slicer on Findlater's cold meats counter ...

He would regale any gathering of one or more with thrilling descriptions of his time as an enforcer for the Irish Hospitals Sweepstakes in Capone's Chicago. Around the table sat the mobsters, thinking Tim Joyce and his boys a soft touch. One of the mobsters, Legs Diamond, as clearly identified by Tim, surreptitiously reached for his equalizer, only to realize, as Tim graphically put it, 'that I had my gat already out, under the table, trained on him. He changed his tune after that, I can tell you ...' Tim Joyce had never been outside Ireland in his life ...

For that reason, as well as his self-obsession, he had no idea about the rest of the world. Oh, he knew it was *there*, he read the papers. An intelligent man, he was fully up to speed on everything that was happening, at home and abroad. It was not happening to him, that was all. When you are the centre, everything else must seem on the periphery.

I was there the day his son Eamonn returned on a visit, from Australia. Twenty-six hours on a plane to London, then another flight to Dublin, followed by a three-hour car journey down windy, country roads to Tullow, Co. Carlow. Tim was watching television when Eamonn came into the room.

'How'ya doin', Dad?', shouted the bold Eamonn, a son of Oz to his flip-flops.

Tim turned around in his chair. 'Oh, how'ya?' he said, and turned back to the television.

It was as if Eamonn had dropped in from down the road.

And yet to those he loved, and I am afraid, to those who buttered him up, there was no kinder, more generous man than Timothy James Joyce. Helen and I could not have bought our first house without his help. I never had a proper talk with him. He had set phrases with which he would open the conversation: 'How are the shares?' or 'Is the rain comin' through the roof?' We never got beyond banter. Tim Joyce never gave his feelings away, and he gave his heart to only one: his beloved Ellie, from Sligo.

She was another Muds Byrne. Sweet-faced and smiling, diminutive and soft-spoken, she, too, lived in a cocoon. She simply never recognized the bad in anybody. For her, armoured by innocence, there was no evil. A devout Catholic, she always seemed to me to be marking time here, until she went to her eternal reward.

Tim did not recognize the existence of death. I expect he thought that the world would stop, when *he* did. Without any intimations of mortality, in his eighties he planted tiny apple trees, fully expecting to pick their fruit, in the fullness of time. Which he did, before he died, aged ninety-three.

Although Tim Joyce never learned to drive, Michael T. Wogan quickly mastered the machinations of the Ford Consul. Well, perhaps 'mastered' is putting it a bit strongly. For instance, the Da never fully grasped the principle of overtaking. He simply did not understand that when you pulled out to go past another car, it was *your* job to go faster, not the other fellow's to slow down. 'That louser!' the Da would shout. 'He won't let me go by!'

There still were not *that* many cars on the road in the Ireland of the late fifties, and a good thing, too. There was no driving test. You simply found a convenient field with a friend who knew how to do it, and, a lesson or two later, provided you paid for your driving licence, of course, there you were, fit and able to take your vehicle on to the highways and byways of Ireland. I got my driving licence that way, and, after a couple of lessons from me in the vast emptiness of Dublin's Phoenix Park, so did Helen.

When, much later we came to live in Britain, I felt that it was the honourable thing to pass a driving test. Fresh-faced, fine-featured and full of confidence – after all, I had been driving for about ten years – I duly rolled up at the Slough Test Centre. And failed. Next time, I took a half-dozen lessons from a local driving school, and passed. Rather like school being more about passing exams than getting an education, the driving test had little relevance to the realities of modern motoring. This never worried Helen. She did not bother with passing the test – she simply waited until the European Union regulations made it possible for her to swap her Irish driving licence for a British one!

# CRÈME DE LA CRÈME

Belvedere College, my new Alma Mater in Dublin, had a high opinion of itself: 'A Belvederian is a Belvederian wherever he goes,' was the watchword of a school that regarded itself as the *crème de la crème* of Irish education. It had an old boys' network that Etonians would envy, and a roll-call of past pupils that would have been the envy of any: Prime Ministers, heroes, archbishops, rugby internationals, Irish and British Lions' captains, James Joyce and Tony O'Reilly. The Jesuits kept pretty quiet about the former, and were quietly proud of the latter.

There was one priest, a Father Kelly, who under the guise of lectures on the Mysteries of Life (sex), extolled instead the virtues of *A Portrait of the Artist as a Young Man* and *Ulysses*. *Ulysses* was on all our wanted lists anyway, for the same reason as *Lady Chatterley's Lover* – they were both on the Catholic Index, an endless list of books banned by the Roman Catholic hierarchy. And when the hierarchy declared something was not good enough, that was good enough for the Irish Government. Right up to the 1960s, the influence and power of the Irish Catholic Church in Ireland can only be compared to the reign of the Ayatollahs in present-day Iran.

I arrived at Belvedere the year after A.J.F. (Tony) O'Reilly left, trailing clouds of glory behind him. Nowadays he is known as an international man of business, a philanthropist, a former rugby star. Then, my peers held him in awe as the greatest schoolboy rugby player of his generation, and an all-round star of the classroom, tennis court, cricket pitch, you name it. I only mention it because with all that, this idol of his peers, this obvious leader of men, was never Captain of School. One can only wonder at the Jesuitical thinking that rationalized *that* decision.

Anyway, in my new black blazer with the silver school crest, I was the new kid on the block. Because of my Intermediate Certificate results, I went straight into the A stream or 'Honours' class. This meant that we followed an 'Honours' curriculum in eight subjects – English Literature, Irish, French, Latin, Greek, History, Geography and Maths – in which particular subject I was glad to join the 'Pass' class, being nothing more than an innumerate eejit. Also, the 'Honours' maths teacher had all the makings of psychopath, so I was glad to see the back of him in favour of the gentle incompetent who was in charge of the dim-wits.

In general, I found the teachers in Belvedere to be gentler, more civilized than the ones I had left behind in Limerick. Unsurprisingly, my studies, having been previously motivated largely by fear, took a downturn under a more kindly regime. Or maybe it was the distraction of building new social bridges, making new friends. That was not all that difficult, so it is not much of an excuse.

To a boy, or more properly, a young man, the sixteen other denizens of the 'Honours' class were all well-motivated, well-behaved, decent sons of the Dublin middle, professional class. They had the confidence that going to a self-confident school imbues. They knew who they were, and what they were going to be: doctors, solicitors, lawyers, quantity surveyors, stockbrokers – just like their fathers.

A long time ago, it struck me that one of the luckiest breaks in my life was that my father was not a professional man. Had he been a doctor, say, or an architect, I would have followed him into his profession. That was my upbringing, my education: conventional, conformist, do the right thing. 'Doing your own thing' is the fashion these days, and I am not sure about it. The people who 'do their own thing' are only free to do it because of the people who 'do the right thing'.

Many of my class became distinguished doctors and surgeons, which, in view of their education, is a tribute to their intelligence and hard work. As you can see, the 'Honours' class pursued a classical education. Chemistry and science were good enough only for the 'Pass' class! It meant that my unfortunate classmates had to start from scratch with anything scientific or chemical in pre-med. Mind you, they were one up with Greek or Latin terminology.

Next to maths, my weakest subject was Irish. I don't know why, because if I had any scholastic talent it was for languages. I would like to think that it was bad teaching, but it was probably due to my old affliction: if it did not come easy, I did not make the effort.

Our Irish teacher in Poetry (that is what they called the fifth form – Rhetoric in the sixth) was a 'native' speaker. That is, someone brought up in one of the remaining areas of Ireland where Irish – Gaelic – was the first language. Tagdh, or Thomas in English, was the little fellow's name. White-haired, kindly, good-humoured, the kind of teacher from whom I would never learn a thing. He was from Kerry, and because I, too, came from the province of Munster, he was expecting great things of me. After my first Irish essay, he handed it back with a saddened expression, and, turning to the class, said: '*Níl sé go ro-the*' – 'He's not too hot.'

Why do I remember *that*, when I have forgotten far more important events? Why do I remember that little flecks of foam gathered at the corner of Tagdh's mouth, when I have difficulty remembering what most of my teachers looked like? Mind you, some you would never forget – they were the stuff of night-mares: Father Murphy, who was given to fits every few minutes; the eyes rolling around his head, his tongue caught between his teeth while he rubbed his hands furiously together. I was so afraid of him that I got sick every morning for a year. Did my parents complain? Of course not. Teachers were always right, particularly if they were priests.

Limerick and Munster stood me in good stead on the rugby field, though. They assumed I would be in the Limerick tradition: tough, aggressive, born to the oval ball. They never really found out the truth. I had grown over the previous summer, and was built like a brick outhouse, so they confused strength and bulk with aggression and there I was, just sixteen, on the first-team squad of one of the two or three best school rugby teams in Ireland.

This, along with my supposed academic abilities, gave me an immediate standing with my peers and the lower orders (any-body under sixteen), so a transition that might have been difficult – country bumpkin to urban sophisticate – went smoothly. I quickly forgot James and Billy and made friends with Frank and Ken. As in Limerick, it was the good old half-man, half-bicycle routine, except that it was a bit further from Ballymun Avenue to Belvedere than it was from Elm Park to Crescent. Still, it was downhill one way. (No wonder that, to this day, my thighs are the envy of Arnold Schwarzenegger … )

## DISCOVERING ELVIS

So the bogman came to Dublin, and became a jackeen. My routine as a schoolboy in the Big Smoke was not all that different from my years in the City of the Broken Treaty. Same school hours, same study pattern, same subjects, slightly longer journey back and forth to school, slightly better bicycle.

The difference was after school, and weekends. I was no longer in and out of the houses of my old friends, and Subbuteo was a vague and slightly embarrassing memory. The closeness and camaraderie of a small town was lost to me – none of my new friends lived nearby. Indeed, in the two and a half years that I spent at Belvedere, I only remember being invited to one other boy's home, and that was for a weekend because he lived so far away from me – ten miles, at least.

I will never forget that weekend: his mother cooked grilled mushrooms and bacon for tea. I had never had a grilled mushroom before – they simply did not exist in my mother's culinary canon. I have never forgotten the taste, like my first Coca-Cola, or my granny's fresh-fried mackerel.

The lady with the grilled mushrooms was my friend Ken's mother. She and Rose became firm friends through their sons' friendship: they would meet in Bewley's Coffee House for tea (never coffee) and visit each other's homes. They never went out with their respective husbands as a foursome; it was a woman – no, a mother-thing. And they called each other 'Mrs Wogan' and 'Mrs Daly'. *Never, never* by their first names. Only young people and immediate family were called by their first names. And I am talking the 1950s here – not the 1850s.

When I started my dazzling career, clerking in the Royal Bank of Ireland for a fiver a week, a couple of years later, all of my colleagues had to be addressed as 'Miss' or 'Mister', even the bank porter. The manager was 'Sir', even though he did wear children's sandals and a suit that appeared to be made out of hopsacking. And you could only wear your rugby club blazer on a Saturday morning. Don't ask ...

Although deprived of the kind of companionship I had enjoyed as a simple country lad, as a dazzling urban sophisticate I do not remember missing it much. Alone, but never lonely, my early training as an only child must have stood me in good stead. Anyway, there was rugby, and the school play, and suddenly – pop music.

The rugby was two days a week training after school, and a match on the weekends, usually against some other Dublin or Leinster college team. I remember nothing of the domestic stuff, but then the main features of the Wogan game were pretty unremarkable: a little leaning on my opposite number in the scrum, and some desultory jumping in the line-out.

I have but a hazy recollection of trips to various boarding schools, their cold dormitories and their dreadful food. It made me appreciate home and mother – and left me with the firm resolution that no child of mine would ever go away to school – nor did they. And was I right? Who knows? The certainties of youth grow ever more worn at the edges with the advancing years, and the most important thing you learn is how little you know.

I do remember the rugby tours, though. Over the Irish Sea by the blessed mail-boat to play English public schools such as Marlborough and Beaumont. Then to Scotland and Edinburgh, to take on George Heriot's school. It involved spending a couple of nights in the house of your opposite number – and I got a boy whose father was an elder of the Scottish Kirk. I remember oatcakes, and what could have been haggis – why do all my memories seem to focus on food? – and my first alcoholic beverage: a glass of cider. What a scapegrace! A wild man, let loose on Princes Street. And it was on Princes Street, Edinburgh, that I saw it. In the window of a record shop – an Elvis Presley LP!

I had always liked music; my favourite movies were musicals and musical stars – Doris Day, Bing Crosby, *Seven Brides for Seven Brothers*, *Oklahoma!*, *Carousel*, all that stuff. The movie I have seen more than any other is *High Society* – but then, what other movie could boast a cast-list of Crosby, Sinatra, Satchmo and Grace Kelly?

My first year in Dublin, we got hold of an old record player, and I bought my first record: 'Zambezi' by Lou Busch. I drifted into trad jazz, with Bunk Johnson and Bix Beiderbecke, while others went for Benny Goodman and Glenn Miller. There was no such thing as 'popular' music, a right old farrago of Kay Starr, Guy Mitchell, Rosemary Clooney and lots of British clones who sounded quite like them, but never quite as good. 'Popular' music was not aimed at 'yoof' – there was no such thing. Nobody had ever heard of 'teenagers', they were just an ugly American rumour. We were marking time …

Then it happened: out of a black-and-white movie drama called *The Blackboard Jungle* came an extraordinary sound-track by Bill Haley and the Comets: 'Rock Around the Clock'. Rock'n'roll! It swept through the youth of America, Europe and the rest of the world like a tornado, and nothing was ever the same again; 'popular' music was dead, youth was on its feet, and dancing in cinema aisles and on the streets outside, stopping the traffic and stunning the adults.

The flames were fanned by follow-up movies featuring Haley and his band, with close harmony groups such as the Platters and other rock'n'roll outfits. The beat went on – Dublin's dance halls elbowed the old band-leader with dinner-jackets, foxtrots and cha-chas – rock'n'roll was king and every night was 'jive' night!

I liked it. It was alive, it was electric, it got you moving. It spoke to the beast inside, in a way that Guy Mitchell with 'There's a Pawn Shop on the Corner in Pittsburgh, Pennsylvania' never could. Even Johnnie Ray, who regularly burst into tears with his impassioned rendition of 'Cry', failed to strike the responsive chord in the way that good old Bill Haley with his kiss-curl did.

And yet, and yet, it didn't quite hit the spot! By now I was listening to AFN, American Forces Network, for my radio inspiration. Irish radio was hopeless, with its mixture of classical, quasi-religious and 'diddly-eye' music. The BBC had never grasped popular music, and indeed, would not, until forced into it by the 'pirates' several years later. So, every afternoon, back from school, I would hop off my velocipede, into the lounge, and on with my buddies from Frankfurt, AFN.

Then, one afternoon, out of the clear blue ether, I heard him. I had never heard anything like it my life. It caused my heart to leap like nothing I have heard since: it was country, it was blues with a driving beat, but it was the singer that caused the small hairs to stand up on the back of the neck – such power, such raw sexuality! I could not believe it! And I didn't catch his name, which sounded strange. I couldn't wait to get to school next morning, but nobody else had heard this mind-blowing record, and I didn't know the singer's name!

It was not until I was walking down Princes Street, Edinburgh, two whole weeks later that the penny dropped: Elvis Presley. I think I must have been the first person in Ireland to hear of him. And he *really* hit the spot …

# FOUR

# OF SPORT AND STARS

So Poetry came and went, without much fuss. Nobody got beaten, we were too big and spotty; detention was the sole punishment which, compared to getting your fingers reduced to swollen numbness, was a piece of cake. I suppose the Jesuits reasoned that we were old enough to realize how important it was to apply ourselves to our studies. Wrong. Only some of us. The work/study ethic was much more developed in Belvedere than at Crescent, and it was new and foreign to me. I drifted through, making new friends, playing rugby, listening to AFN, rediscovering the singing voice I had left behind in the Limerick Church Choir, and taking a lead role in the school production of *The Gondoliers*.

Exams were a worry, but not enough to make me do anything drastic about them, like studying or revising. Good job I didn't smoke, they would have had me down for a waster ...

The wasters congregated in the back room of a newsagent's called Seymour's, a hundred yards down the road from the Belvedere gates. Instead of going home and diving into the books, or joining something worthwhile like the Camera Club, or partaking in manly sporting pursuits, here would convene the rakes of the school, the ne'er-do-wells.

The hard-man 'Harrys' were produced (Harry Wragg, a jockey, – fag – cig) and boldly lit; racing papers were considered; a hand of cards dealt; bad language freely used; the names of innocent women bandied about. And what could the Js do about it? Nothing. They were not foolish enough to inform the parents about their sons' depravity – that might lead to a mass exodus to boarding school. A blind eye was turned – and the more studious, respectable elements in the school were scandalized. An editorial, contributed by one of the swots in the yearly school magazine, bore the stinging headline: 'Smoke Signals In Great Denmark Street – Need We Seymour?' Good, but no cigar. The poker school soldiered on in a haze of blue smoke, and the hard men went on, to a man, to lives of utter respectability.

A couple of years ago, I went back to Dublin, to old Belvedere Rugby Club, to a reunion of the old class, forty years on. They were all there, the sporting giants, the smoking pygmies, the studious, the couldn't-care-less, the successful, the slightly-less-so. There was nobody there, of course, who was not success-ful to a greater or lesser degree. Still, it was a remarkable gather-ing of the nearly sixty-year-olds.

Greyer, balder, fatter, wrinkled, rubicund or wan, they had not changed. They were the same people I had left behind in a Belvedere classroom, forty years ago. The quiet ones still quiet, the show-offs still brash, the comedians still telling jokes, the chancers still making it up as they went along, the hard men slip-ping outside for a quick drag. A couple had sadly lost their wives through death, but there were only two separations and *no* divorces. Holy Catholic Ireland was keeping her grip. Even the class eejit was still an eejit in a green sports coat, exporting snails to France. All the same, no change.

Maybe if more of them had left Ireland? Well, many of them had, to Britain and the US. Can it be that we are fully formed at seventeen; that life with all its troughs and peaks, sadness, triumphs and failures, never really changes the person we have grown to be, by our late teens? Or did we all regress that night, and slough off the carapace of forty years on, to be young men again? Just a minute – who is that sentimental Old Geezer, meandering on to himself? Sorry ...

## DE VALERA'S IRELAND

The summer holidays stretched away to the horizon. No tennis, no table-football now, no friends' houses close by, no Granny Byrne's to go to for holidays. It was not the same just going for tea on a Sunday. Still, I was content with the radio and my books, but certain people felt that a young man of my age should not be sitting around, doing nothing. It encouraged the mind to wander, and, before you knew it, impure thoughts and occasions of sin ... Cricket, that's the ticket. Keep his brain clean with cricket.

Belvedere was the outstanding cricketing school, winning cups, producing rafts of international players, and even the occasional phenomenon who actually got a trial with an English county! All Dutch to me, although I had a passing interest in everything that involved a ball. I know of Hutton, Edrich and the great Compton. Later, much later, I was privileged to know the legendary Compo. He even played in a charity cricket match for me at Taplow – slower, more rotund, more florid than in his glory days, but still with the eye of a hawk, the reactions of a snake. I can still remember him, five yards from the wicket, plucking a savagely hit ball out of the air, as if he were catching a feather. Such class, such grace. As he was in sport, so he was in life.

But at Crescent, we had not played cricket. It was played in Limerick, of course. They would have played beach netball there, if they knew what it was and had the weather – or the beach. Cricket was a Proddy game. The YMCA played it, and a couple of Protestant schools. It was the garrison game to end them all. The Christian Brothers had never heard of cricket, and it certainly did not come into Éamon de Valera's scheme of things for a rural Ireland, peopled by healthy, shiny-faced young men and women who, when they were not saving hay, snagging turnips, cutting turf or hoeing potatoes, were playing hurling in the fields or dancing merrily at crossroads.

I kid you not, that was Dev's vision for Ireland in the latter half of the twentieth century. It nearly did for us. It would have done, for a lesser people. It held Ireland back for decades, just as Franco did in Spain, and Salazar in Portugal.

Did I tell you about the 'Protestant look'? Well, when we were young, we could tell a Protestant by looking at them. We did not have to know their names (that was too easy) or where they went to school (even easier). We could tell by their complexions. They were not like us, ruddy and coarse, they were pale-skinned, fine-featured. You could tell a Protestant a mile away, in Limerick. They did not have Limerick accents, either, which was a dead give-away. They went away to boarding schools, probably in the accursed Protestant state of Northern Ireland! I told Helen about this preposterous visual prejudice which we all shared as kids, and she said: 'Yes. I thought *you* were a Protestant when I met you first. You had the "look". And a funny name ...'

The trouble is, there are still people who think like that, and not just in the top right-hand corner of Ireland, either. The Republic likes to think itself free of religious prejudice, but Catholics have been so much in the majority there that conflict or confrontation was out of the question. Protestants, the Church of England, had to accept that the Catholic Church's role was enshrined in the Irish Constitution. So, no divorce, no birth control, no abortion, and days off on Catholic Church holidays. Still, no prejudice ...

A couple of years ago, while working on *Wogan's Ireland* for BBC TV, Paul Walters (a decent sort, although a producer) and I were in Northern Ireland, driving through Cookstown, Co. Antrim. A clean, busy, thriving little market town, there was a British Army foot-patrol coming cautiously, back-to-back, down the main street, guns at the ready. The people milled about among the soldiers, in and out of the shops, stopping to chat to each other; children played around the wary soldiers' boots.

We stopped the car, unable to take it in at first sight. Paul, English and proud of it, could not believe the sight of soldiers patrolling what he believed to be part of the United Kingdom. He had had the same trouble with the gun-towers at border crossing-points, and police stations armoured like medieval castles. *His* country, looking like East Germany before Gorbachev packed it all in.

As we drove on, after wordlessly watching everyday life freely intermingling with war, I said: 'Of course, Cookstown is a Protestant town.'

My English friend, who had worked with me too long to be all that confident of my sanity, looked at me as if I had finally lost it for good and all. 'A what town?'

'A Protestant town, full of Protestants.'

He was aghast. Growing up in rural Hertfordshire, in secular England, where religious bigotry has disappeared, along with church-going and Sunday School, Paul had never heard of people divided by religion into schools, enclaves and whole towns ...

I did not try to explain the 'Protestant look' to him. A friend of mine, the brilliant Northern Irish comedian, Adrian Walsh, says: 'People are always asking me what Northern Ireland is like. I always tell them: "It's like Beirut, only without the Christians."'

Unfortunately, cricket and I did not get on. Nothing to do with religious bigotry – I just came to the game too late. People who take up cricket at an early age obviously grow accustomed to others trying to take their heads off with a ball as hard as a rock, but, at fifteen, and with an already highly developed sense of self-preservation, I quickly realized that this particular ball game was not for me. Let the Prods play it. Or the 'Castle Catholics' from Belvedere.

I joined the school swimming team. We went to the Tara Street Baths, along with every other school in Dublin. The concept of municipal swimming baths was pretty foreign to Ireland, when I was growing up. Probably because de Valera had not mentioned it as a suitable pursuit for bright-eyed Irish youth.

But what could have been better, after an exhausting evening at the crossroads dancing, than a quick dip in the local county council pool? Probably never much of a swimmer himself, it never occurred to Dev. Anyway, weren't we an island? Weren't there rivers a-plenty? And all the rain?

I don't remember a pool in Limerick – we swam in the river at Corbally. Thirty thousand inhabitants, not one swimming pool. The only one I knew of in Dublin City was Tara Street Baths. There was always the Irish Sea, of course. In the summer only, naturally, and if you fancied freezing to death, or walking four miles out before the water got above your knees.

There was a swimming baths by the sea at Blackrock, and the famous 'forty-foot' at Sandycove, famed for its association with James Joyce and Buck Mulligan, but we were North-City boys, and south of the Liffey was another country.

Even as you entered the door of Tara Street Baths your eyes would smart with the chlorine fumes. After the swim it clung to you, like a feed of garlic. It put you off. It put everybody off. A surprising number of people in Ireland cannot swim. There they are, surrounded by water, incapable of swimming a stroke.

I blame de Valera and the Christian Brothers. But then they get the blame for everything. Why not the smell of Tara Street Baths?

The self-preservation motif, as mentioned above in relation to the dangerous game of cricket, has always been high on my agenda. I have never been on a motorbike in my life. I have never even been on a scooter. Skiing frightens me to death. For a couple of years, Helen and I would take a skiing lodge, with all mod cons, including chef, breakfast, afternoon tea and four-course dinner with wine, in Val d'Isère, Chamonix or Klosters, and bring along the three younger Wogans, all keen black-run artists.

After I had slid backwards into a café full of people at Val d'Isère, I decided to take up ski-walking – 'Langlauf'. This is much more becoming for one of advancing years – level ground and only the gentlest of slopes. Still, I take no chances. When faced with anything that even vaguely resembles a decline, I remove my walking skis, walk down, and slip them on again as soon as a decent amount of level ground is available.

I get no kick from risking life and limb. Who wants to fling themselves from a plane, with or without a parachute? Unless there is something vital missing in your life, why would you bungee-jump? It is not without its own significance that bungee-jumping was invented in New Zealand, a land of scenery, sheep and rugby. Suicide can never be far from the minds of most thinking New Zealanders – I suppose that bungee-jumping is the closest they can get …

## LISTENERS' THEORIES AND ANTICS

Speaking of New Zealand, as it brightly crosses our ken – unless you have been 'finding yourself' in the foothills of the Hindu Kush for the last ten years, it will not have escaped your bat-like ear that there has been a lot of high-sounding talk over the decade, of changes in weather patterns, greenhouse effects, melting of the polar ice-caps, holes in the ozone layer. All this is put down to environmental thuggery: the cutting down of trees in the Amazon rainforest, the fumes of millions of motor vehicles, the profligate use of hairspray and deodorants.

My loyal listener of a dewy morn on Radio 2, however, will have none of it. He, she or it, anorak buttoned to the chin, has a far more plausible theory: the hole in the ozone layer, with particular reference to the Southern Hemisphere, is all the fault of New Zealand sheep. Or, more particularly, the constant breaking of wind of Kiwi sheep. Wave after wave of methane gas, bombarding the stratosphere and beyond, day and night for years, is what has done the damage, according to my man in the cagoule.

Like many listeners' theories, I find it hard to dismiss. Sheep have no place in the lush grasslands of New Zealand, the rich diet does not suit them – they were designed for harder climes. When did you last hear of a sheep breaking wind in the Highlands of Scotland? The furry divils are not indigenous to the Land of the Morning Cloud any more than rabbits are in Australia, or in my back garden if it comes to that. Don't start me off on that tack …

While on the topic of listeners' theories, nobody has ever explained to our satisfaction why, if you are eager to see the world, it is not possible to simply hop into a balloon, go up a bit, say a couple of thousand feet to avoid the large outcrops and tall buildings, and hang about until the world comes around to you. Surely the thing is revolving beneath you, unless we have been cruelly misled? Get up there with a flask of soup and some sandwiches, wait for a day or two, and look! Here comes Hawaii! Drop down, enjoy the sunshine, surf and pineapples, up again, nice cup of tea and a biscuit, couple of hours of shut-eye, and, blow me down, there's Old Blighty coming up over the horizon! What a weekend!

Why can't it be done? We are convinced it is a conspiracy, it would put the travel companies and the airlines out of business. What would Carol Smillie and Judith Chalmers do for a crust? As usual, Richard Branson would be on the pig's back, having cornered the market in balloons. The BBC would be on to a nice little earner with that big red number that you bump into every time you turn on the television.

Before we abandon the balloon motif to a young lad's relentless rite of passage through the four green fields of Erin, one of my Old Geezers (don't look at *me* – it's what they call themselves, my listeners) felt that he should strike a blow for Grey Pride, and make an attempt on behalf of the Well-Stricken-In-Years to balloon around the world. Everybody else was at it, and some oaf had just claimed to have circumnavigated the globe by flying off from Switzerland and landing back in Egypt.

Well, *excuse me*. Had nobody noticed that a target had been missed – by more than a thousand miles? Willie Gofar, for thus did our Old Geezer sign himself, was determined to better this bungled effort – Peterborough to Peterborough, on the nose. In the interest of safety, he planned to keep one foot on the ground at all times.

On a dull Monday morning not too long ago, he set off into a light sou'westerly that barely ruffled the turf. Daily reports reached us of his progress. Disappointment set in early. Progress was slow. It was not the safety foot dragging along the ground that was holding things up. It was Willie's insistence on going home for his tea every evening. Come six o'clock, he would moor the balloon at a convenient lamp-post and set off again after breakfast the following morning. Doomed to failure, Willie abandoned his brave attempt a week later, having reached the outskirts of Kettering. Any further, he reasoned, and he would never have got a bus home in time for tea.

## GREAT FAVOURITES

Rhetoric, or the sixth form, as anybody other than the Js would call it, passed much in the same pleasant, unflurried way that Poetry did. The final state exam, the Leaving Certificate, on which all our hopes and dreams and futures depended, loomed on the horizon, and I could see others fretting about their prospects, particularly the bright boys, who were sure of coming through *summa cum laude* anyway.

Maybe I was too much of a *dummkopf* to realize the seriousness of the situation, but I strolled through the year as I had the previous one: rugby training during the week, big match on Saturday, trip to Edinburgh to play George Heriot's school, rehearsals and performances of *Iolanthe*, out with the Da for a spin in the car after dinner on Sundays, reading, radio.

Sixteen, coming close to my sexual peak as a male, and not a woman in sight. Now, it sounds ridiculous, but then, in Ireland, it was the norm. Belvedere was less enlightened in easing sexual tension than even Crescent. Dances with the nearest convent? Even if Dev himself had arranged a convenient crossroads at his own expense, I doubt if the boys in black would have acquiesced. The nearest convent was Eccles Street, from where James Joyce sent Leopold Bloom on his epic search for a kidney for his breakfast.

I am sure that the place was full to bursting with nubile young pieces of stuff, but in the truly awful Eccles Street uniform they looked like lumps of lard – or, as the Granny would have it, barrels of bread-soda ...

The pictures – there was still the pictures – still with the queues stretching round the block for the Savoy, the Adelphi (pronounced 'Adelphia' by every right-thinking Dubliner) the Metropole, the Capitol, the Royal, the Carlton (pronounced 'Carlington'). Incidentally, the Dublin Zoo has always been known as the 'Azoo' to the natives, and the natives themselves as 'gurriers'. 'Gurriers' or 'jackeens'. Everyone unfortunate enough to be born outside the city's purlieus is a 'culchie' or 'bogman'.

Sophisticated cosmopolitan that I was, or gurrier if you like, my tastes in movie stars had moved on: no longer Doris Day, although she still retained a cheery, bubbly hold on my affections, now it was Grace Kelly. Flawless beauty, cut-glass Boston accent, ravishing elegance, *To Catch a Thief*, *Rear Window* – remember that sequence where she makes her first entrance into James Stewart's darkened room (he's spying on the neighbours)? As she turns on each light, she says her character's name: 'Lisa – Carol – Freemont', each light throwing into relief her beautiful features ...

I interviewed Grace Kelly a year or so before her tragic death. In the good old days of the seventies, before they started fooling around with wavelengths, BBC Radio 2 was on the long wave, and could be heard all over Europe, just like the Light Programme before it. And Grace Kelly used to listen to me! Imagine it – the Palace of the Grimaldis in sunny Monaco, echoing to 'The Fight on Flab'!

I can't remember whether she was visiting Britain as Grace Kelly, or in her official capacity as Princess Grace of Monaco, but when I met her she was alone; not a prince, nor a courtier, nor even a press officer, in sight. One of the women's magazines had heard that she was a fan of mine, and she had agreed to give an interview.

I still cannot believe that she wanted to meet me. This was long before *Wogan* reared its head, or even my Saturday night talk-show, but, as far as I remember, it was the only interview Princess Grace gave. She greeted me at the door of her suite, and a couple of hours passed like a dream, which maybe is why I have only a hazy memory of an idol, middle-aged but still beautiful, with those delicate, patrician features, that elegance untouched by time, that crystal Boston accent, and a laugh that can only be described as 'silvery'.

Sorry, but 'silvery' is the *only* word. She was warm, charming and utterly lovely, everything that I just knew she would be. She talked freely, easily, without any inhibition, and, naturally, I cannot remember a word. All I have ever taken from interviews or conversations are impressions. After a couple of hours, we made our goodbyes, she promising to continue to hang on to my every word across the ether, and I, inwardly, swearing undying affection, and all too short a time later, she was dead ...

Grace Kelly co-starred in my all-time favourite film musical, *High Society*. It is the only film I have actually paid to see more than once. It is the stars that do it for me: never before, and never again, are you going to get Louis Armstrong, Frank Sinatra, Grace Kelly and Bing Crosby in the same movie. Nowadays, it would be like having Tom Cruise, Mel Gibson, Julia Roberts and Michael Jackson together on film. And who could afford that?

When younger, Bing Crosby with his deceptively easy singing style and his similar gift on the big screen, had been a great favourite of mine. I could never have dreamt of meeting him, as I queued for the one-and-nines, but I did. In the early seventies, he dropped in one morning on my radio show, and we chatted. He, too, was everything I knew he would be: full of *bonhomie* and good humour, relaxed and generous with his time.

As I recall (and, as you have noticed, my recollections can be a bit on the misty side), Bing was in London to record an album with Fred Astaire. The word had it that the recording was not going as swimmingly as it might: Astaire was a workaholic, meticulous in everything, as in his dancing: rehearse, refine, rehearse, let's do it one more time. Crosby's style was the antithesis of Astaire's: rely on your talent, do it on your toes, wing it, let's go, I've got a golf date …

## PRO-CELEBRITY GOLF

I am sure for Bing the session with Astaire was just a convenient hook on which to hang his golf bag, an excuse to play some of his favourite courses in Britain. He was certainly involved in some of the first 'Pro-Celebrity' golf matches screened by BBC 2. Later on, thanks to the good offices of my friend Peter Alliss, I spent many happy years with my family at Gleneagles and Turnberry playing in the series. The format was simple: nine holes, famous celebrity and famous professional golfer versus ditto, with Peter as the referee, commentator and interviewer. It took off from the first, getting good viewing figures for BBC 2, and a wide spectrum of viewers, not all of them golfers. It was dropped from the schedules some time in 1986/7, just as golf was really taking off as a popular sport. Go figure, as Bing might say …

I am not sure who the professional golfers were that year in Gleneagles, but Bing Crosby's star opponent was the great American screen actor George C. Scott, fresh from his success as Patton. Two nine-hole matches were played every day, one teeing off at 9 a.m. and the afternoon match at 2.30 p.m. Crosby and Scott were due to engage for the morning four ball. Belying his years, Crosby was on the tee early, eager and frisky and ready to bring the King's Course to its knees. A large crowd of spectators had turned up to cheer on the great men. The problem was that one of the great men was missing: George C. Scott.

There was no panic. George was not known for his time-keeping; indeed, it was suggested that he might be nursing a bit of a hangover, as he had been seen enjoying a post-prandial snifter or several the evening before. Runners were sent to his bedroom, the breakfast room and, finally, to the bar. There he was behind it – well, beneath it, dozing, surrounded by several bottles! He growled at all attempts to move him. All appeals to his finer nature, to his golfing soul, came to nought.

Bing Crosby was sent for. In he ambled, and bending over his erstwhile opponent, crooned: 'George … George!'

The hulking figure opened an eye. 'Yeah, Bing?'

'Whaddya want, George?'

'Two things, Bing …'

'Yes, George, and what can we get for you?'

'A piss, and a plane ticket outta here.'

George C. Scott left for Edinburgh airport within the hour. Peter Alliss recalls him hurling his golf clubs out of the limousine window, as it made its stately progress down the drive.

Another legend of the *Pro-Celebrity Golf* fairways was Leslie Nielsen. He of steel-grey hair, the poker-face, the bow-legs, star of *Airplane*, then the television cop-spoof series *Police Squad*, followed by three movie blockbusters, *Naked Gun 1, 2*, and *3*. Nielsen's act was grace under pressure, or, rather, deep stupidity masked by effortless aplomb.

However, at the time of his appearance on *Pro-Celebrity Golf* he was just one of those faces everybody knew from the movies, but could not put a name on. He played cops, robbers, cowboys, FBI men, in that same expressionless, tough guy way that served him so well later.

One afternoon, in the early seventies, he was sitting with a friend in the Bel-Air Country Club, sipping a light libation, greeting the occasional perspiring golfers as they came in after their rounds. Meanwhile, things had become pretty desperate back at the Pro-Celebs' office. They needed a Hollywood star. The Forsyths, Tarbucks and Wogans were a dime a dozen – they needed 'cred'. Bing was not available, Hope wouldn't do it, Lemmon was busy, Savalas had not even been invented.

Desperately the producer trolled the hang-outs of Hollywood's golfing celebrities and there, cool as you like, on the terrace of the Bel-Air Country Club, he found one. An introduction was effected, the invitation extended. How would Mr Nielsen and a partner of his choosing like to spend a week at the great Gleneagles Hotel in the very heart of the Highlands of Scotland, all expenses paid, with first-class travel from Los Angeles to Edinburgh? Mr Nielsen gave him the old stone-face: 'Why not?'

So, in the fullness of time, a cheery Leslie Nielsen found himself on the first tee at Gleneagles, having already spent a couple of nights at the hotel, enjoying the hospitality to the full and impressing all with his engaging, modest charm.

That morning, Leslie's professional partner was the tall, classically-swinging American, Tom Weiskopf. A manly hand-shake, and Leslie stepped up to the tee. He missed. Never mind, they whispered. Can happen to anybody. Nerves, you know. Even the best of them have nerves under the unforgiving camera's eye. Then he missed again. And again. He took thirty-two strokes for the first hole. After a while, they took the camera off him.

As he stepped up to his ball on the second tee, none of Nielsen's good humour had left him. He winked at Weiskopf, smiled winningly for the camera, and swung mightily. Hallelujah! The ball soared into the Scottish mist. Sighs of relief all around. Even Tom Weiskopf allowed the corners of his mouth to turn up just a tad.

Nielsen's second shot flew off at a right angle, narrowly missing his partner's head, straight into a bunker. Leslie's face lit up. 'Hey! Look at that!' he called to Weiskopf. 'Whaddo I do now?' Tom Weiskopf threw his clubs to the ground, and, without a word, strode from the course, straight to the bar. Shooting was over for the morning ...

It turned out that Leslie Nielsen had never picked up a golf club in his life. There he had been, minding his own business at the Bel-Air Country Club, and somebody had offered him a free trip to Scotland. Well, wouldn't you? For the remainder of the week, he and his partner enjoyed to the full all that Gleneagles had to offer, greeting all and sundry with that affability, that innocent open-faced simplicity that is so much a part of Leslie Nielsen. He was even seen on the putting green, laughing uproariously at his inability to even hit the ball. I think he was doing a lot of laughing on the inside as well.

The list of the great and the good that graced the green swards of Gleneagles and Turnberry was endless. From Sean Connery to Peter Cook, from Douglas Bader to Hurricane Higgins. And the golfers! How else could a poor, pathetic sixteen-handicapper like myself get to play with Gary Player, Lee Trevino, Johnny Miller, Seve Ballesteros, Greg Norman, Nick Faldo? Trevino seemed to play every year. He was good value – laughing and joking constantly with an endless stream of golfing stories, and as the golfers among you will know, an endless variety of brilliant, individual shots.

One afternoon, at Turnberry, he was my partner, and on the third tee, I duffed one off the heel of the club into the heather.

'Oh, blast it!' I cried. (I would have expressed it better – and a deal more strongly – but the cameras were rolling.) 'Lifted my bloody head!'

Trevino did not even look at me: 'Back home,' he said gently, 'Chi Chi Rodriguez gives exhibitions where he hits the ball with a bag over his head ...'

Lee Trevino was all talk and airy badinage on the course for the cameras and the crowd, but as soon as he was back in the hotel, it was straight to his suite, room service and television for the night. Off the course, he never socialized. Maybe something to do with the old pro golfer never entering the club-house – the player and the gentlemen thing. Or maybe he had had enough of eejits like me for the day.

I know it sounds excessively sycophantic, and even unlike me, but throughout the many years that I was privileged to play with the greatest golfers of the day, I never met one that was less than courteous, helpful, good-humoured and generous. It must be the game. Arnold Palmer and Gary Player helped me to celebrate my birthday with a glass of Champagne on a misty morning at Turnberry. Johnny Miller showed me what was wrong with my grip, and Greg Norman advised me to have my clubs put down. They did not hand out much advice on how the ball should be struck to the best advantage, reasoning quite properly that people like me, while theoretically playing the same game, in practice were in a separate dimension.

Never was this more clearly demonstrated than one sunny

day at Gleneagles. On the tee, T. Wogan and Greg Norman versus Gareth Edwards and Tom Watson. Gareth Edwards, the greatest rugby player of his generation – indeed, in the opinion of another peerless Welshman, Cliff Morgan, the greatest rugby player he has ever seen. Gareth, hero of Wales, the Barbarians and the British Lions. A man tried and triumphant in the cauldrons of Twickenham, Arms Park, Parc des Princes, Cape Town, Melbourne and Auckland.

As we stood on the tee, awaiting the cameras, under the eyes of the crowd and those of the two greatest golfers of the modern era, Gareth Edwards whispered, 'You know, I've no feelin' in my legs below the knees ...'

Unbelievably, Gareth Edwards was nervous! After a hole or two, seeing his partner's unease and lack of confidence, the kindly Tom Watson, even then several times an Open winner, took Gareth aside and showed him how to slow his take-back, and get a full turn. Sure enough, for the remainder of the round, Gareth Edwards could not hit his hat.

Peter Cook and I became friends through *Pro-Celebrity Golf*. We played together at Gleneagles, and later at Loch Lomond when Channel 4 revived the series briefly, with Tony Jacklin at the helm. Cook had played the game since a lad, and had a natural talent for it. It was, of course, overwhelmed by his other talents which, according to popular legend, he wasted prodigally. Maybe, but not to himself. Peter put his talent into his life.

As Alan Bennett said at Peter's memorial service: 'Peter Cook regretted nothing about his life. Except, perhaps, on one occasion in America, when he saved David Frost from drowning.'

Frost, an old friend of Cook's from Cambridge Footlights days, who was at the memorial service, took it, as he had taken Peter's jibes in life, in exactly the right spirit.

Bennett went on: 'Sir David Frost invited Peter to dinner one evening. "Next Wednesday, eight o'clock, all right?"

A pause at the other end of the phone. "Sorry, David, can't make it. I'm watching television that night!"'

Gleneagles is an imposing place, with its share of imposing people, or at least people pretty impressed with themselves. As Cliff Michelmore sat down to dine, he turned to the next table, which happened to be four Boston Brahmins, and courteously asked: 'Do you mind if I remove my jacket?'

'Yes, we do,' they said, not being used to such excesses of behaviour in Boston, Massachusetts.

Michelmore was surprised, but not fazed: 'Too bad,' he remarked drily, and took it off anyway.

What these fastidious people made of Peter Cook happily bears thinking about. He arrived with a young lady of dusky aspect, whom he claimed to have met in Hong Kong. She was a striking girl, in every way. Dressed in purple suede with matching boots and pussy pelmet, she danced the night away – usually on the dining room table. She went through the snobs' sensibilities like a knife through butter, while the rest of us looked on in awe and admiration – except Peter, who looked on benignly as if it were the most natural thing in the world.

I am not sure if this wonderful girl from Hong Kong had brought a change of clothes with her because she turned up to play tennis one morning in the purple outfit, complete with high-heeled boots. I, fool that I was, had been expecting Cook. 'Peter's not able to make it,' she said, 'so he asked me to play with you instead.' It was an interesting hour on the courts, but I could not rid myself of the uneasy feeling that I was being watched from behind bedroom curtains, by a certain sniggering person.

James Hunt was another regular participant in the golfing proceedings. Invariably dressed in jeans (which the committee kindly ignored), sneakers and odd socks, he was accompanied – not by some big Teuton with a crook, but by a huge German Shepherd dog. A very well-trained dog, it would lie down with its nose behind the tee-box, watching unblinkingly as its master and his partner teed off. It was all right for James, but the rest of us, already intimidated by the cameras, crowds and legendary golfers, found that two baleful eyes staring up at you from ground level did not exactly help to put the jangling nerve-ends to rest.

The evening before Peter Cook was due to play James Hunt, he promised us that he would bring along *his* pet the following morning. Why should Hunt be the only one with a pet following him around? And, anyway, said Cook, his pet would be company for James's dog. The following morning, Peter Cook turned up at the first tee with his pet, a goldfish in a bowl. At every tee, he would place it carefully just beside the dog's nose.

Ah, memories, memories. Of Hurricane Higgins in a bunker at Turnberry, advising Greg Norman that if he gave him one more piece of advice, Higgins would knock his block off. David Soul (Starsky – or was it Hutch?), reduced to tearing the first grouse of the season apart with his bare hands. The American golfer, Jerry Pate, a self-confessed connoisseur of fine wines, knocking back the Margaux and Lafite like it was water. Jack Lemmon, all good nature and urbanity, and never really with us.

Then there was the night Peter Alliss, myself and our respectable wives rose from the dining table at Turnberry, replete. Peter immediately fell over in a kind of faint. Frightening, particularly if you were the producer, with an eye to the following day's shoot. Peter recovered immediately, but unfortunately nobody would let him get up.

'Lie there! Don't let him move! Somebody get a doctor!'

There was not a medic in sight. Then Charlie Jack, a regular feature at the *Pro-Celeb* – he provided the shirts and pullovers that we were all supposed to wear – had a brainwave: 'Get Sean!' he commanded.

Sean Connery was dragged in from the bar. He looked bemused.

'Peter's not well, Sean! What shall we do?' shouted Charlie.

'Make him lie down and get a doctor,' said Sean Connery, exiting once more for the bar.

How many times must Sean, a simple actor, have been confused with James Bond? How often has he been called upon in a crisis for a Bond-type miracle? Mind you, he does look very *like* James Bond.

Peter Alliss got up and carried on, and I have never seen him fall over since, with or without a couple of glasses bubbling behind his back teeth. I have heard him with a bad chest; all the fault of the grey parrot that his wife, Jackie, bought him one Christmas. Peter caught psittacosis off the feathered friend. Alliss claims there had been no kissing, but I have my doubts …

The Allisses and Wogans have been firm friends for more than twenty years. We have seen each other's families grow up, shared anniversaries, birthdays, barbecues and the bubbly. In a moment of weakness, they even allowed me the honour of becoming a godfather to their youngest, Henry. Henry was named for Peter Alliss's co-commentator in his early days of televised golf, Henry Longhurst.

Longhurst was not only Peter's mentor, he was his idol. From the great Henry, Peter learned not to fill every spare moment on the air with sound; to let the camera speak for itself; to catch the magic moment just before the viewer; to explain but never over-elaborate; to use wit, but be sparing with it. All this and more, Peter Alliss will readily acknowledge that he learned from Henry Longhurst, but, in my opinion at least, he has long since surpassed the old master, bringing his own extra dimensions of observational humour and quirky comment to enliven our viewing of the great game.

Peter Alliss is undoubtedly the premier golf commentator on television, a fact acknowledged even by the Americans, who notoriously think that nobody but themselves can do anything. And not just on television … Peter is now as famed a golf commentator in the States as he is on his home turf, his calm English wit an antidote to the crudity of Gary McCord, the self-importance of Johnny Miller.

It is as well that American television discovered Alliss's talents, just about the time BBC Television was giving up its golf coverage. I say 'giving up' because I am convinced it was not just a matter of being outbid for tournament coverage by Sky Sports TV; the will was not there. Funds had been earmarked for greater things: twenty-four hour news – BBC Choice – carpets for middle-management offices … So went the way of most BBC Television Sport.

*Saturday Grandstand* is now a joke; car-rallying and bowls – with curling to add some spice during the long winter months. The BBC still clings to the jewels in the Grand National, the Open Golf, Wimbledon, the FA Cup Final, Royal Ascot, but for how long? Much of cricket, including radio coverage, has been lost; the Cup Final is shared, the Derby gone. Sky dominates league football, and rugby league. Athletics remains the BBC's domain, probably because nobody gives a hoot until the Olympic Games come around every four years. Even then, only the major track events attract any kind audience. As we have seen, golf has virtually disappeared off the BBC Sports map. It is a shame that terrestrial television viewers only hear the wonderful Alliss and the excellent Alex 'Booshes' Hey, a scant few times a year.

As I write this, the Director-General, Greg Dyke, promises to bend every nerve and sinew to claw back the lost sports ground. I doubt if it can be his first priority, particularly if he is attempting to put his own stamp on the BBC, and dismantle some of the intricacies of the Birt apparatus. He will find the apparatchiks well strapped in to their procedural corsets. It will take some time to loosen the stays ...

# FIVE

# THE MANAGER, THE PORTER AND THE UPSTAIRS CHOP

Unsurprisingly, in view of my failure to appreciate the seriousness of the situation, my results in the final exam, the Leaving Certificate, were mediocre. My parents, as ever, were uncritical, and let me off to Kilkee again to join Billy, my friend from Limerick, and his family, in their cosy rented cottage overlooking the lovely crescent beach. The advantage of such a situation being, as I have said before, that the bather was spared the indignity, nay, illegality of displaying anything untoward, by changing cossies on the beach itself.

It was not all swimming and rackets against the sea-wall this time, though. There were girls. I am not sure, but I think I kissed one. Billy, always more advanced in these matters, claimed to have gone further, even to the forbidden reaches of bra and knickers. I humoured him in his fantasy ... Then, suddenly, mysteriously, I fell ill, very ill. Billy's lovely Australian mother, who had been a nurse, called my parents. Down they came on the long journey from Dublin and back I went with them. I left Kilkee feet first, and, as I mentioned before, I have never been back there since.

It was diagnosed as viral pneumonia, and I was rushed to bed in the Mater Hospital, Dublin. I shared a ward with three other grown-up Dublin men; ulcers had laid them low, and, as soon as the worst of my coughing and spluttering had died down, I found them typical of their ilk: decent, honest, hard-working, good-humoured family men. Milk and white fish boiled to nothingness was their diet, a sovereign treatment for the auld ulcer. Except that, despite having been in there for three weeks, there seemed to be no improvement in their condition.

One day, two of them simply got up off their beds, packed their bags, left the milk-and-fish diet and went back to work, ulcers and all. Just as well; they probably felt better immediately! Only in later years did I learn that milk and boiled-to-buggery white fish was a diet designed to worsen any ulcer worthy of the name. The good holy nuns of the Mater Hospital did not know any better at the time, but they must have been up to speed on viral pneumonia, because I was back in my own little trundle bed at home within two weeks.

## JOB OFFER

Weakened and aimless, the weeks of summer passed me by without any thought of a decision on what I was going to do with the rest of my life. Was it to be university? Medicine? Accountancy? I didn't know. I didn't want to think about it. Who does, when they are barely seventeen? It is all too much, too soon. After a lifetime of having every decision made for you, suddenly you are being asked to make probably the most momentous decision of your life.

Remembering my own suffering at the hands of my elders, I make it a practice never to ask any young person what they are going to do with their lives. I have never asked my children. They simply do not know the answer. If they are like me, they never will. So, without any decision, the time for university entry came and went, as it did for applicants for the professions, or even a job.

What were we to do with the useless little fellow? The Js had the answer: send the eejit back here to us – at least he won't be under your feet. So, back I went to Belvedere College, Great Denmark Street, Dublin, to become a philosopher.

The course was designed for young limbs exactly like me – a bit too young and immature for the outside world, it gave us a chance to retake some subjects for the Leaving Certificate, and at the same time to grow to maturity by dint of careful study of Logic, Ethics, Theology, Theosophy and all the spokes of the great wheel of Philosophy.

Father Schrenk, the gentle German Jesuit who attempted to get us to reach conclusions by reason alone, laid it out on the very first day: 'Boys, after you have read Philosophy, you will never think the same way again.' I have never forgotten his words – because he was right. The gentle one hour a day in

Father Schrenk's company was thought-provoking, stimulating. The rest was a complete waste of time.

As far as I was concerned, I was not repeating any exams. Exams and I were *finito*, a thing of the past – we had never got on all that well anyway. I just did not want to study any more, university seemed a waste of my parents' hard-earned cash. They had spent enough on me. My two fellow-philosophers (we were a small but doughty band) were at least trying – they needed better marks to get into medical school and engineering.

I must have been a terrible distraction to them. All I wanted to do was stroll up and down O'Connell Street and look at the girls, until it was time for rugby practice. I was still young enough to turn out for the Senior XV – a rugged old campaigner of seventeen – and the manly baritone was again called up in the service of Gilbert and Sullivan. Christmas came and went, with Auntie Nellie's turkey once again winning all hearts.

Dear, sweet-natured Auntie Kitty, the second youngest of the Byrne sisters, got knocked down by a car on the Drumcondra Road, was hospitalized for some months, and never really recovered from the shock. She took to her bed, and rarely rose from it. Helen's enduring memory of Auntie Kitty is her perfectly manicured and painted nails peeping over her coverlet. She became increasingly frail, and died in her sixties, but not before my darling Auntie May, who went quickly, the victim of an inveterate smoking habit. Even as I write, I think of how much I owe to her. She gave me the gift of words.

At the time of which I write, Great-Aunt Mag had passed on, but little Muds Byrne battled on, becoming increasingly deaf, which necessitated turning up the hearing aid, which in turn would emit a piercing whistle. 'Muds! Turn that down!' She would nod, smile her beatific smile and get on with her knitting.

Auntie Dinah had long since married Uncle Eddie (another marriage made in Leverette & Frye) and they had two sons. Auntie Nellie, the eldest and, according to herself, the most long-suffering of the sisters, continued to dominate the curtain department of Clery's of O'Connell Street.

Then, out of the blue, came the offer of a job. The Royal Bank of Ireland was looking for clean-living, well-brought-up, middle-class young men who could add up. The Jesuits informed my parents, and in their understanding way, they asked me.

Why not? I had never thought that I would end up working in a bank, but there was nothing else happening in my life. By now, I thought I would like to write for a living, become a journalist. I didn't share this ambition with anybody, of course, and hadn't the smallest idea of how to go about becoming a journalist, so, as always, I took the line of least resistance.

I went for an interview, did a written exam, and a couple of weeks later, was invited to join the bank's training course. Why not? Might as well. And my parents were delighted. All they had hoped for: good, solid, respectable job, permanent and pensionable. Their son was set for life. Much to the disgust of the coach, I walked out on the Senior Rugby XV, leaving a gap in the front row, and, with much greater regret, bade my farewell to my fellow-philosophers and to Philosophy. Along with English Literature, it was perhaps the only school subject I ever really enjoyed.

Long since swallowed up by the much bigger Munster and Leinster Bank and then renamed Allied Irish, the Royal Bank was Ireland's smallest. It had a few branches in the north-western corner of the country, Sligo and Donegal, a few more down the east coast – none outside the Pale – and most of its branches were in Dublin. Which was one of my main reasons for joining up. It didn't matter much to me what I did, but I was not going down the bog to do it. With the Royal, there was a chance that I would end up on a deserted beach in Donegal, but the odds were in favour of a Dublin branch.

We assembled, humble trainees, at the Anglesey Bridge branch, just down the road from my granny's. About twenty of us, mostly Protestants, but then, the Royal was a Protestant bank. Every year, a few Catholics slipped in under the razor wire, for the look of the thing. More and more every year, as Protestants diminished in numbers and Catholics proliferated. Not that anybody ever mentioned religious differences in the Royal Bank of Ireland – nor indeed did it make the slightest difference to anything or anybody in all the four years of my banking career.

All we trainees got on like a house on fire. Why wouldn't we?

Out of school, into a job of guaranteed security and respectability. Even for the well-educated, jobs were thin on the ground in the Ireland of the fifties. Barely a Republic, seeking its place in the world, trying to shake off de Valera's stultifying rural idyll, Ireland was poor. Little or no industrial base and only the safety-valve of emigration to release the pressure on the economy. People were still leaving the country in droves, for America, but mainly for Britain. Only the money being sent home kept the little farms and townships on their feet.

All of which mattered not a jot to the smug new boys in the bank. Every day, smartly at ten, we would assemble, to learn, as best we could, the mysteries of the long book, the typing up and sealing of used banknotes, the adding up of long columns of figures, and, most difficult of all, the counting of notes with the left hand. And it *had* to be the left hand, according to our teacher, a man with a pair of eyes like two boiled eggs.

What gave me heart was the newly acquired knowledge that banks opened at 10 a.m., closed at 12.30, opened again at 1.30, and closed at 3 p.m. And only opened from 10 a.m. to 12.30 on a Saturday! This was not a job, at least, not the kind of job my father worked at. This was a doddle! Throughout my brilliant, brief banking career, I never quite came to terms with how little we worked. The four weeks of preparation for life on the other side of the bank counter came all to quickly to a close, with the dreaded announcement of which branches of the Royal were lucky enough to acquire one of us as a new junior.

As always, being a W, I was last. The chips fell. Most of them around the city, or at least within the Pale, so you had a good chance of seeing home and mother on the weekend. One of the guys (an international-standard hockey player) even got a posting to Head Office! Ernie, a particular friend of mine, got Sligo. I watched him as the colour drained from his face. Old boiled-egg eyes looked up from the list, and smiled as he read Ernie's death notice. 'An envious billet!' he exclaimed. I'm sure he meant 'enviable', but envy in any shape or form was not how any of us were feeling about Ernie.

Now, before anybody, particularly on my wife's side of the family, starts having a go, I know Helen's mother came from

Sligo, W.B. Yeats, and all that stuff … It's a fine town, Sligo, and a credit to itself. It's just that to a Dublin teenager it might as well have been the Gulag. Finally, the hammer came down: 'Wogan – Cornmarket'. Somebody must have been storming Heaven for me. *Cornmarket.* Up in the Liberties, bottom of Thomas Street, near Guinness's brewery and two cathedrals, Christ Church and Dean Swift's St Patrick's. The oldest part of Dublin and fifteen minutes from home by car, if you had one.

I took the bus to Dame Street, and walked up the hill past Dublin Castle. I took the old bike a couple of times as well, and got there in no time, but I could sense the disapproval, even from the bank porter. It was scarcely fitting for a member of staff to be leaving his bicycle tethered to a lamp-post outside the very portals of the bank.

I quickly learned that the manager was an Old Belvederian himself – proving once again the efficacy of the old boy network. The rest of the staff were uniformly decent, courteous and typical. The accountant or sub-manager: about the same age as the manager himself, but never going to get a branch of his own. The cashier: about ten years younger, and in line for his first managership, probably in the wilds of Donegal. Two tellers: like the cashier, the men behind the wire, taking in the cash and handing it out. Two pairs of eyes on the cashier's job during the week, rugby playing, drinking and chasing women all weekend. Senior junior: couple of years in the job, a dab hand at typing up the lodgement dockets, good-natured and worried sick that the arrival of a new junior spells curtains – or Enniscrone. Manager's secretary: unmarried, with few prospects. Secretly in love with the manager. Happy to die in his service. The girls in the machine room: keeping the accounts and the endless conversation going. The elder usually thwarted in love, with no high opinion of men, particularly those she had to work with. The younger, attractive, slightly flirty, with no other interest except men. Not that she would touch anyone in this branch with a barge-pole …

Since I could not bring my bike, and the bus journey took too long, I strolled down the hill to Foster Place, Head Office of the Royal Bank of Ireland, and lunched in the canteen there. It was a little daunting at first, since I didn't know anybody, but people were friendly and the place was heaving with women. Everywhere you looked, secretaries and machinists. The food was no great shakes, relying to a great extent on beans and nourishing stews, but the view made for a pleasant half hour or so, before heading back up the hill to the Cornmarket branch.

Work? I can't remember doing anything that resembled it. Meanwhile, I joined the Old Belvedere Rugby Club, trained in a desultory manner once a week, and played on the weekend for the 3rd XV.

The main thrust of my life *was* the weekend, and hops. Saturday night, every tennis and rugby club worthy of the name, employed a three-piece band and had a hop. Only a few had a Sunday hop, but I went to them as well, and let Monday morning go hang.

The ritual proceeded thus: Saturday afternoon, rugby match. If playing away, a couple of pints at your opponents' club-house bar, and then back to the Old Belvedere club-house for a serious session. About nine o'clock, off to some gastronomic sewer for some ballast, and then, hit the hop. The girls had been there since eight o'clock, chatting, weighing each other up, sipping on the soft drinks which were the only kind of liquid refreshment available. Not that the boys needed any more alcohol by the time *they* arrived. Without exception, it was lapping up against the back of their teeth.

It is to the eternal credit of Irishwomen everywhere that they tolerated being pushed around a dance-floor every Saturday and Sunday by some gobdaw who smelt like a brewery, couldn't put a foot under him, and was virtually speechless with drink. Dutch courage, of course. Sober, we would have been even more speechless. So, you asked a nice-looking girl to dance. If you got on okay, the next move was hers. Up came the Ladies' Choice. Will she? Nah. She asks her best friend's brother, or the boy next door, or somebody she has known all her life. Did you really think she was going to stick her neck out, in front of all her friends, for a total stranger?

Past eleven now, how are we going to get home? Anybody got a car? Anybody know anybody with a car? I knew somebody – Frank. Good old reliable Frank. Any chance of a lift? Decent fellow. Now, not only had you avoided a five-mile walk home, but you had a weapon. Ask her to dance again. How are you getting home? Would you like a lift? Yippee! Then, down comes the guillotine: 'Can my friend come with me? I can't have her go home alone ...' Oh, no! Not the 'friend'! She'll sit there, in the back of Frank's car, on the other side of the new-found love of my life, with a face like thunder, sending out vibrations of disapproval that make even holding hands impossible. 'Goodnight – thanks for the lift.' The friend never utters. Why was there always a 'friend'? And why did she never have a boyfriend of her own? She ruined my life ...

## UNMITIGATED JOY

I must have been all of six months infesting the Cornmarket branch, when news came through of the transfer. The senior junior breathed again, it was me, heading for pastures new: the Phibsborough branch. What a break! Ten minutes by bus from home. Back to Mammy for lunch every day. Save a few quid on meals as well. At that time, I was earning £5 a week, and giving my mother £2.10 shillings (the old money, you know). Even now, I can't believe that I lived a life of drinking, dancing, the pictures and coffee at the Rainbow Café, all on two and a half quid a week.

There was a hint of caution, however. The manager of Phibsborough had the reputation of being a martinet, a man who brooked no eejits. One of the tellers looked down his nose at me and said: 'Phibsborough? You'll *work* there, my boy!' He could talk to me like that because he was a teller, and, to my eyes, pretty well stricken in years – twenty-six or twenty-seven at least.

I bade my farewells to the ancient Liberties and headed towards home; the north side, Phibsborough, the Cattle Market branch. For Phibsborough branch was on the corner of the road down which thousands of cattle were driven every week, from the market to Dublin Docks. I know it sounds Hardyesque, but they were still driving cattle by foot and hand through the centre of Dublin in the late fifties and early sixties. After a few minutes in the bank there, especially on market day, you quickly knew all

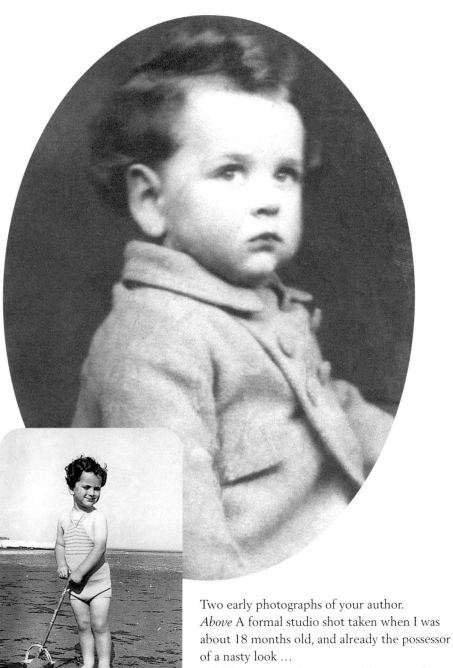

Two early photographs of your author.
*Above* A formal studio shot taken when I was
about 18 months old, and already the possessor
of a nasty look …
*Left* This is me at three years old. It was taken
at Sandymount Strand, a beach on Dublin Bay,
where you could walk halfway to the Isle of
Man before the water came up to your knees.

*Far left* Shopping with my mother, Rose, in Limerick in the early 1940s.

*Left* My maternal grandfather, Frank Byrne. I remember that moustache. As you can see, he left me his legs.

*Below left* Rugby was the game at Crescent College, Limerick. This is me (standing, far right) in the school team.

*Right* Performing in Gilbert and Sullivan's *The Gondoliers* when I was at Belvedere College.

*Below* Another photo with my mother, this time taken in Dublin when I was about 17.

*Left* Helen, Mrs Wogan. This beautiful shot was taken shortly after Mark was born. Helen thought she'd go back to photographic modelling. Luckily for us, after a few weeks she decided she'd rather give her life to her family.

*Below* The family wedding line-up. Posing with my parents, Michael and Rose, and Helen's mother and father, Ellie and Tim.

*Right* With Helen and our children, Alan, Mark and Katherine. This was taken in the mid-70s, shortly after we moved to Taplow.

*Top* The now famous birthday shot of Radio 1 talent taken in 1967. That's Robin Scott, the first Controller, at the back, and if you look closely you'll see all the usual suspects in their better days. As a direct result of this photo I had to resign from the staff of RTÉ, so you could say it's a lucky talisman.

*Above* Early days: this was taken during my Radio 1 show in 1969. Turntables, records … ah, memories …

*Right* Getting to be an old hand – a publicity portrait from 1976.

*Above* The long-running BBC television programme, *Come Dancing*. This was taken in 1977. I was the presenter for almost seven years without anybody noticing, apart from the then critic Clive James who compared me to an automaton. Then he made the mistake of becoming a presenter himself …

*Left* On course for *Pro-Celebrity Golf.* The caddy's name was Jimmy and, as you can see, I could never get a cap to fit me. This snap was taken on the very day I sunk the longest putt ever seen on television, 33 yards, on the 18th green at Gleneagles.

about it. It was pungent, redolent of all that was best in Irish farmyard life.

After a couple of days, I wondered if I would not have been better off down the bog somewhere. It certainly could not have smelled any worse. The cattlemen were bad enough, but it was the Pig Man that inspired real fear. You could smell him coming down the street, and cashier and tellers took evasive action. The cashier, being senior on the desk, found pressing business in the safe. The rest of us simply ducked under the counter. Every week, the Pig Man, smelling like the wrath of God, would enter a deserted bank – deserted that is except for the flies that followed him everywhere. A quick peep over the counter, and there he would be – bemused, alone.

Eventually, struck by the unnatural silence, the manager would come out of his office to see what was up. 'Service!' he would rasp. (Rasp? It was just the way he spoke, and why everybody thought he was a martinet.) An unfortunate teller would have to pretend that he had been searching for something on the floor behind the counter, and take the Pig Man's lodgement. The banknotes smelled as bad as the man himself. It was the toughest work I ever saw anybody do in a bank.

I had been apprehensive of Phibsborough, because of the manager's reputation, but the four years I spent there were an unmitigated joy. The atmosphere of the place resembled nothing so much as the Roseland Ballroom, Templemore, on a Saturday night. It was probably just a lucky conjunction of a few like-minded young men and women thrown together by fate into a small space, but it made life and a boring job, fun.

One of the onerous tasks of the teller, during the occasional *longueur* between customers, was to separate soiled or torn banknotes from the clean ones. Don't ask me how it started, but it became a jolly jape to rush into a teller's box when his back was turned, grab a handful of carefully separated new notes, and tear them into little pieces. Then would come the flinging of the sponges. The damp sponge was the cashier and teller's strong right arm, an absolute necessity in facilitating the arcane art of counting notes with the left hand. There you would be, chatting urbanely with some attractive shop-girl or secretary who had been sent to make her company's lodgement for the day, and a wet sponge would come whistling across the counter and hit you straight between the eyes.

It was not easy keeping your dignity, particularly in the face of hysteria from the young lady. Then would the sponges fly in all directions, the carnage ceasing only with a rasping cry of 'Quiet!' from the manager's office. The accountant, or sub-manager, ignored it all, bent Cratchit-like over the ledger, unless he was hit by a wayward sponge, in which case he would look up over his half-moon glasses and gently admonish: 'Ah, lads – lads!' Chaos would slowly subside, and the bank would become safe for customers again. Never for the staff, though. Another ingenious way to pass the idle hour was to sneak into the teller's box while he was dealing with a (preferably female) customer, and shove the bank broom handle up his backside! Rough, manly fun.

The Royal Bank of Ireland, Phibsborough, was no place for the sissy, nor the faint-hearted. You had to be there by 9.30 in the morning – any later, and you were under the red line, drawn censoriously by the cashier. The theory was that if you came under the line more than once a week, you were in for a pretty stern talking-to from the sub-manager. McBrian, one of the tellers, was always late. Every so often, the sub-manager would remonstrate: 'Aah, Tom – do you think you could get in at least one morning before quarter to ten?'

Those of us in at the appointed hour would gather round a copy of the day's *Irish Times* (a Protestant newspaper – I had never seen one in Limerick) or discuss the latest books or plays. We had rarely read the book or seen the play, but we were review readers, and many a heated discussion on whether Lampedusa was a little off-form with *The Leopard*, or what Pinter was really after with *The Birthday Party*, was broken up by a familiar rasping shout from the direction of the manager's office: 'Is anybody going to open the bank today?'

The porter would fling wide the portals, and in they would come – the Italian fish-and-chips man from across the road, the pub owner from next door, the cattle-jobber, the farmer, the chancer and the relics of auld decency from the once fine houses up the road.

The porter was a small, bandy-legged Scotsman with a German name. His job was to open and close the bank, so he was always first in, and last out. He fetched and carried, tidied and cleaned, and upstairs, in the tiny kitchen, he cooked the manager's lunch. It wasn't part of his job description, nor was going out in the middle of the morning to buy a chop and vegetables. He always kicked the manager's chop around the floor before he cooked it.

As he worked, the porter made strange, musical noises. He did trumpet impersonations, and clarinet, as well as trombone and bassoon. He covered most of the brass section, and much of the woodwind. It was not always a treat to hear 'The Dark Town Strutters' Ball' come ringing from above, as you were trying to add up a long column of figures, and the manager certainly found it a distraction. As the notes rang out, giving any musically inclined passer-by the definite impression that Louis Armstrong was working at the Royal Bank, Phibsborough, the manager would come out from his office, and look plaintively at the ceiling. He never said anything. Who else was going to do him a chop and green peas for lunch?

The porter had a dream: 'Imagine it!' he would say. 'A great theatre, the audience sitting there, the curtains drawn. Then, the sound of a great orchestra: trumpets, trombones, clarinets, French horns, drums, even violins! They would finish, to huge applause, and then, up would go the curtain, and it would just be people on the stage – not an instrument in sight! A whole orchestra of impersonators!'

I never asked him where he thought he was going to recruit all these musical impersonators, or how interest would be sustained after the initial *coup de théâtre*. He was obsessed by the idea, and not shy about bursting into a solo in the middle of the street or on top of a bus.

I suffered a great deal, because a couple of times a week, a taxing duty was required of the Royal Phibsborough's junior. This involved the meticulous wrapping and sealing of £5000 worth of old soiled notes, placing them in a holdall, and transporting them – in the company of our impressionistic porter – to Head Office, Note Department. There, they were exchanged for

£5000 worth of crisp oners, fivers or tenners (the £20 note was rarer than hen's teeth in those days), these to be, in turn, transported back to Phibsborough's branch for the use of eager cashiers and tellers.

Five thousand quid was not an amount to be laughed at in the late fifties; indeed, it would not raise much of a snigger nowadays. Then, it was the equivalent of about £75,000 in today's money. And how did we carry this lump of money, enough to feed twenty-five starving Irish families for a year? On a high-speed motorbike? Under police protection? Armoured car? Trusted taxi, even? No. Myself and the porter walked around the corner and waited at the bus stop for a number 19 to come along. We never changed our routine, and it stuck out a mile what we were carrying in the big black bag.

We had a plan, though, devised by the porter. If accosted with menaces by some toe-rag or gang of corner-boys, we knew exactly what to do. We would hand over the bag and run like hell. We were not being paid to sacrifice our young lives for the benefit of the bank, was how the porter put it, and it was hard to see a flaw in his argument ...

Upstairs, in the back seat of the bus, the porter would pay the fare, which, with due ceremony, the manager had given him out of petty cash. So, we travelled along, down the Phibsborough Road, along Dorset Street, then down North Great George's Street to the Parnell Monument, and the broad boulevard of O'Connell Street, over the bridge into D'Olier Street, past the Ballant Office Clock that Joyce called an epiphany, around by Trinity College (where you had to be a Protestant to attend, or get a special dispensation from the Archbishop, if you were a Catholic) and then the great pillars of the Bank of Ireland, once the Irish House of Parliament in the great days when Dublin was the second city of the Empire.

All the while, in a journey that took about fifteen minutes, the porter would regale me, and whoever was unfortunate enough to come upstairs on the bus, with his musical impressions. Trumpet and banjo figured large in these recitals, and, for all I know, bassoon, flute and euphonium. I never truly drank in the glories of these porterly impressions, being too suffused in embarrassment, and the justified suspicion that kicking up a racket was not the best way to maintain a low profile.

Mind you, the people of Dublin were well used to bizarre behaviour on the buses. For years they were infested by a madman simply known as 'Bang-Bang'. He would stand on the bus platform, with a comb in his hand, and then, pointing the comb like a revolver at some innocent pedestrian or messenger-boy, shout 'Bang! Bang!' in a voice to wake the dead.

Heaven knows how many unfortunate passers-by he reduced to heartburn, the vapours or the shakes over the many years that he terrorized the pavements of O'Connell Street, but nobody ever objected or chastised him. No bus conductor ever refused 'Bang-Bang' a place on his platform, and Dublin thought itself the poorer when he passed away. The Irish love their 'characters' and seem more tolerant than most, of the eccentric or the unfortunate. The Irish (Gaelic) words for someone with Down's Syndrome or a mentally challenged person are *'Duine le Dia'* – 'One of God's people'.

I wish I could say that I viewed the porter's noisy company with amused tolerance, but I was young, still consumed with the need for conformity. The cardinal sin was drawing attention to yourself ... Off the number 19 then, the porter and I, and through the portals of Head Office, thence to the Note Department. The man in charge of the Note Department had a gun, the first real revolver I had ever seen. It looked like a relic of the Great War, which it probably was, but I'll tell you 'Bang-Bang' would have given his eye-teeth for it.

What the man in the Note Department would have done with the gun, in the event of a raid, I never found out. Perhaps, unlike the porter and me, he was paid to die in the service of the bank. Maybe he earned as much as another fiver a week ... I would hand over the bundle of soiled, old notes, and he would give me the new ones. The porter and I were out the door in five minutes, headed for Phibsborough, me with the prospect of separating several hundred half-crowns from florins, he with kicking the manager's chop around before a light grilling.

We were in no hurry. Carrying the £5000 in new notes, in the prominent black bag, we would stroll past the Bank of Ireland,

and on towards O'Connell Bridge. It was a lot easier than the bus journey because not even the porter would commit the heinous social gaffe of whistling in the street. Women did not smoke in the street and men did not whistle. I always assumed these were the Rules of Life, but lately, I am beginning to suspect that they may have been made up by my mother.

We never got past Bewley's, the porter and I. The smell of freshly ground coffee issuing forth from Bewley's Oriental Café would have stopped a horse and four – and probably did in the old days. Lured by odours of Colombia and Java, we would place the big bag of cash carefully under the table, and treat ourselves to a dish or two, the better to fortify our spirits for another few hours at the financial coalface. Bewley's coffee was strong – you could trot a mouse across it – and the porter and I would continue on our way considerably enlivened, a foot or two off the ground from its powerful effects.

We never got knocked over with our king's ransom in cash, nobody ever even approached us for a penny for a cup of tea. It never occurred to me to make a break for the border, even with my £5 a week. The porter could have done with the money as well. He was probably earning little more than me, and keeping a little girl, probably his daughter, in an apartment once pointed out to me, painted pillar-box red. He had a German name, a Scots accent, and had been a car park attendant. He was one of the most mysterious people I have ever met, with or without his musical impressions. None of us could ever work out how he got such a job as a bank porter, requiring as it did the moral values of a Cistercian monk and the endorsements of several bishops and High Court judges. 'A love-child of the General Manager', was our best shot …

## A BENIGN DICTATORSHIP

Everybody was 'Mister' in the bank, except the manager, who was 'Manager'. And the girls were 'Misses' in those days, and I am not talking about the nineteenth century … Married women knew their place: home with the kids. As soon as one of the bank's gals got married, that was it. Curtains to the career.

Commonplace then, how ridiculous it seems now – yet we thought ourselves the very epitome of modernity.

The sub-manager, or accountant, was a decent man called Henderson. Looked as old as the hills to me, but, with a young family, was probably in his early forties. He asked us all to dinner in his house (excluding the manager, that would have been going too far). A bit of bonding, well before its time.

I only remember the occasion because of one tiny exchange: just before dinner, Mr Henderson and I exchanged a few civil words, probably on our favourite topic, the manager's sandals (open variety, worn in all weathers).

'Mr Henderson …' I said.

'Terry!' he interrupted, 'let's drop the Mr Henderson stuff here!'

'Oh, right,' I agreed.

'Yes. Make it A.J.P. …'

It wasn't a democracy, the bank. More of a dictatorship, but a benign one.

I quickly learned that the manager, despite his demob suit, his children's sandals, his sandpaper voice, basilisk stare and foreboding reputation, was a kindly soul who turned a blind eye and cocked a deaf ear to his young and very foolish staff. He must have been aware of the lager-loutism that broke out whenever a pretty girl entered the bank; he must surely have had an inkling of the wholesale groping that went on in the safe; and certainly suspected that a cheap chop could hardly have been that tender, without somebody knocking seven bells out of it. But as long as the books balanced at the end of the day, he ignored it all: the trumpet impressions, the shrieks from the safe, the gratuitous fumbling by all and sundry of his secretary's impressive *embonpoint*.

Every couple of years, inspectors would descend from Head Office to check the books, and make sure that some clever Dick was not siphoning off a pile to the Cayman Islands. This was a tense time for all, interfering as it did with the merry social intercourse and general hooliganism that characterized everyday banking life at the Royal, Phibsborough.

One inspector, a Mr Cairns, was particularly feared for his rigour, and exacting book-keeping standards. I remember him clearly, because a couple of years after spreading alarm and despondency with an inspection at our branch, he did a runner with a couple of hundred thousand quid and a bimbo to some foreign field, and was never seen again.

The bank's business day ended at three in the afternoon. The last customer ushered out, the porter closed the door, and peace descended. By half past three, the cash had been totted up and the books balanced. There was an occasional panic, when the cashier or one of the tellers found himself short of cash. That was not too bad if it was small change or a couple of quid, but worrying if it were more – cash differences had to be made up out of your own pocket, not easy on a bank clerk's salary. You had to hand it over to the manager.

The junior clerks had no such worries or responsibilities. We filled the idle hour with surreptitious games of shove ha'penny (real ha'pennies) before we could decently ask the sub-manager permission to leave for the day. Trying not to disturb the manager, in a trance in his little office, we slipped out at around about four o'clock. We caught a bus to Grafton Street, and were immediately transformed from bank clerks to *boulevardiers*.

## NIGHTLIFE IN DUBLIN

Café society, or more accurately, coffee society, had just hit Dublin. Coffee bars were the thing, and the fluffy cappuccino was king. It was a major social upheaval for the young people of Dublin, who hitherto had done their socializing in dingy bars over a pint of stout. There we sat, bank and insurance clerks, accountancy students and civil servants, every young man and woman in Dublin who was out of the office by four, trying to look like students on the Left Bank.

The Dublin students themselves were in the pubs, a pint of stout representing better value than a cappuccino when you were trying to keep body and soul together on a student's allowance. The young men looked at the young women, and vice versa. Then, after about an hour, we got up, caught the bus, and went home to our tea.

It wasn't the Boul' Mich', it wasn't Las Ramblas, but it was all we had, all we knew; it was life – life in the fast lane. It's important to remember that most of us travelled by bus or bike in those days, and roads were too narrow to have more than one lane. And the Volkswagen was king of the road …

Eventually, the thought occurred to us that we might do a bit more with our time. The other junior clerk, the main protagonist of the Great Shove Ha'penny Championships, had been transferred to Dunfanaghy, the Irish equivalent of Ust'-Kamenogorsk, and the shock had given us all pause. It could happen to anyone. We had to make what remained of our years in civilization count. Also, the new junior was a desperate pain in the rear, whom you could not bring anywhere near a coffee bar.

One of our tellers knew a girl in Head Office who was a member of the Rathmines and Rathgar Musical and Dramatic Society. She said that they were crying out for new, young, male members. We rolled up for auditions: Jimmy the teller, Joe, Joe's brother who was in insurance, his friend Eric, who was in something else, and me.

I liked Eric. At dances, after he had attempted a quick feel and been repulsed, he would say to the girl: 'Do good looks count for nothing then?' She would flounce back to her friends, to tell them of the arrogant swine she had just met, and Eric would turn away with a secret smile. Every week, he sacrificed sex for a laugh. You had to admire it …

We passed through the auditions, not bad when you consider that only a couple of us had a note between us. The next three months were a flurry of rehearsals in the Rathmines Town Hall, preparatory to taking the Dublin stage by storm in *Love from Judy*, an obscure musical which, I think, was the basis for the film *Daddy Long Legs*, which, and again don't quote me, starred Fred Astaire. The R & R had not got anybody like that on their books, but every year they would take to the boards of Dublin's finest, the Gaiety Theatre, with a musical, and, six months later, a Gilbert and Sullivan season.

It was big stuff, and we were right there in the thick of it, up to our eyebrows in the old five-and-nine, dancing, singing, and loving it. After the first night, Joe, who was a romantic, said to me: 'I think we've got a big hit on our hands!' We hadn't, of course, the loud applause was because the house was papered with every relation the cast could dig up. Joe knew that as well as me, it was just something he had heard in the movies, and always wanted to say himself.

Jimmy the teller dropped out after *Love from Judy*; his dancing was worse than his singing. Anyway, he was a poet and a songwriter. We would go to the dances together, and he would try to get the band's vocalist to sing his songs. They never would. It was understandable – Jimmy couldn't write music, so he would corner the unfortunate vocalist in between sets and sing the tune to him. We knew Jimmy was not going about it the right way, but I think he couldn't be bothered with the whole tedious business of submitting stuff to publishers. He liked standing at the side of the stage, buying the vocalist a drink, and humming tunelessly into his ear. He was the same with poetry.

Paddy Campbell was alive then, magnificent poet, magnificently bohemian, if by 'bohemian' you mean filthy dirty, permanently drunk and perpetually penniless. There is a statue of him now by the Grand Canal in Dublin, where he used to walk, or rather stagger. Campbell never wore any socks, but you couldn't tell, because his legs were so filthy.

Jimmy had a poem of which he was inordinately proud, and one evening he tracked down Paddy Campbell in a pub in Harold's Cross.

'Mr Campbell,' said the bold Jim, 'I'd like your opinion on this poem I've written.'

Campbell, three sheets to the wind and smelling like the canal itself, was terse: 'Buy us a drink!' he commanded. 'A large one!'

Jimmy did the needful. Campbell downed it. 'Buy us another one!'

Another ball of malt was poured. Campbell snatched the poem from Jimmy's hand and read it as he downed the whiskey. He put down the glass and the poem, and fixed Jimmy with a cross-eyed glare: 'Shite!' he shouted, in the hoarse tones of Co. Cavan. 'Absolute shite!'

He could have been right, but he might have been kinder to a person who was pouring drink down him ...

I stuck with R & R, progressing in the approved showbiz manner from the chorus to minor roles in *Naughty Marietta*, *Bitter Sweet* and *The Gondoliers*. Life in the bank was never dull, but the amateur dramatics were another glittering facet in the diadem of my life: clerking, rugby, hopping, dancing and singing. And all of it by bus. Well, most of it. There was a great deal of walking as well, particularly if you had been canoodling with a girl on the other side of the city after the buses had packed it in for the night.

A taxi was an extravagance that never came into the equation. Many's the night I trudged for hours from one side of the city to the other, cursing the fact that none of the girls I ever met lived on my side of the Liffey. Lately, reminiscing in my cups, I was bemoaning this fact, when a friend from Dublin said that his young manhood had been tested by exactly the same problem in reverse. He lived on the south side, yet every girl he ever met lived in Glasnevin, Drumcondra or Finglas, on the north side of Dublin. Life can be cruel …

## TRIAL AND ERROR

There were unspoken rules in a banker's life that nobody told you about, mostly centred on that staple of male, middle-class Dublin fashion, the rugby club blazer. How were you supposed to know that the blazer was *de trop* at bank social functions? They didn't tell you until you got there, and you couldn't go back to change. I suppose that it was a little trial that every naive bank junior had to go through, so that he would the better know his place in the great scheme of things.

You could not wear your club blazer to work during the week, either, although, once again, they never told you that until you had committed the heinous gaffe. A patronizing avuncular arm around the shoulder: 'Blazers only allowed on a Saturday morning, I'm afraid, old boy …' Don't ask me why, unless it was a way of keeping things non-denominational. The old Proddy/Catholic thing – you could always tell, from the club or school crest. We could always tell from the 'look', anyway.

And why didn't it matter on a Saturday? Because nobody

cared on a Saturday. Neither the staff, nor the customers, and certainly not me. The bank closed at 12.30 and we were all out of there, like scalded cats by a quarter to one. Saturday was rugby, drink, the hop, unrequited passion and the long walk home.

## PHANTOM BARBECUES

The car was a black Morris Minor, recommended by a friend of a friend of the Da's. I had a look over it, but I knew as much then as I know now about what goes on under a bonnet, and, anyway, it *was* a car. The Da advanced me a couple of hundred pounds, and it was *my* car. A couple of lessons from a pal up in the Phoenix Park, bought the licence, and I was on the road. No more walking the streets of Dublin in the small hours of the morning, no more wheedling for lifts home from hops, no more buses, no more bikes. I had four wheels. The world was my Dublin Bay Prawn.

I could cast my net further afield – to the outer reaches of Dublin's social scene: to Skerries, a seaside resort with a ballroom, north of Dublin, to Bray, beloved of my father, on the south side of Dublin Bay, where the English still holidayed and there was chance, no bigger than a man's hand on the horizon, of a pliant English rose who might do the bold thing.

Saturday nights were spent on the sands of Killiney Bay, searching for the Phantom Barbecue. After the rugby, the pints, and the inevitable failure in the romantic stakes, it was either a party or the Killiney Bay Barbecue. The parties were never any great shakes, just a few fellows like ourselves drinking our own bottles of stout in some suburban kitchen, and there never was a barbecue.

There was the suggestion that there *might* have been a barbecue, some time in the distant past: the charred remnant of a chipolata, the dusty embers of a fire, an abandoned guitarist drunkenly picking his way through what might have once been a Bob Dylan song, but, somehow, we always missed it. Everybody missed it. It was one of those weird experiences that seem to be universally shared – like getting smut in your eye through the open window of a train, your mother removing it with the corner of her handkerchief, and then, for good measure, wetting the handkerchief and taking a layer of skin off your face with vicious rubbing. That seems to have happened to everybody, even those born long after the passing of the steam engine. A folk memory ...

Throughout my interminable young manhood, I never went to a party worthy of the name. All the men were drunk and all the girls were taken. The answer was to take a girl with you, but it was a kind of Catch 22 – how could you take any decent girl to the kind of party that welcomed *you* on a Saturday night?

The only good party I ever went to was the one where I met Helen – and that was useless. It was only good because she was there. There was the usual conspicuous lack of drink, complete absence of food, and the statutory three-piece banging away in a corner.

I nearly didn't go to it – I was a fully-fledged radio and television newsreader by then, and already beginning to weary of the dogs' abuse I was getting from the discerning Irish viewer. The Irish have never been slow to express an opinion, particularly a critical one, and they took to their fledgling television service in heart-warming fashion. Within weeks of its opening night, the plain people of Ireland had decided that their new television service was rubbish, and that went for everybody on it as well. There was no doubt in the mind of the entire population that they could do my job twice as well as me, and most of them were not slow to share this insight with me in pubs, on the street and at parties.

Mike Murphy, a contemporary of mine in the early days of RTÉ, recounts an occasion on which he was quietly and civilly downing a pint in his local hostelry, when he was accosted by a passing member of the Great Irish Viewing Public: 'Are you Mike Murphy?'

'Well, yes I am, actually.'

'You're f***ing brutal, do you know that?' This last sally as the man exited the pub.

Mike rolled his eyes tolerantly to heaven for the benefit of the other customers, and sought some solace in his pint.

The door swung violently open. The viewer from hell had

returned: 'And me wife thinks you're f***ing brutal, too.' A pause. 'And she knows f*** all!'

It was not easy, and I took to going to pubs and public places only in the company of a small crowd who would sort of circle the wagons around me. You were still a target, and sometimes there was no escape. I mind well an occasion in the Horseshoe Bar of the Shelbourne Hotel, one of Dublin's ritziest addresses, and a spot where only the very best of city society came to drink themselves senseless. Helen and I, a number by then, were quietly ensconced at a corner table, with eyes only for each other. However, we were distracted by a minor fracas at another table.

Two ladies of the town had brought their negotiations with a couple of visiting freemen to an unsatisfactory conclusion, and were leaving in what could only be described as a marked manner. Hurling abuse over the shoulders of their artificial furs as they stormed out, one of them spotted me.

'Ah, Jaysus, Mary, look who it is!'

'Who?'

'It's Terry Wogan!'

A pause, while Mary picks her words: 'Thinks he's f***ing gorgeous.'

They exit, laughing merrily, leaving behind a shattered husk of a man, the cynosure of all eyes, who is hoping against hope that a passing earthquake might open the floor and get him out of there …

Helen nearly did not go to the party either, having been let down earlier that night by some madman. A good friend of hers (and now, not surprisingly, one of my best friends), Tom, persuaded her to accompany him, and the rest is my life … There she was, the most beautiful woman in Ireland, with blinding Titian hair, looking about six feet tall, and utterly unapproachable. How did I ever pluck up the courage to cross that room and ask her if she would like to dance?

I took her home in my car. I was still driving the Morris Minor, which had by now acquired a broken passenger seat. Don't ask me how. I had also acquired another passenger, my friend Mick, who had long since passed out in the back. Helen and I left him lying there peacefully and shared our first meal together at Dublin's then most fashionable late-night watering hole: Scotty's, a soup-and-sandwich run by an enterprising Scot.

The menu was spare – you felt the kitchen didn't over-extend itself: ham or cheese sandwiches, chicken or lentil soup. It was just the ballast needed to hold down the stout and get you safely home. A soup-and-sandwich bar at one o'clock in the morning, the most beautiful woman in Ireland, and me? I still wonder at it …

## FOUR-WHEELERS

Dublin was more of a two- than a four-wheeled city, even in the late fifties, so, provided you kept an eye open for the odd bicycle coming up on the blind side, the roads and streets were easy to drive. Which was just as well, in view of the fact that most people had only the most rudimentary idea of what they were doing, myself included. Deserted and all as the streets were, it was only a matter of time before my first accident. It started innocently enough, with a car coming out of a side road, about a hundred yards ahead of me. It might have been all right if it had continued its slow progress, but it stopped. I panicked, failed to take evasive action and, standing on my brakes, drifted inexorably into it at about ten miles an hour.

I leapt out of my car, spitting with fury, until Mick, my friend and passenger, luckily both sober and awake, pulled me aside to gently point out that the accident was my fault. There was hardly any damage anyway, but in a typically average driver's history of small shunts here and there, it is the only one that sticks in my memory. Is it the universal experience again? Do we all remember our first car crash?

I now had a dent on my front bumper, to match the one on the boot in the back. My nearside indicator had never worked properly, requiring elaborate circular motions with the arm through the driver's window when turning left. Whatever happened to hand signals? All you get is the finger these days … I had a perpetual slow puncture on the front nearside wheel, but none of my wheels was the Mae West. In Ireland, the remould was king. The only time anybody ever bought a new set of tyres was when they bought a new car. And *nobody* bought a new car. Every second car in Ireland was a wreck, and the others were not much better.

My great friend and mentor, Denis Meehan, kept the averages up, or down if you like: he had two wrecks. Always parked outside his house (pretty spectacularly wrecked in its own right), the cars, both featuring dead batteries, only ever moved when pushed. I would occasionally drive over, and help Denis charge up his batteries with jump-leads attached to *my* barely surviving battery. Not that we were going anywhere: the car with the working engine had no bulbs in its headlights.

One evening, Denis got called out in an emergency. No time to call a friend for a quick charge-up, he ran out on the road and waved down a passing car. It was a woman driver, eager to help. Denis explained the position:

'I just need a good push from your car, and that'll get me going down the hill.'

'Certainly,' said the obliging woman.

Denis got into his car, put her into first, foot on the clutch, ready for the push. It was only when he looked in his rear-view mirror that he saw the woman had reversed a hundred yards up the road, and was now roaring towards him at 30 m.p.h. He could only sit, watch, and brace himself … The thunderous crash was scarcely noticeable on Denis's wreck, but the woman's car had folded like a matchbox … Denis said she was very apologetic.

The Irish just do not care about cars. Stop in any country town and you will see the filthiest selection of motors anywhere in the known world, complemented by dents, rust, broken doors, exhausts hanging off and boots held down by hairy twine. To the Irish, the car is a thing that gets you where you want to go, not a fashion statement. In country areas, there is little distinction made between the car and the truck. I have seen cattle in the back of Ford Saloons, and sheep in the front seats of Fiats.

Talking of front seats, a couple of years ago a car was stopped for erratic driving by the police, outside Galway. Upon investigation, as the Garda Síochána put it, the offending vehicle was found to have kitchen chairs instead of front seats. They were not tied or bolted down or otherwise fixed to the car's floor. As you may imagine, they slid about a bit on corners, or when stopping, which accounted for the erratic driving. The owners were astonished to be dragged before the magistrate: 'The car seats were so comfortable, we took them out and put them around the kitchen fire. So, we put the kitchen seats in the car …'

There was the odd new car, owned by the successful commercial traveller, veterinary surgeon, cattle-jobber or robber baron. One of the last-named, of my acquaintance, was very proud of his new Jaguar, the cleanest car in Ireland. As he returned to Dublin one evening, he was waved down by an old farm-worker for a lift. People in Ireland still stop for hitchhikers. The old boy, smelling strongly of slurry, got into the front, my friend fretting over his new leather seats.

After a moment, the ancient took an old tin box from a disgusting pocket, and pried a butt of a cigarette loose: 'D'ye mind if I smoke?'

'Not at all,' my friend, all seigniorial civility, acquiesced, 'fire away.'

'Have ye got a light?'

My friend could scarce forbear to smile: 'In front of you there, on the dashboard, press it in, it's a cigarette lighter.'

'Ooh – isn't that powerful? Can you beat that?' said the old man, as he lit up his butt, and then, rolling down his window, threw the lighter out into the darkness.

Some people in Ireland *don't* stop for hitchhikers, any more …

I regret to say that little or no regard was paid to the drink/drive regulations either. It was the drunk on the bicycle that you had to look out for – particularly on the pavement. Every evening, as soon as the pubs closed in Dublin, a great motorized exodus would take place to various locations outside the city limits; these oases were known as '*bonafides*', where a man could drink himself into a satisfactory state of transmogrification until the wee small hours.

One Christmas Eve, my friend Tom popped out to purchase some extra nibbles for the *soirée* his wife was planning for some friends and neighbours that evening. As is the way of it, in Dublin he fell among gurriers, and about five hours later found himself driving up a hill near his home, with the butt of a cigar in his hand.

As he neared the top of the hill, he decided to dispense with the remains of the cigar. Rather than winding down the window, he opened the offside door, and hurled the cigar, at the same time hurling himself out of the door. With one foot inside and the rest of him on the road, the car slid back down the hill, stopping only by crashing into a parked car. Tom picked himself up, put the cigar, which had never left his hand, back in his mouth, and drove home. As his infuriated wife opened the door, Tom stumbled inside: 'Quick! Shut the door! The boys in blue are after me!' he mumbled, before sliding senseless to the floor.

# SIX

# DON'T GIVE UP THE DAY JOB!

Four years in the bank passed in a flurry of fun and good fellow-ship. I started playing golf with a set of razor-blades-on-sticks that someone dug out of an attic. Romance flourished, then withered on the vine; ships passed each other on a Saturday night. I did a couple of holiday reliefs in country towns that convinced me that if ever they sent me permanently to the sticks, it was curtains for the old bank career. As it turned out, the curtain was coming down anyway …

The advertisement was in the *Irish Independent*: Radio Éireann was seeking announcer/newsreaders. Only those fluent in Gaelic and English need apply. Familiarity with French, Italian, Spanish and German would be to the applicant's advantage. A knowledge of music would be no drawback, and, of course, a pleasing voice.

I still can't believe I answered the ad. What in hell's chance did I have? My Gaelic was sketchy, my French and German suit-able for written exams only. Half the briefless barristers and out-of-work graduates in the country would be applying: jobs like this were once in a lifetime. How could I have even imag-ined that a junior bank clerk, with pretty undistinguished exam results, and an unfinished course in philosophy to his credit, had a prayer for this plum?

I sent off for the form, filled it in, and lied about my fluency in languages. Radio Éireann was a semi-State body, half in, half out of the Irish Civil Service, so the advertisements for vacancies had to be placed in every newspaper in the land. Otherwise the jobs could have been filled by sons, daughters, cousins, other relatives or friends of a friend, as was the norm in the jobless Ireland of those days.

Much later, my friend and mentor, Denis Meehan, who, as Head of Presentation, placed the advertisement, told me that there were almost 10,000 applicants for the job. They should have binned me on the first inspection, but for some reason that

I will never fathom, I got a note a couple of weeks later asking me to attend an audition at Radio Éireann Studios, GPO, Henry Street, Dublin.

I told the bank manager that I had a dental appointment for the fateful morning, and, in the fullness of time, found myself sitting in a little room at Radio Éireann with audition script in hand. It contained news items in English, musical introductions liberally sprinkled with French, Italian and German, and screeds of Gaelic. I don't remember being nervous; I was probably desensitized by the certain knowledge that I did not have a chance.

The audition was okay: the English was no problem, and I faked the rest. I have always been a mimic with what my mother used to call 'an ear for languages'. To this day, there are people who think me fluent in four or five tongues. It is a con: just because I sound like I can speak a language does not mean that I know what I am talking about. Many would say that that holds good for my English as well.

I toddled back to my permanent pensionable position in the bank, and awaited the rejection slip. After a decent interval, the envelope dropped on the doormat, and, unbelievably, Radio Éireann were inviting me to join them for a training course, five evenings a week, for a month! There was no guarantee of a job at the end of it, naturally, but there was one vacancy for a permanent post behind the microphone, to be decided by the final audition, at the end of the course. So, every evening, I would finish up at the bank, play the statutory game of shove ha'penny, and drift down to the Radio Éireann studios for three hours of training in the hidden art of radio announcing.

What would I have done had I been anywhere else but Dublin? Supposing I was working in a country branch of the bank, or still living in Limerick? The opportunity of my lifetime would have gone a-begging, and by now, I would be a retired bank official, probably married for years to a farmer's daughter, with five children, all of them priests or nuns, and snug as a bug in a rug. Never mind …

The training course was conducted by Denis Meehan, his deputy Head of Presentation, Brigid Kilfeather, and Liam Devally, announcer and assistant to the Controller in his spare time. All of them became Irish broadcasting legends, with Liam adding an extra dimension by becoming a judge of the Irish High Court. You will have learned by now not to trust what passes for my memory, but I have a vague recollection that there were six of us in the course: a pretty, very bright girl, and five fellas, one of whom was an eejit. There is always one … We were young, eager, with, surprisingly, not a law degree nor a spoiled priesthood between us.

I am sure that it was Denis Meehan's crafty plan to shift Irish radio's presentation, and hopefully the station itself, out of the sub-BBC Home Service-type bog into which it had sunk. Not long after the Irish Free State was formed, Radio Éireann was set up, strictly along BBC lines. Well, who else was there to follow, if you were next door to the greatest broadcasting organization in the world? It became more Reithian than Reith himself: patriarchal, excessively Gaelic-speaking when ninety per cent of the population could not understand a word, well-meaning and boring. It blessed itself and the nation continuously, and carefully trod its appointed semi-State line. I never listened to it – as I have already said, I was a BBC Light Programme/AFN/ Radio Luxembourg man, as were most people of my generation. Rock'n'roll kids, Irish radio to us was an old tune played on an old fiddle. The training course, though, changed my mind.

Denis, Brigid and Liam were all up to date, sharp and quick-witted. And they could teach: we learned microphone technique, intonation, emphasis, phrasing and delivery. We learned to breathe, which is the first thing you forget when faced with a live mike. You watch anybody making their television début: it isn't their face that gives the game away – you will hear it in their voice. And it was *fun*. I knew from that first evening that it was where I wanted to be, what I wanted to do. I had found it, almost stumbled across it: the one thing I could be good at. Most people never get that lucky.

I only told a couple of boys in the bank what I was doing of an evening, in the warren-like studios at the back of Dublin's General Post Office; they were as surprised as I was that Radio Éireann thought me worth training. We kept it from the manager, much as we kept most things; the old boy was better off not disturbed.

Michael and Rose showed no apparent alarm at the new direction that the life of their conventional, well-behaved son was taking, just the usual kindly interest. I have never been a great talker, outside of the job, and I am sure that my poor mother had given up years before trying to get information on anything out of me. Helen, too, abandoned me early on in our marriage. I never talk about what I do, and I have never mastered the arts of chitchat or gossip. My inability to do any more than exchange basic information on the phone is legendary in the family. Information trickles from me like blood from a stone. So I suppose my parents could only hazard an intelligent guess at what I was doing. 'He's learning to be an announcer!' I heard mother proudly tell my maiden aunts, just before I came into the sitting room. They all looked at me fondly, blankly …

We happy band, we RÉ trainees, learned the intricacies of the presentation studio: how to open and close the microphone channel; how to play records; how to introduce programmes; how to read the news. Announcer/newsreaders did it all: record programmes, music recitals, symphony concerts, outside broadcasts, State funerals. They introduced talks, plays, quizzes and men who played the fiddle with a cushion under their feet to stop them banging on the floor. They read weather forecasts, gale warnings, stock exchange prices, the cattle market report and the news.

It was a wonderful month, learning a new game, for which it appeared that I had an instinctive flair, which Denis Meehan seemed to recognize. From the beginning, he must have known that my Irish was not any great shakes, and the rest of my languages pure mimicry, but at the end of the month-long course, he offered me the opportunity of part-time work. Actually, now that I think of it, he offered it to all of us, with the exception of the eejit. A part-time position, with the possibility of permanency at the end of a three-month trial period.

Many of the announcers were part-time on Irish radio, working at the day job, and 'announcing' in the evenings and at weekends. Among them was Gay Byrne, later to become the most influential presenter of the modern era on Irish radio and television. About this time, he had a major breakthrough on British television as a reporter for Granada Television, based in Manchester. His fellow-presenters there included Michael Parkinson and Bill Grundy; Gay would fly to Manchester on a Sunday night, having spent the weekend in Dublin, working as a part-time announcer on Radio Éireann.

I asked him why, and he said something about 'keeping options open'. He worked, ate, slept, dreamt broadcasting; it is a gift, or a curse, that I never understood nor shared. All my life as a broadcaster, I have loved it. I have loved the doing of it, and because I can do it, but I have always loved life more. I have never loved the work enough to live for it. I suppose that I have never taken it seriously, but then, I have never thought that being serious is any more intrinsically worthwhile than being of good cheer ...

So the carrying of perilously large lumps of money and the sorting of half-crowns from two-bob bits in the service of the Royal Bank of Ireland continued, while I announced and news-read part-time for the Irish National Broadcasting Service. I was plunged in headlong: The Cattle Market Report. I have never been as nervous before nor since. The script danced in front of me, as my hands shook; my eyes were having trouble focusing; a cold sweat dappled my brow and upper lip. Then, the green light in front of me lit up: I was on the air. Me! Talking to the Irish nation! I forgot about breathing almost immediately. Within seconds, I was gulping for air, fighting asphyxia. The room grew smaller, the ceiling seemed to be pressing down on me. How I choked my way to the end of the fat-stock prices, I will never know.

I staggered from the studio, half-exultant and half wondering why I had inflicted this terrible, nerve-racking suffering on myself. I suppose that is every actor's, every presenter's 'first night' story. I have never forgotten that feeling – it stayed with me for my early days on Irish television, and, indeed, British television. Over the years, as Lord Macaulay put it, 'the agony somewhat abated', but the memory of fighting for breath as the cold hand of fear gripped the bowels will stay with me forever. And they say that the body has no recollection of pain ...

Now, I was finding the bank work tedious, beginning to pin

my hopes on getting the Radio Éireann job. Not that life in the bank was any less foolish, or eccentric. The Pig Man was still walking into a deserted bank, the porter's trumpet voluntary could still be heard halfway to O'Connell Street, the sponges still flew. Groping in the safe was not what it was, for a while – the star of the show had got engaged and it was several weeks before she was herself again.

Then, the man came for the manager, and lightened my days. He was a little fellow, and you could smell the drink off him long before he came through the door. He picked me out almost immediately, as drunks have all my life. They seem to sense my embarrassment and discomfiture, and are drawn to it, rather like cats who immediately slink up to those who hate them. He ambled across the floor of the bank, and leant against the counter, in the easy manner with which he must have been leaning against the counter in the snug bar where he had obviously spent most of the day, if not his life.

'The manager,' he slurred.

'Yes, sir?'

'Get the manager, you gobshite!'

'Yes, sir. What name will I say?'

'You'll say nothin', you whey-faced eejit. Where's the manager? I'll swing for the little swine!'

By now, this manly badinage was attracting the attention not only of other customers, but of the senior staff, who, as ever, conscious of their position and responsibilities, were looking for somewhere to hide. The cashier had urgent business in the ledger room, the sub-manager made for the safe with all speed. The drunk grabbed for me, and missed.

'I said, where's that bollocks of a manager?' he roared.

By now, he had even the manager's attention. The door of his sanctum opened a fraction, a terrified little bespectacled face looked out. Unfortunately, the drunk, following my eye-line, saw him too: 'There y'are, you little fucker!'

He charged to the manager's door, even as it was slammed in his face. Like a greyhound in the slips, the manager shot through the side door, belying his age, and recalling rather the halcyon days of his youth as fly-half for the bank's rugger team.

With an athleticism that can only be put down to drink, the drunk vaulted the counter, and there followed a chase of which the Keystone Kops would have been proud. In and out of the cashiers' boxes, over tables, round the floor of the bank, in one door and out the other of the manager's office, your man the drunk roaring blue murder, the manager's children's sandals a blur as he sped for his very life. Into the safe, where the sub-manager was hiding, and then out again, twice around the ladies in the ledger room, before the quarry finally went to ground in the loo.

With many a curse, our friend the drunk started to kick the door down, and indeed, hopes were high for his success, but some dumb-bell among the customers had run outside and called a policeman. There's always someone who doesn't get the joke ...

When the dust of the great chase had settled, I asked the porter where he had been. After all, he was supposed to be responsible for the bank's security and the ejection of undesirables. 'Didn't hear a thing,' he said, 'I was practising my French horn. Sorry I missed it, though ...'

## OPENING THE MICROPHONE

I had informed the manager of my part-time work on the radio, but he made no great fuss, putting it down to boyish whim, which would pass soon enough. He couldn't conceive that anyone would be foolish enough to give up the permanent pensionable security of the bank, for the gypsy existence of a radio announcer/newsreader. He was wrong. When they offered me the job, I resigned from the bank without a backward glance. I joined the staff of Radio Éireann in the company of Andy O'Mahony, another failed bank clerk who had been a part-timer for a couple of years.

I wish I could pretend that it was a tremendously plucky move – the kicking over of traces, a reckless, buccaneering leap into the unknown – but a position on the staff of Irish radio was every bit as permanent and pensionable as working in a bank. It was more so: the pension was better, and the pay! The pay! As is the way of mothers everywhere, Rose kept the letter: the rates of pay were £14.7s.2d per week, rising by annual increases of 12s.11d. to £17.11s.8d. at the top of the scale. A king's ransom, to somebody who had been living on a fiver a week. As I look at the letter again, dated October 1961, the last paragraph states: 'It will be necessary for you to take a medical examination, the fee for which will be payable by you.' They were not throwing it around, either ...

The bank let me go without much fuss, and very few signs of regret, and my mother and father were similarly unmoved. I found it remarkable then, and still do, that, given their early circumstances, their struggle to bring up their children and give them the very best, that they never at any stage attempted to interfere, nor even advise caution. All they ever did was encourage. In all my years at school, they never once criticized, nor expressed disappointment at poor results or bad reports. I know my father thought I was lazy – most people were, compared to him. He was right, anyway, and I knew it. I remember few cross words from my father, although I am sure, with his quick temper, he must have clipped me round the ear a few times. And then immediately felt an awful remorse.

I know that, because every time I slapped my sons, which was at least once every fifteen years, it drained me. There I go, thinking I am my father. Well, I am: over the years, I find myself increasingly saying the things he said, recognizing his little quirks among my own, and slowly seeing his face emerge as I look into the bathroom mirror.

That reminds me: I was chastising one of my sons, giving him a piece of my mind on his behaviour, telling him off for not doing things my way. My father took me gently aside. 'Remember,' he said, 'he's not you.' It's the best piece of child-rearing advice I have ever heard, although I constantly had to remind myself of it, over the years when my children were growing up.

We all try to bring up our children in our own image, or, at least, what we imagine ourselves to be. They should think as we think, behave as we behave, act as we would in any given situation. Often, parents live through their children, expecting the children to achieve *their* ambitions, to succeed where they have failed. It is always a mistake. My children are not me. Certainly, I recognize little bits of me and flashes of their mother in their personalities or attitudes, but they are their own people. Hard as it is to grasp, our children may not want the same things we do, may not be the same as us. Do the best you can, and let them be. And, given that life is a lottery, pray ...

At the time I joined, the entrance to Ireland's national radio station was hardly designed to impress: you entered through a side door of the General Post Office, sited in Henry Street, a narrow, busy thoroughfare, off O'Connell Street. Up three floors in the lift, and you were in reception. There, you invariably found a comely receptionist, a couple of decrepit figures in uniforms shiny with use and age – studio attendants, hand-picked for slowness of thought and action – and an elderly member of the Garda Síochána in plain clothes, carrying a Smith and Wesson older than himself. His job was to defend Irish radio in the event of an attempted take-over by an illegal organization, an infuriated taxpayer, or a listener driven beyond the bounds of sanity by sheer boredom.

I never saw the detective's capabilities put to the test in all my years there. Even an insane listener, not to mind an illegal organization, knew that taking over a studio was not much good to you. You might get a couple of words of protest out, but all they had to do was switch off the transmitter in the Dublin Mountains.

Not withstanding the growth of illegal organizations in Ireland since I left, I imagine the man in the hat with the gun is even more redundant these days. Irish radio took the phone-in to its heart some years ago, and it seems as if no opinion is too revolutionary, radical or outrageous to be expressed at length over the air. Even despite the sexual and religious inhibitions under which most of the population were reared, Irish radio these days is a Rabelaisian revelation. No shock-jock in Britain comes even close to some of the boyos on Irish radio. More importantly, Radio Éireann has become the forum of Irish public opinion, and is helping to free the country from the small-minded parochialism, the clinging to the past, the prejudice that for so long bedevilled it.

Then, it was a different story: Irish radio opened bilingually and prayerfully at 8 a.m., long before a soul was stirring in the country. There was news, something for the farmer, a feature on some aspect of Irish life, perhaps a burst of something classical, a programme of popular music requests, then a raft of fifteen-minute long commercial programmes interrupted by the one o'clock news, until 3 p.m., when the station closed down.

Hard to believe in these days of wall-to-wall talk and music, but Radio Éireann put up the shutters for two hours, until 5 p.m., when we opened again with something for the kiddies. News, features, concerts, plays followed relentlessly, until 11 p.m., when we blessed what remained of the listening public, and sent them off to their trundle beds. What a life. I loved it: desperately searching through the prayer-book for the name of the saint of the day; taking a wild shot in Irish at St Chrysostom or Athanasius; feeling like the only person awake in the entire country, as I opened the microphone and started the day for Ireland.

I have never forgotten the thrill of it: driving through the deserted streets of Dublin at seven o'clock (they get up a lot earlier these days), down the dark corridor, with its empty offices and studios, and at the very end, the only lights, the lights of the continuity suite. Just the engineer and me. And a million radios out there, listening. *To me.* The wonderment wears off, of course, and a good job, too. Otherwise you would end up a basket case, thinking that the world out there is clinging to your every word, that what you have to say is important.

The megalomania of the radio broadcaster – you can hear it every day on any radio station you care to listen to. Radio lends itself to the madness more readily than television, because people react to radio in a much more positive way than they do to television. Radio stimulates the brain, the imagination, it provokes reaction. Television, by providing the picture to go with the thought, stunts the imagination, makes it redundant.

With a current audience of nearly seven million every day for *Wake up to Wogan*, I can receive up to 500 e-mails, 100 faxes, and as many letters and postcards. In the course of the programme, the instant audience reaction can be another hundred e-mails and faxes. I have done television programmes for up to 20 million viewers, and never heard a dicky-bird from one of them. Yes, I know, maybe they like me better on the radio – but not that much ...

If you are not careful, this kind of public reaction can make you think that they are out there in their tens of millions, ready to follow you anywhere. Then a listener writes in to tell you that they phoned the BBC with a query about the show, and the BBC replied: 'Wake up to Wogan? Is that a radio show?' You may have 7 million listeners, but there are another 50 million out there in blissful ignorance of your very existence. Forget this, and you forget yourself. And when you do what I do, you have got to cling very tightly to the wreckage.

Think about it: here is an outwardly sane human being, who goes to work in the morning, secure in the knowledge that he will entertain millions of people for two hours every day by talking to them. Playing a bit of music as well, but mainly opening his big mouth. How far short of the full shilling do you think you have to be to believe that? Which is why I try not to think about it too much. There are people in padded cells with far less grand delusions ...

## AN UNFORGETTABLE LESSON

We would sit and talk in the continuity studio, the two news announcers, the boy broadcasters, the two failed bank clerks, Andy and me. By inclination and study, he was a philosopher. Deduction rather than induction, reason rather than emotion, cause rather than effect. Implication and inclination. Andy could talk around a subject for hours and I was happy to listen.

One morning, as I sat there in the studio, Andy was delivering deep philosophical thoughts and then bursting into hoots of laughter at the sheer pretension of the piece of classical music being broadcast to the great Irish public who were going about their business, ignoring it. He had introduced the piece ponderously, as you were supposed to with classical music. Oh, yes, it was being played for the public at large, but nobody expected them to understand it. Still, it was probably doing them good ...

That was the attitude to broadcast classical music then. And there is still a touch of it about. Does anybody *really* care about Köchel ratings on a *Desert Island* disc?

The music played, and Andy talked. Distracted by the music's interruption of his finely honed dissertation, he absent-mindedly reached out, and lifted the needle from the gramophone record. He continued to talk freely, and it was some seconds before I could interrupt long enough to point out that he had just reduced Irish radio to silence. All over the country, people were wondering why it had suddenly gone quiet, and probably welcoming the respite.

As the seconds of dead air raced on, Andy and I collapsed into hysteria. After what must have been well over a minute (a lifetime on the radio, particularly if it is a silent minute), he pulled himself together long enough to put the needle back to the approximate point on the record at which he had removed it.

Once more, music was heard in the land. We sat back and waited for the sky to fall. Nothing. Not one word of complaint, neither from the public nor our boss, nor even an engineer. Radio Éireann was off the air for ninety seconds and not a soul in the country noticed. It was a lesson I have never forgotten …

## SEVEN

# SO MUCH TO SAY,
# SO LITTLE TIME TO SAY IT

Radio Éireann's newsroom was all Ireland's source of information – and the Irish like their news. Limerick, with all of 20,000 inhabitants, had two daily newspapers of its own, the *Leader* and the *Echo*, two Cork newspapers, and three national dailies. Hungry, but informed – that was us. The RÉ newsroom was up a rickety flight of stairs, in the very attic of the GPO. Heavy with smoke, and redolent of a million pints of stout, it was a chattering maelstrom of typewriters, telexes and journalists in varying stages of decay.

The somewhat intimidated tyro newsreader – *moi* – was instructed to perch himself near the senior sub-editor, who would collect the news as it came in from the avaricious news-hounds, and hand it over, after checking it for errors and omissions, to the eejit whose only job was to read the thing. A gob on a stick ...

As the time for the broadcast grew nearer, I would take as much of the news as was ready, and off with me downstairs to the studio. Often there would only be a couple of sentences to go before what would have been an extremely embarrassing silence, when the door of the studio would burst open, with scant regard for the finely tuned listeners, or indeed the nervous wreck of a young newsreader, and in would come Charlie, the other sub-editor, with the rest of the news, or at least the next few pages.

Charlie had a high complexion due to drink, and this was not helped by having to charge up and down flights of stairs at the last minute. As our brave newsreader read on as if nothing had happened, Charlie would sit himself heavily down next to me, wheezing. I am sure that most of the Irish public who were listening closely enough to care, were convinced that I was a candidate for the sanatorium, with a chest like that ...

The journos were an easy-going, good-natured mixture of

hard men from the print, and youngish ex-graduates who had joined Radio Éireann expecting to go somewhere, and found themselves on the roof, with no chance of going anywhere but down. Still, it was typical of Ireland and the Irish in those days: everybody wanting to be liked, everybody wanting to get on with everybody else. The ultimate accolade was: 'Sure, he's a decent fellow.' This encomium would always be followed by a qualification: 'Pity about the drink ...' Or 'the wife', or 'the family', or 'the bad breath ...'

Years ago, that greatest of broadcasters, Alistair Cooke, shrewdly identified this peculiarly Irish syndrome. Cooke said that the best conversations he had ever had were in Neary's pub in Chatham Street, Dublin. He claimed that he could hear them yet, although many miles away in Manhattan.

'D'you mind that Alistair Cooke the other week?'

'Ooh, don't be talking!' would come the retort. 'What a man! What a brain! And the turn of phrase!'

'Ah,' would pipe up another voice, 'you wouldn't hear the like of it anywhere for fine-sounding talk ...'

'No, indeed,' would acquiesce a voice from the corner, 'and a fine-looking man, with a broad knowledge of literature and the arts.'

'Oh, be the hokey, yes, a grand man altogether ...'

And then, Cooke said, there would be a pause, a grave pause, while men drank deeply of their stout. Then, from the back of the bar:

'D'you mind the way he picked his nose?'

It was not until I began my career in Britain that I worked with people who manifestly could not have cared less about me, and what is more, did not care if I knew it. A professional relationship, rather than a personal one, doesn't suit the Irish, and, frankly, has never really suited me. I have to like people I work with, and it has to be mutual, if it is going to work for me. It would not be worth getting up at 5.30 every morning if I didn't work with one of my best friends, Paul Walters, or the bunch of degenerate newsreaders, John (Two Sheds) Marsh, Alan (Voice of the Balls) Dedicote, and Fran (Anybody's) Godfrey, who daily infest my Radio 2 morning ramble through the absurd. Let's not forget, either, the studio managers who feign amusement and manage to stay awake through the mindless tedium …

People look back now to the seventies as a Beltane – Beautiful Age – of British broadcasting, particularly of the British Broadcasting Corporation; and although not as hamstrung then by process, procedure and attendant bureaucracy as it sadly has been recently, it was capable of great politeness. For instance, it was one of the unspoken rules of Radio 2 that producers and presenters should not become too 'close' to each other. This was probably an old Reithian hang-over designed to prevent the producer losing his judgement or having his authority vitiated by excessive friendship, or even, dammit, affection …

So there you would be, producer and presenter, working well together, coping with each other's foibles, knowing each other's strengths and weaknesses. Then, bingo! Out of the clear blue ether, your producer would be moved to another show, and you would be given someone you hardly knew, with whom you had got to spend the next six months building a relationship and a whole new way of working – and keep those ratings up.

I suppose of its very nature, any broadcasting organization, up to its armpits, as it should be, with volatile, egomaniacal creatives, must be eccentric. And Radio Éireann certainly was. Where else, while an announcer was in the middle of a scene-setting piece for Strauss's *Die Fledermaus*, would another announcer sneak into the studio on his hands and knees and set fire to the script? From the bottom of the page?

Have you any idea how it feels to be broadcasting to the nation on something you know absolutely nothing about, only to see the script disappearing into ashes in front of your very own eyes? Leaving you speechless, while some gobdaw with no sense of responsibility lies shrieking with laughter at your feet?

I often wonder what the Irish listening public made of the strange silences that would occur from time to time on their precious wirelesses. Did they throw the set, cursing modern technology, at the cat, or, worse, the granny? Or did they turn the thing up, only to be deafened seconds later when certain announcers had pulled themselves together and blamed 'technical trouble at the transmitter'?

It was as nothing to slowly pour a carafe of water over a person's head as they were reading the one o'clock news, nor to unbutton a lady announcer's blouse while she was giving a long continuity announcement her all …

## THE AULD DIDDLEY-EYE

Meanwhile, in the little music studios upstairs, men were thrashing away with fiddle and bow and the music our fathers loved … Personally, I have never liked it much, the auld diddley-eye, and I liked it even less when I had to announce it in Irish, and sneak into the studio halfway through 'The Priest in His Boots' with a cushion for the fiddler's right boot which was threatening to bring the floor down as he kept time.

It was a sadistic mind that designed those little studios for music: the fiddle, the bodhran, the banjo and the tin whistle were one thing, but watching the studio attendants, all of them well past their peak, trying to hump a harp, or, even worse, a grand piano up the windy, rickety stairs, taught one much about man's inhumanity to man. I am sure it has marked me, and is at least partly responsible for the way my stomach turns over when, at any Irish function in Britain, before you have even had time to digest the *petits fours*, you are surrounded by hundreds of young people battering the floor with their version of *Riverdance*.

What in the name of all that's holy, did the Irish in Britain do for after-dinner entertainment, before *that* Eurovision Song Contest in Dublin when Michael Flatley, Jean Butler and a dancing horde brought the house down? Fine and dandy it was then, and not without its own significance that the only musical item millions of viewers can remember, after decades of the Song Contest, is the *interval* act. This, however, is no reason to go inflicting various interpretations of the thing on unsuspecting diners and their digestion.

As I keep trying to tell all who will listen (a group that diminishes even as I speak), the diddley-eye was never part of *my* tradition: banjos and fiddles were played on street corners by disreputable-looking men with a few coppers in a cap at their feet. Nobody I know ever went to Irish dancing classes, or sang 'They're Cutting the Corn Around Creeslough Today'. That kind of stuff was far beyond the town's barricades, on the other side of the Pale ... On the other hand – or foot – the present Mrs Wogan was a denizen of Irish dancing classes in her youth. She was sent home for lifting her legs too high. The whole point of Irish dancing, before Flatley and Co. caught us by the scruff of the neck, was not to show your knickers ...

The musical tradition of Dublin Town was Edwardian come-all-ye's or Tom Moore ballads. The only genuflection in the general direction of the Irish musical tradition were the stage-Irish songs of Percy French: 'Are You Right There, Michael, Are You Right?' A radio programme on Radio Éireann, sponsored by a music retailer and publisher, Walton's, had as its slogan 'If you do sing a song, sing an *Irish* song ...' *Their* idea of an Irish song was, 'My goodness, My gracious, My Name Is Ignatius, Ignatius the Leprechaun', performed by Charlie McGee and his Gay Guitar, or the Irish actor Noel Purcell intoning a ditty that began: 'Grafton Street is Heaven, with coffee at eleven, and a stroll round Stephen's Green ...'

## THE RADIO ÉIREANN PLAYERS

The commercial, or sponsored, programmes, when I started on Irish Radio began after the one o'clock news, and finished at three in the afternoon when the station closed down, and people could go and have a decent drink.

The programmes were fifteen minutes long, and extolled the virtues of everything from sausages to dry-cleaners and processed cheese. One of them was a drama of everyday Irish country-folk, called *The Kennedys of Castlerosse*, which had the virtue of keeping a number of starving Irish actors in work, and was, in fact, the forerunner of a successful Irish television country-folk serial, *Glenroe*, which in turn was the inspiration for British television's *Emmerdale Farm*.

Don't say that there is not the odd nugget of information buried in all this ... I have a distinct recollection of Val Doonican singing the sausage commercials: 'It's Donnelly's Sausages for you …' Catchy enough, but without the magic of 'I. I. F. B. C. It's Imco for Better Cleaning!' I suppose copywriting was only in its infancy in Ireland then.

Up the other end of the corridor, past reception and the guard with the gun, there was another corridor, with more studios. These were brighter, more lately refurbished, and the home of Irish radio's band of permanent thespians, the Radio Éireann Players. Apart from Anew McMaster's touring troupe – who, like Sir Donald Wolfit's in Britain, brought Shakespeare to the great unwashed the length and breadth of Ireland – and the holy of holies, the Abbey Theatre, permanent, or even occasional, work was very thin on the ground for the Irish actor. So, a berth in the Players was something along the lines of the Holy Grail.

The Players were an extraordinary mixture: Young Turks, old soaks, refugees from McMaster's gypsies, relics of Lord Longford's Gate Theatre; all Restoration foppishness, clipped English and hair a tad too long. Then there were the mountainy men with thick Kerry accents, and Gaelic speakers from the Claddagh in Galway. They did everything from the Irish rural dramas of Keane and McMahon, to Ibsen and Sheridan, with O'Casey and Shakespeare and Synge to keep everybody on their toes.

It was a treat to make the opening announcement, then listen and watch some of Ireland's greatest actors at work. They were raffish and roguish and careless of everything except: 'the work, love …' One or two worked better with a little lubrication; a few lines early on, with a gap until, say, page 84, allowed ample time for a couple of pints in the pub across the street before return-ing, refreshed, to the piece …

## IF IT WASN'T FOR THE DRINK …

The smell of Guinness was heavy on the work by lunchtime, and I don't remember much dramatic stuff being done after that. Indeed, most of Radio Éireann's best work, in programmes, administration, engineering, music and drama was done before the pubs opened. In particular, the Tower Bar – the Broadcasters' Annexe as it was known – was, at any given time, as full of RÉ's staff, as the radio station itself. Situated as this bar was, directly opposite the door of RÉ, some script and feature writers must have done their best work there, because no one ever saw them leave it, not even during 'The Holy Hour'.

This sacred time, between the hours of 2.30 and 3.30 p.m., every afternoon, was when the pubs of Ireland shut their doors and put up the shutters, at the behest of a kindly Irish Government, the better to enable Mine Host of the tavern and his weary staff to refresh themselves, and recharge their batteries for the long day and evening of pulling pints, and pouring balls of malt, that lay ahead.

In the Tower Bar, as in every other pub in Ireland, due deference was paid to the edict; doors were locked, shutters closed, lights dimmed. However, the clientele was still inside ... 'A drink while you're waiting, gentlemen?' was the civil enquiry, as the talk and the drinking continued, unabated.

Broadcasting's a dangerous game, if you are a drinker. Broken hours, time on your hands, easy enough to cross the street for a pint and a chat to break the monotony. It was accepted, and in no way regarded as abnormal, that people drank before, after and during broadcasts. There was no stigma attached to being a drunk: 'Ah, Johnny – the best announcer in Radio Éireann, if it wasn't for the drink ...'

In case you think the booze/broadcasting syndrome was particularly Irish, I found it to be exactly the same in the BBC, when I first went there to work. The BBC Club in the Langham, just across the road from Broadcasting House, performed exactly the same function for certain actors, announcers and producers as did the good old Tower Bar of Henry Street, Dublin.

## LANGUAGE AT ITS BEST

Further down Henry Street, if you turned right, you were in Moore Street, which housed another tavern for the thirsty, Madigan's Pub. This was a pub for the hard man, the broadcaster who was making no pretence at work; this was a pub for drinking, not talking. You could not hear yourself think, for a start. Moore Street was famous throughout Ireland for its street-traders.

The dirt and smell of the place was remarkable enough, but the language was spectacular. People walked up and down the street just to listen:

'How much is that cod?'

'Two-and-six a pound, missus.'

'Two-and-six! For that little bit?'

'Listen, missus, whaddya want for your ha'penny, Moby Dick?'

And: 'Looka that carrot! That reminds me of my Seán!'

'Wha', the size of it?'

'No, the dirt of it …'

Once you became well known, you walked there at your peril!

'Ah, lookit! It's Terry Wogan!'

'Gaw, he's very fat, isn't he?'

Rosie, the Queen of Moore Street, had a pot perpetually on the boil at her stall. Any left-over scrag-end of meat, cabbage-stalks, onion-skins or past-it potatoes were hurled indiscriminately into the bubbling maelstrom. It kept a lot of poor people fed in the hungry years, but nobody, not even Rosie, had the nerve to give the cauldron a stir. You might easily disturb whatever unspeakable presence had been sitting, seething, at the bottom of the pot for all that time.

The dealers of Moore Street were all women, and straight out of *Juno and the Paycock*, *The Plough and the Stars* and *The Shadow of a Gunman*. Sean O'Casey must have used an earlier generation of Moore Street shawlies as his inspiration, just as Brendan Behan, a familiar figure in Madigan's (and every other local pub) did, later.

The girls were in Madigan's more often than they were at their stalls, and it was not the place for a quiet jar. It was there that you could hear the Dubliners' use of the 'f-word' at its creative best. Noun, verb, adjective, adverb, gerundive – they covered the spectrum with it. The expletive is used more frequently in Ireland than the rest of the English-speaking world put together, but the Irish don't use it in the same vituperative way as elsewhere. In Ireland, and Dublin in particular, the 'f-word' is used to add colour, emphasis and variety – it has no sexual, offensive nor aggressive connotations whatsoever. To call somebody a 'f***er' is not to demean them – it may well be affectionately meant.

Many words that are meant to wound in Britain have a different force in Ireland. Take 'whore', for instance. As was explained to me by a distinguished man of letters, Augustine Martin, 'whore', pronounced 'hooer', is a compliment in Ireland. 'You're a terrible hooer!' is high praise, marking you as a lovable rascal, and a desperate man altogether. On the other hand, if someone calls you a 'whore' in the received English pronunciation, that *is* an insult …

Words like 'gobshite' are more difficult. They can be complimentary, or of the deepest opprobrium – it all depends on the delivery. It is a minefield, but a couple of years of steady drinking in Madigan's of Moore Street could probably help – provided you kept your mouth shut in between pints.

## RECORDS PLAYED FOR SEX!

It was on the corner of Moore Street one day that I saw Larry Cunningham. Larry was one of the biggest names in Irish showbusiness, the lead singer in one of the country's most popular showbands. The showbands were a peculiarly Irish phenomenon – touring the country in their buses, playing in every town and village, every 'Ballroom of Romance'. The countryside was studded with these concrete barns of places in the middle of nowhere, with exotic venues: 'The Las Vegas' in Templemore, or 'Dreamland' in Muff.

The most successful bands worked every night God sent, up and down the country – Donegal one night, Wexford the next. The good ones put on a show of extraordinary variety: country music, ballads, cover versions of all the current hits, Dixieland, jazz, comedy routines, foxtrots, sambas, and, of course, the slow waltz, to end the evening with a hopeful grope. On foot, on bicycle, or if your father was a 'big' farmer, by battered banger, the young people of Ireland, starved of music, entertainment and sex, swarmed to see and hear the showbands.

In the fifties and sixties, the only places where young Irish people could socialize were the ballrooms. A lot of money was made by the proprietors, and by the showbands and their managers, most of it, cash. For a long time, the top Irish bands were raking in more money than any British pop group, with the possible exception of the Beatles, but they certainly worked for it, seven nights a week, fifty-two weeks of the year, a life given over to band-suits and buses.

Clipper Carlton were the showband who really started it all, in the early fifties, then the Royal Showband (who went on to be a Las Vegas lounge act), the Freshmen, the Dixielanders, the Capitol, a hundred others. Among the biggest were Big Tom and the Mighty Mainliners, a name that might raise a few eyebrows in today's drug-conscious culture, but carried no stigma then in Kiltimagh, Crossmolina or Haulbowline.

Big Tom *was* big. A big soft country boy with a border accent, and a slow way of speaking. He didn't do a lot on stage, either, apart from standing there, but he had a deep voice like Jim Reeves, and that was good enough for the plain people of Ireland.

The current king of country music, Vince Gill, reminds me a lot of Big Tom. A bit of a gobdaw, with no idea what to do with his hands, full of awkward charm, and the kind of farm-boy innocence that makes you believe that butter would stay untouched in his mouth for weeks on end.

As befitted his demeanour, Big Tom was not big into rock'n'-roll. The heart-rending country ballad was more his scene. Songs about dogs who passed away, sons killed in the war, and women who went to the bad were meat and drink to him, and his audience. Then he produced a record, 'Gentle Mother'. Its opening line was: 'Will I ne'er see you more, gentle mother?', so you can probably gather that it was not exactly up-beat. More of a dirge.

But what caught my imagination was the publicity photograph that went with the record: a simple snap of Big Tom standing by a gravestone with a bemused expression on his face. The record went to Number One in the Irish pop charts and stayed there for weeks.

Where showbands found the time to make records while traversing the country day and night was a mystery to me, until my meeting with Larry Cunningham.

Larry was up there with Big Tom in the popularity stakes; his 'Lovely Leitrim' had taken the charts by storm some weeks previously. Larry was another who did a mean Jim Reeves, and anybody else in a cowboy hat. He saw me first, and greeted me. Which was just as well, because I would not have recognized him with a blood-stained handkerchief covering his mouth:

'Larry,' I said, 'what the hell happened to you?'

'Ah, sure, not to worry,' came the muffled reply, 'I've just had a few auld teeth out at the dentist's.'

'You'll want to watch that – take a couple of aspirin, go and lie down for a couple of hours.'

'Yerrah, no,' said the voice behind the handkerchief. 'Sure, I've got to go off to the recording studio now to put down the tracks for the new LP.'

Hardy blokes, the showband boys.

Although the records they produced were mostly cover versions – copies – of country hits from Nashville, they sold well to the fans and were important for keeping the band's name on the radio, and in front of the public. The Irish market was not big enough for the record companies to employ salesmen, or pluggers, to promote the record, so it was left to the bands them-selves, and their managers.

One morning, I was sitting alone in the announcer's little office, when one of the showband managers stuck his head around the door:

'Ah, the very man!' he exulted. 'Have you got Joe's new record?'

'No.'

'Well, there it is for you now. You'll give it a spin on *Hospitals' Requests?*'

'Well, I …'

'Ah, good man yourself. And here's a little something for you.'

He dropped a box of twenty Players' Navy Cut on the desk, and exited, smiling. Payola, Irish style. And I didn't even smoke …

A good ten years later, I was presenting the afternoon shows on BBC Radio's 1 and 2 when the great Payola Scandal broke over the BBC. 'Records Played For Sex!' screamed the headlines. Apparently, a number of BBC disc jockeys and producers, with the connivance of a record-plugger, had got entangled with some call-girls. It was not clear how many records had got played for sexual favours, but it did for the careers of a couple of producers, and at least one major disc jockey.

On talking to my friends at the BBC, what galled me was that I was about the *only* disc jockey who had not been propositioned. Me! With a daily show on BBC Radio's 1 and 2! I probably would have run a mile, but it might have been gratifying to have my moral fibre at least tested.

## A RICH AND VARIED LIFE

As befitted a national broadcasting service designed along the lines of the mighty BBC next door, Radio Éireann had its own choir and symphony orchestra. The Radio Éireann Singers recorded their recitals in various small halls around Dublin, usually in front of a small crowd of their relatives, and people who had come in to get out of the rain. The symphony orchestra did most of its best work in slightly bigger halls in front of much the same kind of a crowd. As one of the people who introduced them, and did the announcements in between, I was up to my armpits in fine music. I heard enough Schubert to last me several lifetimes, and could rattle off a series of Mozart Köchel ratings like a machine-gun.

It was a rich and varied life, at least compared to sorting florins from half-crowns, and was even less like work than the bank. It was full of characters, like Denis Meehan. Not that I have ever met anybody remotely like him, before or since. He was also known as Donncha Ó Miocháin. Everybody had two names in Radio Éireann, an Irish name and an English one, although some, more Irish than the rest of us, were known only by the Gaelic version.

This was a hang-over from the Civil Service, where everything was done in Irish and English. Lip-service in the Civil Service; to the old, lost ideal, the guttering flame that was the native language. Sadly, much as the Government, the Education

Department and various vested interests promoted Irish, it never captured the affection of the population. Maybe because in many schools, it was battered into the pupils as a penance, rather than a labour of love ...

Radio Éireann had almost as much news in Irish as it had in English, and, indeed, when later the television service RTÉ started up, the practice continued, despite the fact that ninety per cent of the viewers had neither the smallest idea, nor interest, in what was going on.

As late as the late seventies, RTÉ's premier newsreader, Charles Mitchel, was made to read the news in Irish. Charles was an ex-actor from Hilton Edwards/Micheál MacLiammóir's troupe at the Gate Theatre: tall, elegant, with a grand English accent well suited to the Restoration comedies in which he specialized. Even after extensive courses in the native tongue, Charles Mitchel speaking Irish was eerily like Winston Churchill speaking French: 'Prenez garde! Je vais parler français ... '

Denis Meehan was of medium height, well made ('a barrel of bread-soda', my granny would have called him), with prematurely grey hair, ruddy complexion, a severe expression in repose, and a smile that made him look like a demented cherub. His attitude to life could, at best, be described as cavalier. And without him, I would now be a retired bank clerk. He heard and saw something in me that was not apparent to most, and throughout the all-too-brief years that I was privileged to know and work with him, he was never less than a great friend, adviser and advocate.

He was Head of Presentation at Radio Éireann, in charge of a motley crew of staff and part-timers who included ex-bank clerks, teachers, army officers, civil servants and various legal eagles keeping body and soul together while awaiting a chance to soar. Enunciation, pronunciation, interpretation – Denis Meehan knew it all, and what's more, he could teach it. Anything I know of microphone technique, I learned from him – indeed, anyone of a generation of broadcasters who dominated Irish radio and television for twenty years could, and would, say the same.

He looked like an unmade bed. I have never met anybody who cared less about his appearance. His trousers were ever at half-mast, and the braces that held them up could be seen through the holes in his cardigan. He loved to eat, and nobody could skin a chicken like him.

Whenever I was on an evening duty, he would busy himself in the office until my time was up, and off we would go for something nourishing. Not that Ireland was exactly a gourmets' paradise at the time. There is a story of an English couple lost in the depths of the Irish countryside, who, as the shades of night fall, sight the lights of a tavern.

'Sit anywhere ye like,' says the waitress, 'and what would ye like to eat?'

'Well,' says the Englishman, 'since there's no menu, I think I'd like some smoked salmon to start – what about you, m'dear, the same? Yes, two smoked salmon, and then I shall have a fillet steak, medium rare, with a Béarnaise sauce – what about you, darling? Lamb chops – yes – and some green beans with, I think, Lyonnaise potatoes. A bottle of Cabernet, and cheese to follow? Yes, I think so – and, of course, coffee …'

Having meticulously noted the details, the waitress wordlessly slips away. Within a minute, she returns, empty-handed: 'Himself says that if we had that kind of food here, we'd be eatin' it ourselves …'

My BBC Radio listeners send me many a tale of gastronomic adventures in Ireland – this one of a morning in a pub in Donegal.

'What'll it be, sir?'

'Oh, it's a bit early, I'll just have a coffee – a black coffee.'

'Certainly, sir, a black coffee it is.'

The coffee is poured and being ruminatively sipped, when the barman reappears: 'Would you like a drop of milk in that?'

Another listener reports on a bed and breakfast in Co. Galway.

'And what would you like for breakfast?'

'Well, I dunno, let's see – I'll have two fried eggs and beans on toast.'

After about half an hour, back comes the waitress: 'Two fried eggs, we didn't have any beans, so he's done you some peas on toast …'

There were good eating places in Dublin: the Russell and the Hibernian Hotels, Jammet's, a turn-of-the-century French restaurant, the Red Bank for shellfish and journalists from the *Irish Times*, the Dolphin for steaks and country-folk. All a bit pricey, but below that you were struggling.

Denis Meehan and I favoured the Trocadero, run by a Greek called Eddie. Well, he said he was a Greek, and he did turn out a flavoursome kebab, but there were Italian influences at work in the kitchen with cannelloni and various spaghettis much in evidence, and for the conservative, chops, steak, peas and chips.

One of Helen's earlier boyfriends only *ever* ordered steak, peas and chips, when they went out to dine. He had fast cars and plenty of money, but she could not stand his diet … I mind well an evening at the Trocadero, when Denis and I, having ordered the cannelloni and kebabs, were cogitating on the wine-list. A Cabernet Sauvignon? A Merlot? Perhaps a Shiraz? A hearty Barolo? The waiter, never much for suavity, could take no more. 'And what'll it be for booze, gentlemen?' he enquired impatiently.

The Irish never made great waiters … Cynicism, perhaps, or, more likely, false pride. The Irish waiter feels he is as good, if not better, than the paying customer, and makes that quite clear. The relationship is based on friendship, the meeting of equals. Certainly, it has nothing to do with being anybody's servant, and who do you think you are, anyway?

Denis was married to Sylvia, an attractive woman who shared his sense of humour, his intelligence and his attitude to life. Tidiness was not at a premium in their home. Happiness and laughter were the things that mattered. Sofas with the stuffing knocked out of them, carpets with more holes than Denis's cardigan, chairs with three legs leaning against the wall. You were better off sitting on the floor, except that you were always in danger of being run over by three children and a baby. I was proud to be godfather to that baby.

I am not sure if there was not another sofa in the front garden, but outside the front gate were Denis's pride and joy, the two wrecked cars. One of them was a Morris Oxford. 'Great lights on the Morris,' he would say. 'It was always given up to them.' It was the kind of thing he said with a straight face, and if you took it at face value, more fool you.

He would launch into pseudo-Joycean stream-of-consciousness nonsense at any sign that you were taking yourself too seriously, and he had memorized large tracts of the writings of Flann O'Brien/Myles na Gopaleen (another civil servant with two names). 'The Irish for the jumping,' he would quote, 'wherever you go, it's hats off and *grá mo chróí* to the jumping Irishman ...'

I know, *I know*, only funny if you have read the books ... You had to *be* there ...

Although nobody bothered to do listener surveys in those far-off days, there was no doubting that the most popular programme on RÉ was *Hospitals' Requests*. Apart from the sponsored programmes, it was really the only show on the network in which you could hear popular music. It was an announcer's job, and came around, in strict rotation, every four or five weeks. Some of the announcers could take it or leave it – to them it was a chore, sorting through the thousands of cards and letters and building a two-hour programme that went out live every Wednesday around lunchtime.

Lunchtime was always the biggest listening time of the day: working men and schoolchildren went home for lunch, and, of course, the woman of the house was at home. Nowadays, with our speed of communication and improved transport, *nobody's* at home for lunch – and certainly *not* the woman of the house – unless she's the cleaning lady or the child-minder.

I *loved* doing *Hospitals' Requests*, I would have done it every week, if they had let me. It was the beginning of everything for me; from the very first, I realized that ad-libbing off cards and letters in between records was something I could do with ease. And nearly forty years on, I am still doing it ...

The trouble with any request programme is the requests. If you leave it to the honest, yeoman listener, you will get the same thing, week in, week out. And *Hospitals' Requests* had long since fallen into the rut. 'The Nuns' Chorus', 'Blow the Wind Southerly' and the Tulla Ceili Band were staples of every show.

Nobody ever told the listeners that 'The Nuns' Chorus' was not a hymn by saintly virgins, but a cry of frustration for the attentions of Casanova. Perhaps it was better that the patients never knew. After all, most of them were being looked after by nuns; it might have given them the wrong idea. By far the most popular request was for Father Sydney McEwen's rendition of 'Bring Flowers of the Rarest'. You see, it was a holy song, and, of all things, a holy priest singing it.

Recently I went back to Dublin to guest on one of Gay Byrne's last *Late Late Shows* on RTÉ, the world's longest-running chat-show. Halfway through, Gay introduced a choir to sing a song that was the most requested on his radio show: 'Bring Flowers of the Rarest' … I knew then why I'd had to get away all those years ago. I couldn't wait to see the back of 'Bring Flowers' on *Hospitals' Requests*, and, if it came to that, 'The Nuns' Chorus' and the Tulla Ceili Band.

So, whenever my turn to present the show came around, I sorted and sifted until I came to non-specific requests: 'Please play something nice and cheerful for Sam McGettigan in Ward 4, Portiuncula Hospital, wishing him a speedy recovery, from You Know Who …'

That meant I could play something of my own choice. The programme became my choice of music, not theirs. All my spare time was spent, not across the road in the Tower Bar snug, but in the gramophone library, listening, noting, timing. Hour upon happy hour, what a way to spend your day. People began to respond to the different approach. A letter to a Dublin paper:

*A word of thanks to Terry Wogan. With his cheery good-humoured banter, he has given this programme a 'new look', and one listens to him as much as one does to the records …*
An ex-patient.

Emboldened by this kind of reaction, I pressed forward with an ever-racier, more modern choice of music for the infirm and the ailing. The Clancy Brothers and Tommy Makem, Irish-Americans in Aran pullovers, had become greatly popular with their brand of lively, virile Irish balladeering, and I included their latest, 'Isn't it Grand, Boys?', in the show. Perhaps I should have listened more closely to the words. No sooner had I played it for the sick people of Ireland, than RÉ's telephone lines were jammed with complaints. Another letter to the papers followed:

*What was the mentality of the friends of hospital patients last week when they requested a record which referred in the first verse to a coffin, and went on about the withered flowers upon it, and included the lines 'Isn't it grand, boys, to be bloody well dead?'*

You can't win 'em all – any more than you can with the old ad-lib. While playing the song 'The Spanish Lady', the needle got stuck in the record groove. How archaic that sounds now ... With a cockiness that deserved to be put down, I opened the microphone channel and chuckled, 'Ah, I appear to be stuck in the middle of the Spanish Lady ...' That's how you learn to keep the brain a nano-second ahead of the tongue ...

A few years ago, on a visit to Dublin, I heard a two-way request programme between Australia and Ireland, uniting the exiles so far away with their loved ones at home. Heavy-handed banter was involved.

Dublin presenter: 'Next, we have a request for Olivia Newton-John. She's a lovely girl, isn't she?'

Australian Jack-the-Lad: 'Well, she's a Sheila with a great pair of legs!'

Dublin presenter: 'No, but legs apart, what do you think of her?'

On the same visit, I listened to a radio outside broadcast of the Tour of Ireland cycle race, with the link-man handing over to various reporters along the route:

'Now, over to Mick O'Reilly in the Phoenix Park!'

Silence.

'Well, we don't appear to be able to contact Mick at the moment, so over to Sean Mooney at the North Circular Road!'

And so on around the various reporters until it was time to go back to our missing man in the Phoenix Park again:

'All right, let's hear if we can join Mick O'Reilly.'

Silence.

Then, just as the link-man is about to give up the ghost, a voice: 'Hello? This is the engineer. Mick's not here ...'

Outside broadcasts and sports coverage were very big in my day on Irish radio: Philip Green did the Association football, Fred Cogley the rugby (English names for garrison games, you see) Seán Óg Ó Ceallachain, the games of the Gael. But the king was Michael O'Hehir. He did the hurling, the Gaelic football *and* the horse-racing.

Nobody, not even the legendary Patrick Moore, could cram more words into a single breath than Michael O'Hehir. He invested everything upon which he commentated with pace, excitement and thrills. Half of Ireland clung to his machine-gun delivery on the radio every Sunday afternoon. He continued to do the commentaries when Irish television started, making no concession to the fact that we could now see the game as well as he could, and persisting with the rapid-fire, edge-of-the-seat delivery, although everyone could see that the game was not worth tuppence … At horse-racing commentary, he was non-pareil, and indeed, one of the BBC's regular commentators on the Grand National.

One sunny afternoon, Michael was presenting and commentating on the television coverage of a meeting from the Curragh, the Mecca of Irish race-courses. He set the scene from the paddock, as the horses for the first race paraded around him:

'*Dia Dhuibh, a chairde Ghael* – Good afternoon and welcome to another great day's racing from the glorious setting of the Curragh of Kildare!'

The camera tracked in, from long panoramic shot to close-up of the great O'Hehir. Even as it did, Michael's free hand, the one not holding the microphone, flashed across his chest, to his heart. Now in close-up, Michael looks at the camera, hand on heart without a word. It is unheard of – Michael O'Hehir is silent. His expression is one of pain, of pleading … The camera stays on him, the director as transfixed as O'Hehir himself, and a half a million Irish viewers.

As the great commentator stands mute, speechless and growing ever more wan, the terrible suspicion grows. In the outside broadcast control van, the penny finally drops:

'Get the camera off Michael!' shouts the director. 'He's havin' a heart attack!'

Off the camera zooms, to a long shot of the course, the stands, the bookies, anything ... As he sees the camera move off him, Michael O'Hehir himself moves for the first time. Swiftly, the hand on his heart moves to his mouth. He smiles, and begins to talk again. It is a miracle ... a miracle that he caught his false teeth as they flew out of his mouth on the word 'Kildare'. A miracle that he did not brain the director for keeping the camera on him so long, when all he wanted to do was get his teeth back in ...

## SO MUCH TO SAY ...

As I grew in age and broadcasting experience, mainly I suspect, through the good offices of Denis Meehan, I got involved in outside broadcasts myself. The first was RÉ's coverage of the funeral of the second President of Ireland, Sean T. O'Kelly, or Seán T. ó Ceallaigh, for the usual reasons.

Sean T., as he was known, and genuinely loved by the Irish, was a little man who favoured a Homburg hat and a Crombie coat. I never saw him in anything else, apart, sadly, from his coffin. As the funeral cortège wended slowly past my vantage point at the top of Dorset Street, I must have done a fair job of describing the journey scene and the dead-marching soldiery, because nobody said, 'You'll never do another funeral as long as you live.' Although, come to think of it, I haven't ...

My only view of Sean T. when he was alive was at international rugby matches, or big Gaelic games at Croke Park, when he would enter, to be introduced to the teams. The crowd, as ever, displaying the Irishman's total lack of respect for any kind of authority, would chant: 'Cut the grass! Cut the grass!' Heaven alone knows what they would have shouted had the poor man had a limp, or some disability other than his shortness of stature. I suppose he got off lightly: this was a man they liked ...

The biggest outside broadcast ever staged by Radio Éireann was for the visit of President John F. Kennedy in June 1963. The Golden Boy was touring Europe, and could not have passed up on a chance to visit the land of his forefathers, and pay homage at the simple bothy in Wexford from whence his ancestors had joined the great exodus of the Irish to the Land of the Free. It was not going to harm the Irish vote in the States, either ...

My commentary position, as the President drove in an open car from Dublin Airport to Áras an Uachtaráin, the President of Ireland's residence in the Phoenix Park, was at the bottom of Dame Street. Painting pictures with words, I was to catch John F. as his motorcade swung around by the pillars of the Bank of Ireland, past Trinity College, founded by Queen Elizabeth I, and then on through the teeming, cheering crowds past my vantage point, before swinging right, across the Liffey and on to the Park.

I was ready, pale but determined: 'Thank you, Padraig. Yes, I can see the outriders, and there, the car carrying the young President, as he smiles and waves to the laughing, cheering crowds! And there he goes ... As I hand you over to Jim Murphy ...'

As the motorcade swung around by the Bank of Ireland, I saw Kennedy lean forward and tap his driver on the shoulder. The motorcade and the President shot down the street and by me, in about twenty seconds ...

So much to say ... So little time to say it ...

# EIGHT

# ON BLOWING A TINKER OFF HIS MISSUS

In case you came in in the middle, the GPO, the General Post Office, which housed Radio Éireann, is of great historical importance in Irish history. It was at the GPO in 1916 that a few brave committed men declared an Irish Republic, in the teeth of the mighty British Empire.

The commemoration of that historic declaration is to be seen on a plaque within the GPO, by the statue of the legendary Ulster hero, Cuchulainn. Here, Patrick Pearse and his Volunteers, with James Connolly and his Citizen Army, fought for several days, before being finally overwhelmed by the artillery and superior gun-power of the British Army, and taken away to their executions (a fate Éamon de Valera escaped, because of his American citizenship).

It was those executions that, according to W.B. Yeats, gave birth to 'a terrible beauty', and led directly to Ireland's eventual independence. With that peculiar mixture of sentimentality and cynicism previously referred to, it was commonly said, while I was growing up, that if all the people drawing pensions on the basis of Service to the Cause in 1916, had actually been present, the British Army could never have won the day, because it would have been overwhelmed by sheer weight of numbers …

On the fiftieth anniversary of the Easter Rising of 1916, it was natural that Radio Éireann would cover the celebrations and commemorations that marked the great occasion. Despite my few brief words on the speedy President Kennedy and the slower passing of President O'Kelly, I was chosen to describe the scenes on the big day, as the full might of Ireland's armed forces marched proudly past the spot wherein was born the 'terrible beauty' – the pillars of the GPO.

My commentary position was directly opposite the reviewing stand, and my task was to describe the march-past of Ireland's finest. It would be foolish to give the impression that we are talking Red Square here, or anything remotely resembling Munich Rallies. The Irish Army has never been large, and, at the time, had probably no more than a dozen artillery guns, four armoured cars and two small tanks to its name.

The Irish Navy was similarly strapped, with two corvettes. There was some talk of taking these on the parade, but wiser counsels prevailed, on the basis: a) it would leave old Ireland's shores a prey to all manner of piracy and b) it was only the water that was holding them together.

There was no sign of the Irish Air Force, although its couple of Second World War Spitfires would certainly have added to the occasion. Perhaps I am wronging the pilots, they may well have done a fly-past without anybody noticing …

So, knowing that the military end of things might not be all that much to write home about, I briefed myself fully on the dignitaries of Church, State and County Council who were to grace the reviewing stand. It was to be the very cream of Irish life: President, Taoiseach, Archbishop, down through Ministers of State, Ambassadors and Bishops. Even prominent ballroom proprietors and showband managers had been allocated seats at the back.

The parade started at Dublin Castle, and on my headphones I could hear my fellow-commentators describe the panoply and glory of it as the parade passed their observation posts and made its triumphal way towards O'Connell Street and the GPO. Through College Green it marched, past cheering (or being Dublin, possibly jeering) crowds and on to O'Connell Bridge, and over the Liffey. Meanwhile, the commentator whose job it was to describe in glorious prose the focal point – the crux – of the whole damned thing, namely me, was breaking into a cold sweat and watching the scene swim before his very eyes.

The President was on the dais; there too, the Prime Minister; that must be the Archbishop – but the rest – where were the rest? The reviewing stand was full of people, but I did not recognize a single one! Where were they, the great and the good, the people with two names? Where were the people with the Fáinne badge (Irish speaker, and proud of it) on one lapel and the Pioneer pin (non-drinkers, and even more cocky) on the other?

All I could see opposite me were nonentities, and a few I took to be hooligans and corner-boys. Later, it transpired that the bright spark whose task it had been to send out the invitations, had not. Who knows the whys and wherefores, and who cares? As Ireland's Armed Might swept past the GPO, in full and colourful detail, I – painting pictures with words – described all that could be seen, and a great deal that could not, particularly in the way of dignitaries. It must have given some folk a nasty turn, as they sat in front of their wireless with a nice cup of tea, to hear themselves named and described as taking the salute at the GPO in Dublin.

If you had come from the Bridge end of O'Connell Street, you would have passed the GPO (with or without a salute) on your left, had your eye – distracted by the Floozy in the Jacuzzi statue in the middle of the boulevard and then on the right – seen the impressive façade of the Gresham Hotel. There it was that RTÉ, the Irish Television Service, celebrated its opening night, on New Year's Eve, 1962. The 'T' stood for 'Telefís', a brave attempt to translate a modern term into an archaic idiom.

Excitement had been at fever pitch for the best part of a year. The Minister had appointed Eamonn Andrews, as Ireland's most distinguished and famous broadcaster, Chairman of the RTÉ Authority. Studios had been built (well, half-built), executives appointed, programmes commissioned, schedules thrown back and forth, newsreaders auditioned. (I failed. So did Andy O'Mahony. And Gay Byrne.)

Rafts of chancers arrived on every mail-boat from Britain, America and the Antipodes. Anyone who had ever been within walking distance of a television studio elsewhere was in. People who had been scene-shifters, studio attendants and cleaners in the BBC, Granada, NBC, CBS or Community Television, Omaha, Nebraska were suddenly floor managers, cameramen and even directors.

An obscure American was appointed Director-General, and every last penny was flung at the opening night, live from the lovely ballroom of the equally lovely Gresham Hotel, gem in the diadem of the grandest thoroughfare in all Europe, O'Connell Street, Dublin.

Only Irish pluck and bravura could have countenanced such an opening: a major outside broadcast conducted by personnel and equipment that had never before been tried or tested in real programme conditions.

Of course it went well – why wouldn't it? There were glorious moments that will stay forever in the memories of those privileged to watch that grand opening. All was glitter and glamour in the ballroom, as Eamonn Andrews flung the thing open for Ireland's approval and delight. The RTÉ Orchestra played some fine old Irish airs to the applause of a select and well-turned-out audience; Brendan O'Dowda, who always looked as if he could do with a shave, sang a couple of Percy French crowd-pleasers, with his hands in his pockets, and then, risking all, the cameras took us outside the very portals of the Gresham to O'Connell Street, ablaze with light and life.

A particularly picturesque touch was added by the snow being driven up the street by a gale-force wind. It was blowing directly into the faces of the Number One Army Band, giving its all from a stage in the middle of the boulevard. Another tenor, Patrick O'Hagan (father of the twice *Eurovision Song Contest* winner, Johnny Logan), was deputed to join the band with pleasing ballads and come-all-ye's.

Yet once again, with that splendid lack of any sense of dignity, or occasion, to which I have already referred – the jeering of Presidents at football matches, the booing at plays in the Abbey, which caused Yeats such distress that he leapt on the stage and castigated the audience for 'letting themselves down, yet again' – the crowd did just that and it made the evening for all right-thinking viewers.

Even as Patrick O'Hagan, wrapped against the winter chill with a great-coat over his dinner-jacket, opened his mouth for the first few bars of 'Danny Boy', a shrewdly aimed snowball came hurtling through the air, and, by virtue of a direct hit, brought that grand old ballad, and indeed the balladeer, to an abrupt halt. He and the band started up again, but it was all over – and everybody knew it. The snowballs flew from all directions, hitting bassoons and euphoniums alike, knocking over music stands, striking the unfortunate O'Hagan, still trying to sing, but with his back to the audience and the cameras.

When a particularly well-aimed volley rendered the conductor semi-conscious, wiser counsel prevailed, and we were taken back into the warmth and safety of the ballroom, where mild panic ensued as Eamonn Andrews ad-libbed bravely, while they tried to get the orchestra back from the bar.

By now, they had moved the radio journalists from their eyrie in the attic in the GPO, to join their television counterparts in the spanking new, nearly finished Television Centre at Montrose, in the southern suburbs of Dublin. Continuity still came from Henry Street, but the news was now read from a little studio just off the newsroom at RTÉ, Montrose.

For security reasons, the newsreader was required to lock himself into the studio, while, for the same reasons, outside, sat a man from the Special Branch of the Garda Síochána, with a large Smith and Wesson protruding from his braces. He was usually a man near retirement called 'Bat', the Irish diminutive for Bartholomew, or Bartle, or possibly even Bartley. Well, nobody was going to call him 'Batty', not with the Smith and Wesson sticking out from the braces.

Bat was an old IRA man, as were many of his generation in the Gardai, and had fought with the Republicans (de Valera's side) against the Free State Government during Ireland's desperate Civil War that followed Partition. He was a jolly man, whose only cause for discontent was that 'long drink of water up in the Park', his way of referring to his one-time idol and leader, Éamon de Valera (Dev), who had succeeded Sean T. O'Kelly as President of Ireland.

I could never quite work out why he, and many like him, such as Helen's father, Tim, became disenchanted with Dev. Maybe because at well over six feet, there was not much point in shouting 'Cut the grass!' whenever he appeared at a football match.

The studio outside which Bat sat and guarded me in the name of the Republic and freedom was no more than a little box. You locked yourself in, sat down with your script, switched on your microphone and when the 'On' light flashed, off you went. Claustrophobia was not an option, particularly during the main news bulletins, at one and six o'clock. They went on for half an hour at a time, and woe betide you if you were taken in any kind of fit, whether it be coughing, sneezing, choking or bleeding to death.

I only mention the last, because it happened to me. Halfway through the first five minutes of the one o'clock bulletin, the first drop of my life's blood dripped from my nose and obliterated half of the next sentence. I wiped it away, but the drip turned into a steady flow, and, within seconds, the desk looked like an abattoir. There I was, alone in the world, with the plain people of Ireland hanging on my every word, my life ebbing away in a torrent in front of me, with no prospect of succour, least of all from a man with a gun asleep in a chair on the other side of a locked and bolted, reinforced steel, soundproof door.

The blood flowed. I wiped it off the script as best I could with a soaked handkerchief. The news must go on! I switched off the microphone at the end of a sentence, and shoved two corners of the hankie up both nostrils and held them there with my left hand, while I turned over the pages with my right, and read on for another twenty minutes, until half past one.

I staggered from the studio like Lady Macbeth, but not a word of sympathy did I get. Laughter and jeering: 'We thought you were a bit nosy for the last twenty minutes …' Nowadays, when people remark upon my lack of nerves in the radio studio, I smile and tap the side of my nose. Not too hard: I don't want to go through that again.

## HOUSEHOLD NAMES

Despite having abjectly failed in our auditions in front of a panel that knew more about snipe-shooting than newsreading, or indeed television, in no time at all, the radio announcers were reading the news on the new baby, Irish television RTÉ Bealach a Seacht (Channel Seven).

We all had a go – Denis Meehan included. It came as a shock; I had never seen him in a suit. He cleaned up nicely. In even less time we were household names – the kind of instant celebrity that only television can bestow. You can work your proverbial off for years on radio without ever impinging on the consciousness of the Great Unwashed. A voice shouting in the wilderness, a duck farting in thunder …

Although well into my second incarnation on BBC Radio 2, after nearly six years, at the time of writing this, I still have people writing into the show saying: 'I've just discovered you on the radio again. I wondered where you'd got to …' This, despite presenting the allegedly most popular radio programme not only in Britain, but in Europe. (Don't shout it too loudly; Radio 2 is the BBC's Best-Kept Secret.)

It is important to keep this in mind, when the e-mails, faxes and letters are flooding in at the rate of 500–600 a day. You never get that kind of reaction on television, and the popular radio presenters can easily exacerbate their already rampant megalomania by deluding themselves that the world is hanging on their every word. Not so – 7 million is about 10 per cent of the population, and 90 per cent of them are probably listening for ten to fifteen minutes at a time, and that only above the roar of traffic, children and the little woman.

It is the remaining ten per cent that cling to your every word, that react by mail, fax and Internet. Thank God for them: without that bunch of anoraks, loonies and incredibly funny people, I would sit before the microphone every morning speechless, mumchance, without an idea with which to bless myself.

That ten per cent clinging loyally to the wreckage is the difference between success and failure: a successful presenter's audience profile is usually made up of ten per cent love, ten per cent hate, and the rest – the eighty per cent – the huge majority of the listening and viewing population, could not care less about you one way or the other.

These people never read the long, tedious profiles of show-business personalities that clog the magazine sections of the Sunday newspapers. They skim through the first couple of paragraphs, then move on. I am convinced that they never read the long, tedious, shrieking-for-attention pieces that pass for television criticism these days, either. Even the ten per cent fanatics do not read them: television critiques are only read by people who actually work in the medium. Why should anybody read a critique of something they have already seen, and made up their own minds about?

This is a point I put to the late Sir David English, a great tabloid editor. He said: 'A good television critic reflects the prejudices of our readers. He endorses, validates their views …' So, if you do not agree with the view of your newspaper's television critic, you are reading the wrong newspaper.

So there we were, the faceless wonders of Irish radio, suddenly transformed into the new playboys of the Western world. Letters began to appear in the newspapers:

'I've read "My Man of the Year" in the *Sunday Review*. As we have not a BBC aerial, I can't say anything about it, but here goes for our own Irishmen:

'*The Man I Would Most Like to Be with on a Desert Island*: 'Terry Wogan, Telefís Éireann newscaster. The most attractive man I know of, with his gorgeous smile.'

And before you start with the cat-calling, read on:

'*The Man I'd Like for a Life Partner*: Andy O'Mahony. Kind, gentle and always delightful …

*The Man I'd Like to Be Able to Turn to in Trouble*: Gay Byrne, a real darling and a real man …'

My kisser was all over Ireland's newspapers and magazines. A critic described me as 'a debonair, competent TV newsman on top of his job'. I was twenty-four …

I learned quickly that fame costs – particularly if you were still playing club rugby on a Saturday afternoon. The usual good-natured gouging and mauling took a nasty personal turn: people seemed to be making a point of singling me out for brutality and maiming. I don't think that it was because they were particularly critical of my television performance – I think it was more the satisfaction of being able to say to their loved ones: 'D'you see that eejit readin' the news with the black eye? I gave him that …'

For much the same reason, it became impossible to go for a sociable pint in the newly fashionable 'lounges' (all strip-lighting, plastic and uncut moquette), where Dublin's young adults congregated to eye each other up. Some young one who had taken a fancy to you on the television would get all worked up, the boyfriend would feel the need to assert his proprietorial masculinity, and there you were, invited outside to participate in three knockdowns or a submission to decide the winner.

This was marginally better than the sycophants and fawners, but it was the end of the 'lounges' for me. And, indeed, pubs. I have never leant on a bar since. For the same reason, I never go shopping in supermarkets. The present Mrs Wogan takes a very pawky view of this, totally failing to understand that it is not because I don't want to go to the supermarket with her, it is just that I can't. Fame has its advantages, too.

## HITTING THE *JACKPOT*

The fan mail and the 'Letters to the Editor' continued to roll in, and RTÉ decided that it would get its money's worth out of me. A quiz-show called, pretty shrewdly, *Jackpot*, was lacking its front man, Gay Byrne, who was wilting under the constant back-and-forth between Manchester and Dublin. Who else to step into the breach but the 'debonair' boy wonder? Actually, *anybody*. I hadn't a clue what I was doing, and it being RTÉ, nobody bothered to tell me. I had never seen the show and hadn't the faintest idea about the rules, or anything else.

That was the way it was in those early days of Irish television. Stick a bit of powder on 'em, stand 'em in front of the camera, and hope for the best. Whenever anybody over here asks me if I ever get nervous doing television, I smile the aforementioned quiet smile, and remember *Jackpot*. It made me nervous for years. It was not really until the success of *Blankety Blank* on BBC 1, a good fifteen years later, that I felt able to relax and be myself in front of a television camera.

It was horrific.

A television critic called Brian Devenney was kinder to me than any critic has been since:

*Terry Wogan's début in* Jackpot *nearly ended in a débâcle after the time-up signal failed to ring a bell for him ...* [I had had no idea that we had reached the end of the programme] *There was something extraordinarily insensitive in the way he was left to appear in vision as suffering from a first-night blackout!*

Despite the débâcle, I continued with the show, and it went from strength to strength, regularly topping the TV ratings. Being a live show, it continued to have its hairy moments: if a contestant answered a question correctly, they could take a gift, or wipe out a point scored by the opponent. 'Delete or Dip' was the catchy title of this round. I asked the question, the lady contestant got it right.

'Delete or Dip?' I queried.

'I'll Dip,' says she.

'Fire away!' says I.

She reached into the box in front of her: 'There's nothin' in here!' she said.

'There must be!'

'No. Nothin'.'

A silence followed, broken only by the sound of the production secretary scurrying down the ladder from the control room with the prizes that she had forgotten to put in the boxes.

## ROMANCING HELEN

Olive White, the original hostess of 'Delete or Dip', left to marry her beloved Kits, and in the fullness of time have four delightful children and live in Fowey in Cornwall. She was replaced by the equally lovely Suzanne MacDougal, who had to endure the same kind of press speculation that Olive had gone through: 'Is it romance between Terry and Olive/Suzanne?'

Well, it was. Romance, that is, but *not* with Olive nor Suzanne, lovely and all as they were. I had found someone even lovelier, at that party I mentioned earlier. Helen and I started seeing each other regularly, in between her trips to Paris, London, and up and down every fashion-show ramp from Dublin to Donegal. We went to the cinema, the theatre and the opera.

I particularly remember the opera: she and her good friend Maida had gone to the box office of the Gaiety to buy the tickets, and, while in the queue, had met two charming older men, who would not countenance the ladies paying for their tickets. No! They should have a box in which to enjoy *La Traviata* to the full, at the gentlemen's expense!

The girls were all excitement as they recounted the old boys' generosity to Jack, Maida's boyfriend (and subsequent husband) and myself. It is a tribute to our stupidity, and the enduring innocence of decent Irish girls, that we suspected nothing as we took our seats in the luxurious box, and awaited the curtain and a feast of fine music. As we made ourselves comfortable, the door of the box opened. In walked the two old boys. As they saw Jack and me, they were visibly shaken. 'Ah, for Jaysus sake!' exclaimed one. The other put it more strongly, but I shall spare you …

It was probably one of the most uncomfortable evenings of my life. I can still see the disappointment on the two fellas' faces, thinking that they had lined up two birds in a box, for a night at the opera, and the girls had brought the boyfriends …

We went, all decked in our finery, with a few of my friends from the newsroom, to the Press Ball. Someone pressed a gin upon me, and the night went downhill from there. I don't remember much about the drive home, but Helen clearly remembers the car weaving in and out of the trees that line the pavement of Waterloo Road, Dublin.

On a wing and a prayer, we parked outside Helen's house in Rathmines, just in time to catch her mother leaving for six o'clock morning Mass. As Helen lowered the steamy window, her sweet and gentle mother looked in. 'Would Terence like to come in for a cup of tea?' she asked. Even as she did, Terence opened his door, and threw up on the road.

Not auspicious, but, after a decent interval of several weeks, Helen eventually did invite me to have lunch with her at the Joyce ancestral pile.

It was a blazing August day, as I entered the lounge, the sun streaming in through its large picture window. There was a roaring fire in the hearth, and, over it, a figure huddled in an overcoat and scarf. 'Who's that?' I whispered. 'My brother Martin,' Helen replied. 'He's got a bad chest …'

Helen cooked the lunch, further endearing herself to my finer feelings, which have always been sited in the general area of my stomach, and, in the finest Irish tradition, while the women busied themselves washing up, the men, Timothy J. Joyce and Michael T. Wogan, sat around the fire.

Tim's conversation was, as ever, largely about himself, and I listened and watched as he slowly talked himself to sleep. He nodded off and I sat back gratefully. I might have flung a few Z's at the ceiling myself, if Tim had not frightened the daylights out of me by leaping forward in his sleep. Even as he leapt, his false teeth flew from his mouth, heading for the fire. With a speed of reaction – and hand – that reminded me of the great Compton in the slips, Tim plucked the flying teeth out of the air, inches from the flames, and pinned them back into his mouth, before slumping back into his chair, snoring heavily. To this day, I will swear that his eyes never opened.

'Going together', 'courting', 'doing a line', that was Helen and me, in popular Irish parlance. Weeks turned into months and attraction into love, but never 'the bold thing'. In common with 99.9 per cent of unmarried Irish couples, we didn't go 'all the way' – frustrating, but exciting and romantic, too.

This generation looks unbelievingly, pityingly, at we poor unfortunates who never consummated our relationship until our wedding night: 'How did you know you were going to be compatible?' Trust me, *we knew* ... Any mistakes, any shortfall in sexual technique, well, we made them together – probably still making them, thirty-five years on.

Anyway, there is a case to be made for self-control: romantic love hardly existed before the Crusades of the twelfth century. And what brought it on? Deprivation and the chastity belt. With lord and master gone for several years to free the Holy Land from the Saracen, milady of the manor was left to fret, untouched and unsatisfied. The gap in the market was filled by strolling musicians and poets: the troubadours, who sang of sundered loves, broken hearts and joyful reunions when the wars were o'er. Romance and courtly love were founded on the non-fulfilment of the sexual urge. To paraphrase my mother, you could say that 'Romance flies out the window when sex walks in the door ...'

We had been romancing, Helen and I, for almost a year when the opportunity arose for her to work in Paris, for the great fashion house Pierre Balmain. She didn't want to go: her French was poor, she had never been there, she didn't want to leave me, she'd be lonely! Of course, she really wanted to go, but wanted me to push her, which I did, and she had a marvellous time.

From the beginning of our relationship, we have been secure in each other, each unafraid to let the other go. Helen's heart is true, so when she returned with tales of Russian émigré princes, and glamorous nights by the Seine, my heart filled not with jealousy, but envy. The restaurants, the food!

As if it were nothing, she let slip that some *boulevardier* had taken her to La Tour d'Argent. My mouth watered at the very name. 'La Tour d'Argent! Spare me no detail, tell me *all*!' She described the décor, the napery, the china, the Seine flowing gently beneath the windows of the great restaurant, the merry banter of her suave companion. 'Yes, yes,' I would cry impatiently, 'but the food, the food! What of the *canard pressé*?'

Even then, I was an avid, nay, slavering reader of food and cookery books, and knew of La Tour D'Argent's legendary pressed duck, each one numbered, like a rare whisky. 'You had the pressed duck?' 'No,' said Helen. 'It was a Friday so I had fish ...'

Subsequently, for reasons that have never been fully explained to me, the Roman Catholic Church loosed its hold on the stomachs of the faithful, and declared that you could eat what you wanted on a Friday. Don't ask why the change, why it was suddenly all right to do something that had been forbidden for a hundred years by the rigid Catholic Church restriction that put whole generations of Irish people off fish forever. Not me, my mother couldn't, wouldn't, cook it ...

Then, Gay Byrne got engaged to Kathleen Watkins, a wonderful harpist and one of Irish television's first 'continuity girls'. In case you came in late, continuity girls were attractive young women who introduced the programmes on television. They are long since out of date in Britain, it is all done by faceless voices now. Television has not got any better, just quicker.

Doubtless backed up by the opinions of a thousand focus groups, the word is, that since the invention of the zapper, and the subsequent erosion of the necessity to get up out of your chair if you want to change the programme, the attention span of the average viewer can be measured in seconds, and very few of them. Therefore, they say, we have got to keep it moving.

They are probably right. We all understand the visual shorthand of television and movies these days, so there is no need to spell everything out. Although, sometimes, when watching the news, it is hard to believe that the message has got through to everybody. For instance, what about the ridiculous convention of the 'establishing shot'. Why do we have to have a sequence of, say, Michael Portillo, walking towards the camera, before we get the shot of him talking to the reporter? We all know who Michael Portillo is, we have seen him a thousand times, yet here he comes again, walking down the street ... For some people, the penny never drops. Sorry, but what is the point of putting blood, sweat and tears into a book like this, if I can't get the odd niggle off my chest?

Gay got engaged to his lovely Kathleen, and the fat was in the fire. The Irish public knew of Helen's and my liaison through our being pictured at hooleys and the odd mention in the gossip columns. I was still regarded as an eligible bachelor – a newspaper cartoon of the time has two young women looking at a TV screen which reads, '*The Fugitive*', a popular American series. One of the girls is saying to the other: 'Which reminds me – Terry Wogan's still on the loose!'

Following Gay and Kathleen's good news, someone burst into verse in a Dublin newspaper:

> *A short while ago we were all pleased to see*
> *That these two top favourites of Irish TV*
> *Were to wed in the summer, this couple so fair*
> *And we'll see them off with a wish and a prayer.*
> *And we hope this engagement will serve as a spur*
> *To entice Terry Wogan to go and choose her.*
> *And since fortune's wheel turns, for one and for all,*
> *We hope he will find her – we'll see in the fall.*

The pressure was on. The writer obviously wanted me to run off with *Jackpot*'s hostess, who 'span the wheel', Suzanne MacDougal, but Helen's father had other ideas. Not a man for elaborate word-play, he greeted me one evening with the simple, yet effective: 'When are ye givin' her the ring?'

I laughed it off in a manly way, but it took me aback. Life was good. I was ensconced snugly at home, under the lash of my mother's pan and skillet, but warm, comfortable, loving and inexpensive. I had more money than I had ever dreamed of, a car, adulation, success, and a girlfriend that caused other young men to faint in the streets. I modelled Aran sweaters in magazines: 'Terry Wogan, the gay bachelor compere of RTÉ's *Jackpot* ...'

'Crowds of women and young girls jammed Drogheda's West Street this morning and traffic was halted for a time as Telefís Éireann's Terry Wogan opened Power's new supermarket ...'

Marriage? Frightening. I was young, in my prime. They loved me. And I loved Helen, and she wanted to get married.

There was only one thing for it: the ring.

I went to the 'Ring King', and he gave me a tray of his best stuff. No, honestly – thousands of pounds' worth of diamonds in the back of my old Morris Minor with the broken passenger seat. It was like carrying the bank's money all over again.

I took the tray over to Helen. She didn't really like any of the rings. I said, 'Ah, well, we won't bother for the moment, then,' a line that she has thrown back in my face ever since. I got another tray, and she found a ring she liked. She was not about to give me another way out.

Helen's model agency leaked the news to the papers. I denied it, so did Helen, but the game was up. We went quietly, to the roar of the Irish newspaper headlines: '1965 Wedding For Terry And Helen!'

## SKULDUGGERY

Meanwhile, back at the ranch: *Jackpot* was still topping the ratings, but, unbeknownst to me, a typical bit of television skulduggery was going on. The executive producer was planning another quiz-show, *Quicksilver*.

As is the way in television, nobody told me. They didn't have to, of course, and nobody likes confrontation, but it might have been good manners, rather than have me find out by reading the newspapers that *Jackpot* was being replaced.

Spool on thirty years and the BBC does exactly the same thing to me, replacing *Wogan* with *Eldorado* ... *Plus ça change* ... At least the BBC knew that it had loused up – and gave me an apologetic dinner. RTÉ didn't pretend to notice, not even as the newspapers printed the complaints: 'One of the big mysteries of this season's TÉ programmes has been the unexplained absence of Terry Wogan. What is the point of building up a personality into a household name, and then dropping him?' *Plus c'est la même chose*. Letters flowed into the Editor's postbags and RTÉ gave me lots of other television work, but, naively, I was hurt, disenchanted.

I began to write letters to the BBC and commercial television in Britain. I got called for auditions and screen tests, and Helen and I had a couple of lovely weekends in London, but although the tests seemed to be well received, nothing ever came of them.

I thought I might be barking up the wrong tree, so I sent a tape of my radio work to the BBC Light Programme. It landed on the desk of the Assistant Head of the Gramophone Records Department, a man of military bearing with a handlebar moustache, Mark White. When he tried to play it, he found that the tape was back to front. Any normal busy executive up to his armpits in tapes from budding broadcasters would have binned it. Not Mark White. He re-spooled the tape, listened to it, and offered me a job. Along with Denis Meehan in Ireland, I owe more to Mark White than anybody else in British broadcasting.

Mark offered me *Midday Spin*, a half-hour programme of records played in the BBC studios in London, and presented by me on a line from the RTÉ studios in Dublin. He sent one of his best men, Derek Mills, over to see me. We went for a trip around Dublin Bay in a friend's boat, and I sent him back the next day full of food and drink.

Derek was to become one of my best friends, both inside and outside of the BBC, along with his wife Doreen Davies. They, in turn, were to become two of the major moving spirits of Radios 1 and 2, further down the line.

A charming, boyish chap called Johnny Beerling produced

*Midday Spin.* He went on to become Controller of Programmes, Radio 1, and a successful one, before Margaret Thatcher frightened them into changing it from Britain's most popular music station into something for the birds. Thatcher could not see the point of BBC Radio duplicating commercial radio's output; she threatened to do away with Radio 1. Matthew Bannister took on the task of making the station more esoteric. He sacked its most popular disc jockeys, and lost millions of listeners in the process. The sad thing was, that even as he did so, Margaret Thatcher got the push ...

*Midday Spin* did not set the world alight, but it didn't frighten the horses either. The Gramophone Records Department offered me more work – a couple more series of *Midday Spins*, a programme of Christmas records. I did these from London, with a producer called Peter Chiswell, a South African given to making 'Beep-Beep' noises like the RoadRunner, and drinking like a sailor. After recording the show, we downed what must have been a barrel of port in a Soho bar. I barely made the plane home the following morning.

## THE VERTICAL PLAN

Back in Dublin, I continued with the radio announcing, the newsreading, the music programmes and the television. *Round-about Now* was described as 'a summer miscellany', a series about which I remember precisely zip, apart from the producer/director, a man with three names: at Trinity, Dublin, he was Michael Bogdanovich; producing me, he was Bogdin; and when he finally ended up at the National Theatre, London, having people take their kit off in *The Romans in Britain*, he was Michael Bogdanov.

I have never known whether the use of the three names was designed to keep him one hour ahead of the posse, or due to his wonderful sense of the ridiculous. Probably the latter, which would account for his short-lived career with RTÉ!

Meanwhile, Gunnar Rugheimer, an American/Swedish hardman, had taken the helm as Controller of Programmes, Irish Television. As always in television, the new broom sweeps clean, or at least brings down a few cobwebs, and Gunnar had a bright idea: the 'Vertical Plan'. This had two immediate pluses going for it, at least as far as Mr Rugheimer was concerned. Firstly, nobody knew what it meant, and secondly, it made all other plans appear horizontal, or supine.

The plan, as far as I ever understood it, was to give each weekday night (RTÉ didn't start transmitting until 5 p.m.) a character of its own, with a host that would enhance its characteristics. I was to be Mr Friday, and all this long before Chris Evans was even born ... So, every Friday, up I would pop into the sitting rooms of Ireland, describing in glowing detail the delights of the evening ahead. Then, in between programmes, I would present five- to ten-minute magazine items: comedy, music, a quick interview or two.

If there was a light entertainment show to present, there I would be again. I was all over Friday night, like a cheap suit. The only thing I didn't do was read the news, which probably was the only thing I could have done properly. It was all live – and, if you were of a nervous disposition, life-threatening.

As you have probably gathered, meticulous preparation and painstaking production were not the characteristics of early Irish television, and the magazine items, not to put too fine a point on it, were cobbled together. Only the sheer talent of people like Eamonn Morrissey and Frank Kelly kept the comedy cameos from dying like dogs, but the musical items were a law unto themselves.

I remember introducing a lovely young guitarist, perched fetchingly on a stool. Even as I spoke her fair name, there was a tremendous crash. Out of the corner of my eye I saw stool, girl and guitar up-ended on the floor. The camera stayed with me, the floor manager gave me two fingers, and it was not his way of asking me to leave. You probably have not experienced the *frisson* that goes with having to speak to the nation for two minutes, without a thought in your head. These were days long before the Blessed Autocue, and you really were on your own ... I covered the two minutes, in what only can have been gibberish, and was relieved to see the floor manager make a circular motion with his hand – the wind-up – finishing post in sight.

Just then, someone discovered that the guitar was broken

beyond repair. The floor manager smiled wanly, and stuck another two fingers in the air. 'Did I get nervous doing live interviews on *Wogan*?' 'Doesn't seven hours of live television on *Children in Need* fill me with dread?' Throw it all at me. Give it your best shot. Nothing anyone can do can come anywhere close to the effect of those two fingers on the pit of my stomach, all those years ago.

I can't remember what happened to the Vertical Plan – it must have petered out, and Gunnar Rugheimer along with it. Years later, I met him again, at the BBC, where he was Head of Purchased Programmes – he bought all the American stuff, like *Dallas*. And that was where I once more figured in Mr Rugheimer's plans. Rightly or wrongly, I was perceived in the BBC as the main architect in the runaway success of *Dallas* with the British viewing public.

This rumour had started on my Radio 2 morning programme, with a few observations from me concerning the apparent fact that, although richer than Croesus, the Ewing family of Dallas had only one telephone – in the hall; that they had walk-in wardrobes, but only wire coat-hangers; that nobody ever touched a morsel of food at breakfast; that there were only about twenty people at the lavish Oil Barons' Ball; that wedding receptions appeared to be held in the driveway by the garage; that characters like Miss Ellie and Digger Barnes kept getting new heads; that every time they sat around the swimming pool, there was a wind strong enough to blow a tinker off his missus. The listeners, bless 'em, responded; *Dallas* became a cult, and then a full-blown ratings-winner.

The thing of it, said Gunnar, was they had bought a *Dallas* spin-off series, featuring the Poison Dwarf's dad and black sheep of the Ewings, Gary. It was about middle-class, upwardly mobile Americans, rather than filthy rich ones. It was called *Knots Landing*, and they would like me to give it the kind of boost I had given *Dallas*.

I refrained from mentioning the Vertical Plan, and did my best, but *Knots Landing* never had the *Dallas* magic. It was a run-of-the-mill daytime American soap-opera, that, indeed, went on to great soapy success in the States, but never really took off here. I could do little with it – it didn't have the scope, the scale, the sheer grandiose foolishness that made *Dallas* so awful, and so wonderful. I suppose you could apply the same principles to the *Eurovision Song Contest*.

## WEDDING BELLS

By now, the die was cast. We had named the date 25 April, 1965. I had asked the brother to be my best man, and Brendan – an old pal, and fellow-veteran of a thousand Saturday nights – to hold my coat. Helen had her best friend, Maida, and her younger sister, Miriam, as bridesmaids. Various ushers and matrons-of-honour were appointed, Helen's local parish church lined up, and the Country Club, Portmarnock, selected as the venue for the grand reception.

And 'grand' was the word. This was Timothy J. Joyce's big day, and he was going all the way, and damn the torpedoes. To anyone else it was Helen's big day, and could even be considered mine as well, but to Tim, around whom the world revolved, it was his. After all, he was paying for it, and the sky was the limit.

The wedding breakfast selected was the very top of the range, at 17s.6d. a head. Only the finest of wines were countenanced and there was to be a free bar. Only the very wealthy or the very foolhardy have a free bar at an Irish wedding. Drink brings out the worst in the Irish, and free drink is asking for trouble.

Before the big day dawned, we had to find somewhere we could rest our weary heads together, as we set sail on matrimony's frail barque. Helen and I looked at houses, but, as is our wont, or certainly mine, not for very long nor very hard. We found a pretty little dormy bungalow beneath Killiney Hill, with a view of the sea from the back garden if you looked very hard through the trees.

It was to be our home for only four years. We thought it was for life. I wonder if it would have made any difference to our happiness if it had been? I doubt it. I could be happy with Helen anywhere. I did not really know that at the time, of course. Oh, I knew that she was beautiful, kind, gentle, good-humoured, steadfast – all the qualities that a man could possibly want in a woman

– and she was a wonderful cook, but did I really appreciate her then? Certainly not as much as I do now.

The Big Day dawned. It rained. The brother and I got togged out in the rented finery, I kissed my tearful mother, and we headed for the church. It was chaos: thousands of people, mostly young girls and auld biddies, swarmed all over the church, its grounds and the Rathmines Road, holding up the traffic.

Brian and I ran the gauntlet of cheers and jeers, prayers and exhortations: 'Good luck, Terry.' 'God bless you, son!'

'Isn't he gorgeous?' 'You're only an eejit, d'you know that?' 'Are you breakin' that suit in for a friend?'

We made it inside the door of the church. Sanctuary? Not likely. The crowd followed us in, crowding in the pews, standing on the benches, crushing up the aisles. The ushers were over-whelmed, the invited guests had to battle their way to their seats. Helen was late, a bride's privilege, particularly when you have to fight every inch of the way from the church door to the altar rails.

She looked ethereally beautiful, enhanced by an ivory skin that was a little paler than usual. Struggling your way up the aisle to your own wedding can take it out of a girl, and, as we knelt before the priest, she took hold of my hand in a vice-like grip. I thought it was because she was afraid if she let go, she would lose me, but it was really to stop herself falling over in a faint.

She remembers little of the ceremony – all I can remember is the choir, organized by my friend Cecil Barror, and Liam Devally ringing the rafters with his tenor. I remember walking back down the aisle with my beautiful new bride on my arm, while what seemed like half of Dublin applauded and cheered: 'Isn't she lovely?' 'Me life on you both!' 'Have yiz got an umbrella? It's lashin' rain outside …'

It stopped raining by the time we got to the Country Club, Portmarnock, but the reception is even more of a blur. I know we ran the gamut of the wedding photos, because I have the evidence in front of me, but the day passed by me like a dream.

The free bar was a hit from the start, and most of the guests were three sheets to the wind before they sat down to dine. They were also a good hour and a half late sitting down, but that is always the way in Ireland. Talk and drink takes precedence over food, and rightly so.

The only sober people were Helen and myself, both too nervous and overwhelmed to enjoy ourselves, and Brian, who had telegrams to read and speeches to make. That is the thing about an Irish wedding, there are always plenty of speeches. The priest, the bride's father, the groom's father, the best man, the groom, and anybody from the body of the hall who feels the urge to let fly.

In my experience, only the Swedes have more speechifying at a wedding – and they are not above dragging passers-by in off the streets to say a few words.

All that talk can be a bit wearing, but it is preferable to some English weddings I have attended – especially the nobby ones, when all the money is spent on the location, usually a smart Park Lane Hotel and the Champagne. This leaves only enough funds for a few desultory nibbles; nobody gets to sit down to a square meal and a friendly chat, and the speeches are few and pathetic. Can it be that people do not want to make a fuss, just in case 'things don't work out'?

When Helen and I married, that was *It*. There was going to be no turning back, no running away, and if 'things didn't work out', we knew that we had to stick with them, until they did. And we have. There have been hard days, there have been disagreements, arguments, slamming of doors, cries of frustration, but never fisticuffs. She has hit me with a three-iron, but only because I was trying to show her where she was going wrong with her golf swing.

As the cliché has it, we have never let the sun go down on our anger, always ended up laughing in each other's arms. I suppose, in common with most married couples, we have always agreed on the really serious issues, and only fallen out over the most trivial ones: the loss of a sock, the lack of a hanky, the creases in a suit …

Timothy J. Joyce was in his element at the wedding reception. It was his party, and he enjoyed every last minute of it. He spoke freely when called upon, and when not called upon.

He stood up between speeches and during them. He interrupted my father's speech, for which neither Michael nor Rose Wogan ever forgave him, and sang 'This Is My Lovely Day' every time anybody proposed a toast.

People sang from their tables, as the mood took them – Helen was forced to sing 'My Love Is Like a Red Red Rose' by her mother, who, despite her gentle reticence, could be very determined. While we were courting, I would sometimes go back to Helen's house on a Sunday evening for tea, which usually turned into a 'musical evening'. Helen's mother would insist on all the family singing, even those without a note in their heads. I simply hid behind the curtains or under a chair.

I find nothing more embarrassing than the awful Irish habit of calling for a song at every social gathering. It is excruciating – painful for the victim, and worse for the listeners. Why the Irish feel that they have to put themselves through this agony is beyond me; I know everybody else is as embarrassed as me – I can see it in their eyes, yet they applaud and cheer: 'Good man yourself! Give us another one,' and we are off again, into purgatory. It is masochism masquerading under the guise of Irishness – the awful price we pay to keep our reputation of *bonhomie* and good fellowship. The *craic* – self-conscious Irishry at its worst.

Helen and I slipped away, with the free bar still humming, the guests pink with drink, the women with their hats askew. We caught a plane to London, where I repaired to the Gents to shake the last of the confetti out of my underpants (some of the ushers had got a little over-excited while bidding the couple farewell) and then on to lovely Torremolinos for the honeymoon.

It must have been two in the morning when we got to our room in the ultra-modern, Moorish-ish Hotel Al-Andalus. The room was spacious, with a view of the Mediterranean from its balcony, but there was a drawback – a serious one. I had ordered a large double bed, as befitting the glories of a wedding night, and what stood before me? – two singles! I stormed down to reception, but it was too late in the day or night to do anything about it.

So, next morning, as my child-bride and I sat on our balcony with the full Continental breakfast before us, two giggling chambermaids lashed the two single beds together, and honour was satisfied. We came back to our dormy bungalow in Killiney, and settled down to live happily ever after.

## PAIN AND GRIEF

Denis Meehan appointed me senior announcer, which put a number of other noses out of joint, but it meant nothing. I had no more influence nor authority – it just took some of the work-load off him.

The days, weeks, months hummed along happily: announcing from Henry Street, newsreading from the Television Centre, the odd freelance series on radio and television. The BBC continued to give me work, and I presented the prestigious *Housewives' Choice* on the Light Programme, again with my words coming from Dublin and the music from the BBC in Broadcasting House, London. Helen did a little modelling and photographic work here and there. We planted roses outside the front door; she cooked me delicious dinners; and bliss was not the word for it …

Helen was five months pregnant, when I began to get the pains. I thought my body might be coming out in sympathy with her, but I went to the doctor as a precaution. He could find nothing wrong with me. I remember going for a day's golf with the lads, and having to stop the car to throw up, with the sudden pains in my stomach. I went back to the doctor. He pressed about my ample abdomen (bliss can put on a lot of weight) and pronounced me fit.

It was not even a hysterical pregnancy. What it was, was an appendix; and one fine Saturday morning, when I was getting ready to go to Lansdowne Road for a rugby international, it burst and I doubled up in agony. The ambulance could not come for me, because I was at home and not an accident case out in the street. I offered to lie outside my front gate, but, in the end, the doctor who earlier could find nothing wrong with me, drove me across the city to the Mater Hospital, where the surgeon removed what was left of my appendix.

I woke up looking like one of the Borg from *Star Trek*, with tubes issuing from every orifice, and one from a hole in my stomach, which had not been there previously. Peritonitis is what happens when you let appendix pains go too far, and it can be fatal if it is not treated in time.

As I woke, the surgeon who had performed the operation came into the room. 'I was so worried about you, I left the rugby match before the end,' he said. I tried not to laugh, because it hurt. One night, as I lay in my hospital bed, I heard a tremendous bang. Next morning the papers were full of it: some eejit, in the holy names of the saints and martyrs of Ireland, had blown up poor old Nelson's Pillar.

Helen's time came, and with both of us beside ourselves with excitement and anticipation, she went into the nursing home to have our baby, our first child. She had a terrible, terrible time, hours and hours in labour, with me increasingly worried, in and out of the ward, holding her hand, helpless …

Eventually, somehow, the ordeal came to an end, and our Vanessa was born. Beautiful, pale, fragile, born with a serious heart condition, she was taken from Helen almost immediately and placed in an intensive care unit. I took Helen home a couple of days later without her baby and it broke her heart. I nearly broke my hand, smashing it into a wall, in grief and frustration.

Vanessa never came home, she died three weeks later. We blocked it out, and, even after all these years, we still can't talk about it. We have had three beautiful, healthy children around whom our whole lives revolve, and yet … and yet … the pain has never gone away, and I know that Helen and I will carry that terrible sense of loss to our graves.

## REPLACING THE PIRATES

I broke new ground on Irish radio with a midday show called *Terry Awhile*. Some title, but I was young. It involved music and live, unedited, unexpurgated phone calls. People would write in to ask me to call up someone – anyone from their granny to the local madman – and I, like the eejit I was, would then phone them up live on the air.

It is commonplace now – the staple, the bread-and-butter of every local and national radio concern from the Skelligs to the

Orkneys – but then it was ground-breaking, as well as parlous. They talked too little or too much; they were catatonic or hysterical; they didn't believe it was me, so they treated what they thought was one of their friends having a laugh to a tirade of abuse and bad language.

It was pitiful, but it was priceless – SAS training for the radio. Of course, anyone who engages the public live on air is asking for everything they get: Bunny Carr, another former bank clerk, who, like myself, had drifted into radio, had a weekly show on RTÉ in which he visited obscure locations all over Ireland, and talked to the local characters:

'So, Mary, you've lived in Lisdoonvarna all your life?'

'I have so.'

'And you wouldn't live anywhere else?'

'No.'

'Have you ever been to Lahinch?' [About fifteen miles away.]

'No.'

'Ennis?' [About thirty miles.]

'No.'

'Limerick?' [About forty miles.]

'No.'

'Well, Mary, that's extraordinary. Where apart from Lisdoonvarna have you been?'

'Chicago. I went there last year to see my nephew ...'

Things can go wrong when you wander outside a warm studio. I have done many an outside broadcast for BBC Radio 2 of a morn: St Brelade's Bay, Jersey, with the early-morning sun dancing out of the waves, seemed like a good idea, but once you have painted the picture with words, it can be a tad boring with only a seagull to talk to; and what about Great Yarmouth Promenade with its funfair? – except that my programme starts at 7.30 a.m. and the funfair didn't open until 9 a.m.

I sent a tape of *Terry Awhile* to my mentor at the BBC, Mark White, this time the right way round, and he invited me to come over to London for an audition for a new nightly show, ten-till-midnight, *Late Night Extra*. It had music, news, reports, interviews, features, and was designed to put both the BBC's new babies, Radios 1 and 2, to bed at the same time.

The BBC had finally persuaded the Government that the off-shore 'pirate' stations, that had grown like seaweed in the mid-sixties and captured the ears of every young pop music-lover, were not a good thing. Their enthusiasm, youth, and wall-to-wall, ship-to-shore pop music had revolutionized the listening habits of the younger generation, but they were not paying anybody, as they bobbed about in the Irish Sea and the Channel. Neither music publishers, songwriters, singers, nor the Exchequer were getting their accustomed pound of flesh.

It was not much of a picnic for the underpaid disc jockeys either, throwing up over the side in between records. Record companies loved the pirates, though; they were helping to sell their discs by the million. So it was all right for the BBC, the Music Publishers Association and the Performing Right Society to say: make the pirates walk the plank, but who was going to fill the aching pop music-less void? Who else?

In 1967, the BBC stood on its head. It introduced a new network to replace the pirates in the hearts and minds of the young: Radio 1. And since we were into numerals, it abandoned the Light Programme, the Third Programme and the Home Service. As Lord Reith did hand-springs in his grave, those worthies became Radios 2, 3 and 4 respectively.

The avuncular and clever Robin Scott was handed the baby Radio 1, and all the pirates who could swim ashore were recruited into the ranks of respectability. All the new disc jockeys were paraded in front of the press, and the new millennium of British radio had begun.

Everybody has seen the famous picture, taken on the steps of All Souls Church, opposite Broadcasting House: Tony Blackburn, Kenny Everett, John Peel, Jimmy Young, Ed Stewart and a raft of famous piratical faces that blazed briefly, and were gone. And there in the middle row, in his best grey suit, your man. The audition had gone well, and they had offered me *Late Night Extra* on Radios 1 and 2, every Wednesday night.

# NINE
# THE GREAT LEAP FORWARD

The new job meant flying from Dublin to London every Wednesday lunchtime and back every Thursday morning for £35 a programme, which did not leave much after you had deducted air fares, hotels and meals, but I didn't even have to think about it.

I had asked the BBC to clear it with RTÉ in Dublin, but they overlooked this. After the famous photograph of the New Jocks had been plastered all over the Irish, as well as the British newspapers, I got an ultimatum from Kevin McCourt, the Director-General of RTÉ: they would kindly allow me to work out my six-week contract with the BBC for *Late Night Extra*, but from then on I must focus all my broadcasting efforts on Ireland.

This was reasonable enough; RTÉ could not have their senior radio announcer freelancing for another national radio station. Again I did not have to think about it. I resigned from the announcing staff of RTÉ. After marrying Helen, and leaving the bank, it was probably the third best move of my life! And I never even thanked Kevin McCourt ...

All the same, it was only a six-week contract with the BBC, and I had precious little else: *Terry Awhile* once a week, and the odd bit of television. And Helen was pregnant again ...

Radios 1 and 2 got up and running, and I started my weekly commuting to and from the Big Smoke. *Late Night Extra* hit the ground running, to uniformly favourable reviews, and, with producers like Bobby Jaye, Richard Willcox and Martin Fisher, was the greatest of fun to work on. Bobby would often drop me back at my hotel on the Cromwell Road after the programme, and, years later, confessed to me that at that time he was not at all happy with my ambitions to work full-time on British radio and television.

As a senior light entertainment producer, he knew just how

difficult it would be for me to make any more than the tiny ripples I was making then.

'I really worried about you,' he said a couple of years ago, 'happy family and career back in gentle, easy-going Dublin,' [which shows how much he knew about Dublin] 'regular work on the BBC – I couldn't understand why you wanted to risk it, throw it all into the rat-race here.'

Don't ask me. I just knew that I was on my way. Failure and its consequences never occurred to me – they never have.

I suppose because I have never been out of work, never known the misery of the dole queue, or the frustration of waiting for the phone to ring, the traditional insecurity about the job has never impinged. It must be the reason why I have never been afraid to take risks with my career, and my family's lives. I am not a physical risk-taker: I never minded flinging myself into a rugby scrum, but skiing, bungee-jumping, sky-diving, or even climbing on to the ladder to fix the Christmas tree lights, are activities I leave to better men.

With my broadcasting career, however, I have stuck my neck out farther than most: leaving my permanent, pensionable post with RTÉ; upping sticks, wife and baby son to Britain on the basis of a six-week contract; walking away from *Blankety Blank* at the peak of its popularity; taking on a live three-nights-a-week chat-show at peak viewing time; returning to the daily morning show of Radio 2. Dammit, I was brave. Dammit, it didn't seem so at the time. It never has. I just never thought I was going to fail. Whenever things have gone wrong (and nobody gets it for free), I have ignored it as the idle wind and moved on.

## IN THE MONEY

Back in Dublin, my friend Oliver Barry, one of Ireland's most successful showband managers, asked me to present a sponsored radio show built around his various music acts, and, pretty soon, a couple more sponsors asked me to do their shows. Suddenly, I was earning more money than I had ever dreamed of: over £6000 a year, according to my accountant.

We got rid of the old Riley Elf, and I bought a Sunbeam

Rapier. I started to do two nights a week on *Late Night Extra* – Friday as well as Wednesday. Three nights in a London hotel would have beggared me, even allowing for the less than salubrious accommodation I was frequenting. Luckily, our good friends, Kits and Olive Browning (remember – *Jackpot* hostess, Miss Ireland; married to Daphne du Maurier's adored only son?), gave me free board and lodging in their beautiful house, an old converted tithe barn, in Taplow, Bucks.

It was not entirely free board and lodging – I had to play at least three hard-fought Subbuteo table-football matches with Kits in the course of each stay, occasionally accompany them to Stamford Bridge to watch Chelsea, and smuggle in a bottle of whiskey and a bottle of vodka every week 'neath the eagle eyes of the British and Irish customs.

That was not the worst part of travelling between the two islands: foot-and-mouth disease was rampant among British livestock at the time, and seeing as how agriculture was still the most important industry in Ireland in the sixties, the Department of Agriculture and Fisheries was taking no chances. Every time I got off the London plane at Dublin Airport, I was sprayed with a fine mist of chemicals. I and my clothes smelt like a halibut for days. It went on for the best part of a year, but I never caught foot-and-mouth disease, so it must have worked …

When Alan was about a year old, we thought we would have a holiday, and left him in the tender care of our friends Maida and Jack. We took three weeks touring through France, Switzerland, Italy, and back through France again, via the Côte d'Azur. We had a marvellous time, sunshine, good food, interesting people, yet it turned to dust when we went to collect Alan. As Helen took him in her arms, he heaved a huge sigh. It sounded like he had been keeping it in for three weeks, and it went through me like a knife. That was the last time we took a holiday away from our children.

Alan lives in London now, but he was always a home-boy. We could never have sent him away to school, it would have broken his gentle heart. He hated his years at Warwick University, reading psychology and philosophy, because it took him away from home, and he was miserable teaching English in

Murcia, Spain, for nearly a year. He is happy now – independent and successful – but the important things for him will always be home, hearth, family and the friends he made at school and university.

## AN UNMITIGATED COCK-UP

Around this time, Sheila O'Donovan of the Stanley Barnett Agency became my first-ever agent/manager, and I quickly made friends with the junior, Paul Lang. Paul, another ex-Jesuit lad and a former head boy at Beaumont College, became one of my best friends. He also became the editor of BBC TV's *Grandstand*, the biggest sporting programme of the age, was poached by ITV Sports, married Nina, and died suddenly of a pulmonary embolism in his early thirties, just before his son Nick was born.

I was godfather to Nick, who, last time I saw him, at nineteen years of age, had just come back from a year in the Canadian Rockies and was heading out to the Swiss Alps, happy to be a ski-bum or a chalet cook, whatever, before settling down to life's more mundane rigmarole. I miss Paul, but still see him in his son's smile.

Sheila O'Donovan got me my first television job, a beauty contest from some West End stage. I was terrible. I didn't get any better at beauty contests over the years, either. I don't know why, but they never commanded my full attention. Maybe it was the smell of sweat, perfume and fear – and *that* was only Michael Aspel! He was the best at it: I could never quite come to terms with Miss Bristol or Miss Oldham, and when the late, funny Ray Moore and I used to do Miss UK or Miss Great Britain or even Miss World together, it was a big, silly laugh from beginning to end.

It was not easy to keep a straight face around Eric D. Morley, for whom these beauty contests were a good deal more important than the Second Coming, and who ran them along the lines of a Nuremberg Rally. He always announced the winners in what he called 'reserve' order, which didn't help, either.

I particularly remember making an unmitigated cock-up of Miss Great Britain, in Blackpool. I think what put me off was ordering a pie for lunch, and finding it devoid of meat. Potatoes and gravy, those were the constituents; I still can't believe that people could eat such appalling rubbish. It is a measure of the importance I attach to such things that I can still remember that pie, and have completely forgotten almost everything else about my television career.

Maybe I have got it right ... David Vine and I were sharing the gig, and my job was to interview the poor contestants on stage, on camera. They were terrified, although hardly as frightened as I was, having mixed up their name cards, and having not the slightest idea of their names or where they came from. Not only that, I hadn't a clue whether they were kind to animals, wanted to work with children, or save the whale.

I don't know what it is that stops you turning tail, and running away at times like this: standing there in front of the camera, bathed in flop-sweat, gabbling in fright. They say the body has no memory of pain, but I remember that, just as I remember the pie ...

The lovely and quick-witted Jenny McAdam won that contest. I know that, because she co-presented *Come Dancing* with me for a season or two. And, no, we never danced together; we were just good friends, our friendship cemented by endless car and rail journeys up and down the country to compere the likes of Home Counties South against Scotland, or Wales versus the Midlands. Thrilling encounters, all part of the longest-running television light entertainment show of all time.

I have only hazy recollections of the train journeys, but remember that a fierce battle was entered into between my agent and the BBC, on the matter of fares. Apparently, the rule was: producer travels first class, presenter (otherwise known as 'the talent', or 'hobbledehoy') second class, or steerage. It was an immutable rule, written on stone by BBC Contracts.

We fought long and hard to overthrow it, having to invoke the ultimate sanction of refusal to sign the contract at all, until the clause was changed. I hope Carol Smillie, Gaby Roslin, Dale Winton, and all those others who now travel first class at the BBC's expense, are suitably grateful.

# COME DANCING

This programme's executive producer was pipe-smoking, kindly, good-humoured Barrie Edgar – one of the best and nicest people with whom I have ever worked. A gentleman, a type that, despite everything you may hear, the BBC still breeds: John Getgood, Will Wyatt, David Hatch ... No, hang on, they have all taken early retirement ... Trust me, there are other pearls among the swine, but I won't embarrass them – you will know who they are by how I refer to them in this weighty tome.

The producer/director, Ken Griffin, was another gent, and we made a happy team. BBC Radio 2 was very understanding when it was impossible for me to get back from a *Come Dancing* location in time for my early-morning radio show. Often, I would present the programme from BBC Radio studios in Glasgow, Edinburgh, Norwich or Cardiff, but I can also recall hammering down the motorways of Britain at all hours of the morning after a late TV recording, falling into bed, and getting up a couple of hours later to hammer again up the M4 to Broadcasting House for my 7.30 a.m. start on Radio 2.

Still, I was a young man and I loved it! Does it make me a foolish old man, to admit that I still do? (I have just broken the second rule of broadcasting: Never Ask A Question To Which You Don't Know The Answer. What is the first rule? Never Eat Anything They Send You ...)

*Come Dancing* got viewing audience figures, at ten o'clock in the evening, that a scheduler these days would kill for – eleven million was not unusual. It was the colour, the movement, the glamour, the competition between the countries and the regions. It was Frank and Peggy Spencer, the formation teams, the flash of tempestuous knicker during the Latin-American that kept the public, and particularly those wearing only dirty raincoats, glued to the box.

It certainly was not the presenter. It never is. I introduced *Come Dancing* for at least seven seasons, in front of millions of viewers, and, at the end of it all, the public was still firmly convinced that it was introduced by Peter West, the show's original presenter. I made all the impact of a blancmange, but it was fun;

I saw the country from Paisley to the Mumbles, from Leeds to Torquay. I saw the inside of every ballroom from Sauchiehall Street to Purley.

Speaking of Sauchiehall Street reminds me that passions ran high during the various regional confrontations, and nowhere higher than in Scotland. The Scots treated me like one of their own, but they could never abide Peter West. They blamed him for a narrow defeat that they had suffered some years previously. To the Scots ballroom-dancing fraternity, Peter was up there with Edward Longshanks in the unpopularity stakes.

Heaven knows how he offended, but on the night it happened, Peter West had to barricade himself inside a dressing room, while an incensed mob of Scots ballroom dancers, some of them wearing 200 yards of tulle sewn by their mothers, bayed for his blood. He left Scotland under a cloak and an assumed name, and never had the nerve to go back there again ... It can be a rough old game.

Throughout *Come Dancing* I never put a pump under me: I never learned the Dashing White Sergeant, the Gay Gordons, the Fylde Waltz or the Military Two-Step.

I could never understand how the judges differentiated between the dancers. The good ones all looked the same to me: the men pale but determined, heavily Brylcreemed, insurance/bank clerks to a man, although I do remember one being described by the commentator as 'a plater from Sheffield'. The girls were glorious: yards of material, inches of make-up, legs up to their armpits, secretaries, shop-assistants, hairdressers. Where did they go? Do they still dance at home in front of their embarrassed children? Is there anywhere left to dance, the way they once did? Why am I asking all these Old-Geezer-type questions?

## OFF TO THE BIG SMOKE

The trips back and forward to London added *frisson* and colour to my already happy life with Helen and Alan, but I knew that it could not go on for ever. So, I sent Mark White yet another tape, of a more up-to-date *Terry Awhile*. This time, he really stuck his neck out for me. One of Radio 1's biggest stars, Jimmy Young, was taking the month of July, 1969, off, and would I like to take over Jimmy's show for that month? Has the Pope a balcony?

Once again, Kits and Olive, now known as 'Hacker' (don't ask!), came up trumps. They were off on holiday, too, and offered us the use of their lovely home for a month. It was the biggest break so far, and we took it. Helen and Alan came over for the month with me, and this time my commuting was the other way around, flying to Dublin to record my sponsored radio shows.

I had to learn to work a 'self-operational' desk: play my own records and tapes, operate the microphone, open and close the faders. A nice man called Roger Pusey gave me a whole half hour of instruction. I have never been able to do it properly since, but I have never cared. From the start, I always knew that the technical thing was secondary, far behind what was really important: what you said when you opened the mike. I listened to the other disc jockeys, the ex-pirates – Blackburn, Cash, Brady, Rosko. They were fading the music, blending the jingles. They were smart, sharp, slick. Not me, never would be.

I also noticed that, amusing and bright as they were, they were not really communicating. It was not a dialogue with the listener, it was a monologue to an audience. Letters and cards were read out, but they were not funny, quirky; in the main they were sycophantic. The audience had quickly gathered that the way to get their names mentioned, or their dedications played, was to butter up the host: 'Dear Tony/Dave/Pete, we think you're wonderful and your programme is great …' It didn't seem to me that that was the way friends communicated! Friends don't compliment each other; the admiration is taken for granted, along with the affection. Friends josh, insult, send each other up.

From day one on the Jimmy Young show, it was that kind of reaction I was looking for. Of course it didn't happen in the space of a month, with a new boy they had hardly heard of, but I must have made the right noises. Helen, Alan and I had hardly returned to Dublin and the roses round our door in Killiney, when Mark White made another offer: take over the afternoon slot shared by Radios 1 and 2, in October.

The contract was for a whole six weeks, and they would pay

me a handsome £135 a week for my trouble. It was a lot less than I was earning in Ireland, and six weeks was nothing. If I failed, it would be back to dear old Dublin with my tail between my legs and muted laughter behind my back.

I rented a little furnished house in Farnham Common, near Burnham Beeches, Buckinghamshire. We put a few necessities in the back of the Sunbeam Rapier, and our little family said goodbye to Killiney once again. It was only supposed to be for six weeks, but it was goodbye for good. We never went back to live in our pretty little dormy bungalow again. Helen, Alan and I took the ferry from Dun Laoghaire to Liverpool, like so many millions of Irish immigrants before us, and then the long road to London.

The house in Farnham Common was no great shakes, and I am sure that if Helen had picked one it would have had a great deal more charm. It was years before she told me how lonely and homesick she was during those first few weeks, but she didn't want to upset me. I was full of my new show, happy and optimistic about our new life, the career in British broadcasting that had opened up for me in the space of a couple of months, so I never noticed how unhappy Helen was.

Loyal Maida came over from Dublin for a week to cheer her up and we saw lots of Kits and Hacker. Slowly, resiliently, Helen began to make new friends from the people around her. It has always been one of her gifts to make friends, to bring people together. She built a life for herself and brought me along with her ...

I could spend the morning with Helen and Alan, then off to Broadcasting House for my 3 p.m. to 5 p.m. slot on Radios 1 and 2. I was usually home again by six o'clock. Those were the days when the M4 worked, carrying the amount of traffic it was designed for, and west of London was the most accessible location for the commuter.

It is a different story nowadays, of course, with millions more vehicles and every motorway in the country congested from six o'clock in the morning. I could not do the three-to-five slot now from where I live, twenty-eight miles west of the capital. It would take me at least an hour to get in, and two and a half to get home again.

The only reason I am still doing a daily radio stint, apart from the fact that I love it, is that my early-morning Radio 2 show means that I can travel in and out at off-peak times. I see the jams as I travel against the rush-hour traffic. Rush hour! It is bumper to bumper from seven to ten o'clock in the morning, three to eight o'clock in the afternoon and evening.

Some commuters spend up to five hours a day in their cars. I don't know how they do it, but then I have never lived to work. And I don't eat to live. Which is where 'The Fight on Flab' came in. I can't remember exactly how or when it started, perhaps I picked up on the then infant trend of diet and exercise, but it was the making of me and my afternoon radio show.

'Fight the Flab' is common parlance these days, but we were breaking new ground on popular radio. A boffin was brought in to draft the exercises. I read them out at 4 p.m. every day, and within weeks it seemed as if half the female population was flat on its back, panting. I moaned and grunted in sympathy, of course, without ever moving.

It always astonished me that we did not get a dozen solicitors' letters with every post, from unfortunates who had done themselves mischief while following my flab-fighting exhortations. I did get many letters telling classic tales: one housewife, embarrassed at the prospect of putting her youngsters off their tea by lying on the kitchen floor with her legs in the air, repaired to the privacy of her hallway for her contortions, and was somewhat taken aback at a crucial moment to see the watery eyes of the postman, gazing at her through the letterbox.

'The Fight on Flab' became something of a national institution – later the BBC even published a slim volume of the esoteric acrobatics. I, in turn, for such is the nature of an ungrateful public, became the target of much hysterical abuse about my own figure – as indeed I still am, uncomplainingly, to this day.

Throughout the muck and bullets, I stoutly maintained that there was no point at all in fighting the flab if you did not have any to fight. It was suggested that the best way to find out if you needed to lose weight was to jump up and down, naked, in front of a mirror. If anything wobbled or flopped that was not designed for the purpose, then rigorous exercise was to be recommended.

There is always one, of course: a woman wrote in to complain that she had been jumping up and down naked to her heart's content, when her husband had returned home unexpectedly. Getting the wrong end of the stick completely, he immediately tore off his clothes, and joined in the homely fun. Now, she was pregnant, and what was I going to do about it?

The press began to notice me: 'Terry Wogan is possibly the last of the faceless DJs, a pleasantly chubby-faced man ...'

And I was saying some pretty stupid things myself: 'I would not regard myself as a disc jockey. I would prefer to be known as a compere or a communicator ...'

Pretentious, *moi?*

## ON THE MOVE

Meanwhile, on the house and home front, we had found a detached, four-bedroomed house to rent in Burnham, Bucks. Twenty pounds a week, and making a hole in my weekly wage, but worth it.

On New Year's Eve 1969, we put the kitchen sink, Alan and a goldfish I had won for him at a fair, in the back of the Rapier, and were off to another new home. The lights were on in every house in the Fairway, Burnham, as we unpacked our bits and pieces, and I have never forgotten the kindness of our new neighbours, Thelma and Stan. They knocked on the newcomers' door, and invited us to join their New Year revels. We didn't accept then – Helen had already popped a duck in the oven, and when that happens, nobody leaves – but the good family Clough have been friends of ours ever since.

We made lots of friends in our year in Burnham: Les and Betty Taylor, and John and Marjorie, who lived just behind us. We went there for musical evenings: John would play his mighty organ, and Marjorie would provide the rhythmic accompaniment with a couple of brushes on some upturned saucepans. Eccentricity, I realized, was not the exclusive preserve of the Irish. And Helen was pregnant again.

I was still keeping the wolf from the door, and my earnings up, by flying to Dublin every second weekend and recording half a dozen sponsored programmes for RTÉ. Every other weekend, Helen and I would employ a baby-sitter for Alan and go out on the town. Clubs? You're kidding; even then we were foodies. We tried a new restaurant every second Saturday night: L'Escargot, Au Père de Nico, Terrazza. I don't remember a restaurant with an English name.

I moved agents, without rancour, and joined Harold Davison's string of DJs that included Tony Blackburn and Jimmy Young. We put our Irish house up for sale in February, and in March I came third in the *Reveille* Awards. Tony Blackburn was first, Jimmy Savile was second and I, only five months in Britain, was third.

A couple of weeks before, I had made my second television appearance on *The Golden Shot* with Bob Monkhouse. (I pretended it was my first – nobody remembered the beauty contest débâcle.) I was being invited to premières, I did a public appearance in Barking. I am sure that was the one where I sat in the back of an open cart, acknowledging the apathy and bafflement of the good burghers, who hadn't a clue who this so-called 'celebrity' was. I waved anyway, and a little boy ran up to the slow-moving car: 'Are you Emperor Rosko?' he enquired.

It still happens. I am proud to help out at our local play centre for handicapped children, a marvellous facility staffed by patient saints. I like to help on open days, welcoming people, walking around, signing autographs. Recently, true to form, a young handicapped boy suddenly came hurtling towards me with an autograph book, stopping inches from my nose. 'I don't know who you are!' he shouted.

Mark was born in Queen Charlotte's Hospital, a healthy, happy little baby, the image of his brother. Helen brought him home to the Fairway, Burnham, to me and two-year-old Alan. It was another blessing, another consolation for the loss of Vanessa.

Mark was an attention-seeking little chap, adventurous, creative. He grew up to be the most extrovert of the Wogan clan, and his recklessness got him into a little trouble. The foolishness of youth, unremarkable, even normal for most teenagers, but, of course, he was my son, and a couple of minor peccadilloes were plastered all over the newspapers. We even had the paparazzi parked outside the gates for a couple of days.

It was embarrassing for all of us, most of all for Mark. It drives him yet: he wants, by his achievements, to make it up to us. I keep telling him he doesn't need to, but it may help him to do great things. All he really needs to do for us is to keep making us laugh …

With only a year to spend in our rented house, we had to look for more permanent accommodation. On the weekends that I was at home, we searched assiduously through the far corners of Bucks and Berks: Gerrards Cross, Amersham, the Chalfonts, Beaconsfield. Then in October, we found what we were looking for, down by the Thames, among the river folk of Bray. A lovely Edwardian house on a third of an acre, with its own garden down to the riverside, and a mooring. By December, we owned it, we had to, we needed a roof over our heads by January.

We flew back to Dublin for Christmas to spend it with our families: Helen went with the two children at the beginning of the week, and I followed on Christmas Eve, just as my father had done for countless Christmases, from Limerick to Dublin. For full many a Christmas, well after Katherine was born a couple of years later, we lumped and humped across the Irish Sea loaded with presents and all the paraphernalia of a young family.

It was joyous, but it was a good job we were both young. Even when we got there we hardly settled in one spot long enough to down a Brussels sprout. Visits to the maiden aunts, to friends, lunch with Helen's family, dinner with my Ma and Da – it got even worse when Helen's mother and father moved house to Co. Carlow, a good two hours of country roads from Dublin.

In the end, we called a halt, in the interests of my wife's health and sanity. Occasionally nowadays, we have my brother Brian and his family over to us for Christmas, and, when she became a widow, my mother Rose came often. Even Helen's dad, the mighty Timothy, when he became a widower, joined us for the festivities, but in the main our Christmas has usually been just the five of us: Alan, Mark, Katherine, Helen and me.

You can keep your dysfunctional families; it is our favourite time of the year: excessive, extravagant, full of generosity, caring and love. Call me a sentimental old fool; call me anything you like – as long as you call me in time for the scrambled eggs, smoked salmon and Champagne on Christmas morning ...

At the time of writing, none of our family is married or even affianced, so Helen and I treasure these Christmases together with our children. When they marry, as they will, it will all change, and things will be different. I am sure they will be just as good – I know they won't be better.

In the next year, we settled in with our fellow river folk in Fishery Road, Bray, little thinking that four years later, we would move house again, away from the Thames, up-country. Contrary to what you may have read in what is euphemistically known as the popular press, we did not move because Michael and Mary Parkinson had moved in just down the road, or even because Rolf Harris had joined the crowd, just a few moorings down from ours. We moved because we knew that the orchard on one side of us was to be sold, and we would lose our precious privacy.


## GOING EURO

I started work on *Come Dancing* in the glamorous setting of the Locarno, Coventry, and that year, 1970, seems to have been full of public appearances: Hull, Bradford, Southend – beauty contests, bingo halls, supermarket openings. And, hallelujah! On 1 April, I flew to Dublin to commentate for BBC Radio on the *Eurovision Song Contest*! Thirty years ago ... I loved it then, I love it now.

I did a few years on the radio side, and then took over the television commentary on the *Eurovision* in the late seventies. Apart from *Wake up to Wogan*, it is *the* programme by which most of the British viewing public identify me. It is the television programme that brings me the most critical acclaim, the most praise from the viewer. It may well be something to do with the fact that I am never seen, but I would prefer to think that over the long, weary years, the *Eurovision*, the viewer and I, have aged in the wood together. We have soldiered on through dungeon, fire and sword.

In the beginning, we smiled when others took the thing seriously enough to confuse it with a real song contest. Later, we chortled inwardly as the critics lambasted it for the rubbish that we always knew it was, and finally we had our moment of quiet satisfaction as the *cognoscenti* came to the realization that the *Eurovision Song Contest* was for laughing at. Kitsch, *schlock*, a great international conglomeration of musical mediocrity, but fun.

People have always taken the *Song Contest* at different levels: there is the *Eurovision Song Contest* fan club, Europe-wide and thousands strong, who turn up in great numbers at every contest, take a stand in the hall, and disseminate *Eurovision* literature with the fervour of Mormons. They are up to their shoulder pads in facts and figures: who won, when, where and how? Who came second, twentieth, third and why? They leave train-spotters for dead in their anoraks.

To them, the *Song Contest* is not just serious, it is a way of life, a reason to be. So, as you can imagine, they are not all that crazy about me. Like many Europeans, indeed most of the European entrants to the *Eurovision*, they think it is a real song contest.

I suppose that when you listen to what passes for pop music in most European countries, you can hardly blame them. Have you ever heard a good French pop song? What *is* that Johnny Halliday like? Do you know a German crowd-pleaser? Have a look at some of the stuff they do on German TV. The men are still in *lederhosen*, the girls are wearing gingham and plaits, and the accordion is king.

The fado still rules Portugal, and the Spaniards are getting more, not less ethnic. The Italians won't play any more, because nobody will recognize the fact that their music is the best, and they should be allowed to win every year. The Scandinavians sound strange, as do the Dutch; the Greeks, Turks and Israelis bring a breath of the souk, but it is foreign to the Northern European ear, and it is going to take some time for the new boys, the Eastern Europeans, to worm their way in.

The fact is, pop music is an Anglophone thing. Popular music, as we know it, came to us from the United States of America.

Their music in turn came from the Scots and Irish immigrants, and the Negro slaves. The fusion of music in the New World produced the blues, jazz and then pop. The language it was sung in was English. Pop has to be sung in English, no matter how jingoistic that sounds. You cannot sing pop music in Swedish or Serbo-Croat. That is why European pop does not sound right to us – it is why the *Song Contest* sounds ridiculous to British viewers, and why they find it funny, when the rest of Europe does not.

In 1973, Abba entered the Swedish National Song Contest with an entry entitled 'Waterloo', sung in Swedish. It came nowhere. The next year they entered the same song, this time singing it in English. It won, and went on to win the *Eurovision* itself, in Brighton, 1974. The following year, the European Broadcasting Union (EBU) decreed that all songs had to be sung in their native tongue. That put the kibosh on the Scandinavians' chances, although they have won a couple of times in the intervening years, saw off the Dutch and the Germans, who have won once each in about twenty years, and banjaxed Spaniard, Portuguese, Greek, Turk and Israeli alike. Don't even ask about Johnny Icelander ...

It helped the UK's chances enormously, or would have done if anyone else in Europe had liked the UK. As it was, it all played right into the hands of Ireland, who could sing in English, and were also small, charming and had never made war on any other country in Europe. And, let's be fair, the Irish being much more Euro-minded than the British, had a better idea of the kind of music the international juries might like to hear.

The international juries were often accused of partiality: tactical voting – voting for neighbouring countries or for those to whom their country is or ever was allied. Disgraceful. The EBU finally took action in 1999 – away with unseemly bias! Leave it to the public. The plain people of Europe would be upright, unbiased, fair.

You all saw what happened: same old story, only more so. Greek voted Cypriot, Cypriot voted Greek. Denmark voted Iceland, Iceland voted Denmark. All the Slavs voted for each other, as did the Scandinavians. Every Turkish *Gastarbeiter* in

Germany got on the blower, and the Turkish entry received *douze points* from Allemagne. And you will never guess what Germany got from Turkey … *Plus ça change*, then.

And why, as a better man has said, not? Well, I have to admit to getting a little over-heated at the shameless bias of it all. Although, as I have said, not to everybody. The Irish, who you would expect, above all others, to view it with a tinge of cynicism, took it very seriously when they were winning, seeing it as a kind of assertion of their growing pride and confidence. The French only pretend not to take it seriously; the Germans can't pretend. And if only the Spaniards could be persuaded to take the gypsy from their musical soul, we might get a warm location for a change.

Although, come to think of it, Israel was warm enough in 1999. It is an enduring memory, and a reminder to me of how lucky I am in life, that Helen and I found ourselves in the Old City of Jerusalem on a warm May evening. As we ate and drank, we watched Manchester United win the European Champions League, back-projected onto one of the city's ancient walls.

Whenever and wherever I go to a *Eurovision Song Contest*, I am accosted with the accusation: 'Why do you poke fun at the *Song Contest*? If you don't like it, why do you do it?' They just don't get it. I love the *Eurosong*; I love it for its grandiose awfulness, its manifest foolishness, the flaw at its very heart: bringing the peoples of Europe together on the wings of a song, when all it demonstrates, year after year, is how far apart everybody is, at least musically.

It was always my ambition to introduce the *Eurovision*, and that dream came true in 1998 at the NEC, Birmingham, when Ulrika Jonsson and I had the privilege and pleasure of bringing the contest, on behalf of Britain, to a half a billion viewers worldwide. It will always be the most thrilling moment of my television career, as I opened the show to a fanfare of trumpets, and the roof-lifting enthusiasm of the 5000-strong audience. Old Geezer that I am, my memories of nearly thirty years of *Eurovision Song Contests* have become blurred, blended into each other, from my very first one in the Gaiety Theatre, Dublin, to the one in 2000 in Stockholm, or, as we know it, A Hundred Different Ways With A Herring.

I remember the time before in Stockholm, just after the Portuguese revolution, when Portugal's entry sang their song armed and in combat gear, with a red carnation sticking out from the barrel of each gun. I remember the number of occasions the Irish and Israelis shared a hotel between them, while the rest of us were accommodated as far away as possible in the interests of security.

I remember the security around the hall in Luxembourg, when Black September ruled the terrorist roost: Uzis everywhere, special forces, armoured cars, and inside the hall, a warning that if any member of the audience stood up to applaud, they could well be shot. I had a reporter behind me, just in case an untoward international incident happened, in which case, he was to take the microphone from me and give the balanced BBC newsman's view. They did not want any girlish hysteria from me, thank you very much.

I have been hysterical, of course – if not at the songs or the dresses, then the interval cabaret. We have had clowns, we have had mime acts, we have had acrobats and jugglers. You see, as far as the rest of Europe is concerned, variety never died.

We have had 'spesh' acts; my all-time favourite was a William Tell extravaganza that involved elaborate preparations and flashing lights, as the arrow flew a complicated circuitous route to finally impale a golden apple on a little lad's head. The preparations took at least ten minutes, and all went well in rehearsal. On the big night, however, the arrow missed. We saw it miss in the audience, and hundreds of millions of viewers saw it miss on their television screens. The director, however, fearing the worst, had kept a tape of the rehearsal, and seconds after we saw the arrow miss the apple, we saw it strike home straight and true. It is the kind of thing that keeps you coming back.

The greatest interval act of all was *Riverdance*, in Dublin, a few years ago. Over the years the Irish have made a wonderful job of the *Song Contest*. As they might say themselves: why wouldn't they? Haven't they had more practice than anybody else? Everybody loves going to Ireland; perhaps they should set up a permanent *Song Contest* there.

Some years ago, we all stayed in Killarney, and drove every day to the site of that year's contest, in Millstreet, Co. Cork, a tiny village without a hotel to its name. It did have a huge equestrian centre, where the contest was staged, the brainchild of a local entrepreneur. He insisted that the inhabitants paint their houses, fix their roofs, clean up their gardens, so that the place would be a credit to themselves, and to him.

All agreed, but, as in every village, everywhere, there is always one. He was not going to paint his house for the benefit of a lot of foreigners. If it was good enough for his father, and his father before him, it was good enough for him. The entrepreneur organized a raffle among all the villagers – the prize, a weekend, all expenses paid, in Dublin. Strange as it may seem, the difficult villager won! Off he went with his wife to Dublin. And when he came back, guess what? Hadn't his house been newly painted?

A wonderful man called Michael Devine drives me about whenever I am in Dublin for the *Eurosong*. On the big night he organizes a police motorcycle escort for me. You ought to try it: zooming through crowded streets, crashing through red lights, rocketing over roundabouts to the shriek of police sirens, as the boys on the bikes bring everything except yourself to an unceremonious halt.

Then straight through the gates, and up to the door of the hall. A smart salute and off my escorts go. Actually, they are off to collect the President. Michael, somehow, persuades them to do me first. Don't ask. It's Ireland …

It is entirely Irish, too, that some years previously, at another *Eurosong*, we hailed a taxi to take us to the Royal Dublin Society Showgrounds, where the contest was being staged that year:

'Where to?' said the driver.

'RDS.'

'Ah, Jaysus! You would! The place full of coppers and me without any road tax!'

There was also the year when Ronan Keating of Boyzone, probably Ireland's most famous face, compered the show. Afterwards a security woman would not admit him to the after-show party. He had not got a pass, and she didn't care who he was.

I know that there will come a day when I have to pass the *Eurovision* baton to a younger, better man or woman, but not just yet. They'll probably have to carry me out screaming …

## UP WITH THE LARKS

The BBC put up my weekly stipend, and, by the end of 1971, I was earning almost £2000 a month! I stopped flying back and forward to Dublin to do the sponsored programmes, but still kept the Irish door open, with a weekly request programme for Irish radio from London, and a weekly column for the *RTÉ Guide*.

We made lots of new friends over the year, notably the Clancy family, to whom we have remained very close. We settled by the river and I bought a boat. It is true that the happiest days of your life are when you buy a boat, and the day you sell it. All I ever did with mine was chug it up and down the Thames between Bray and Boulter's Lock in Maidenhead. I never went through a lock; I took one look at the heaving and pulling involved, and turned my little craft for home.

As proof that we never learn from our mistakes, I bought a speedboat in the marina at Caboroig, Alicante, Spain, when we had a house there. Speedboat engines are like lawnmowers: all right when they are running, but leave them for ten minutes and you can never get them started again. And all that palaver with mooring, tying up, untying again.

As you will know by now, I am not the Mae West at the old preparation; my old fault – if it does not come easily, walk away. I walked away shortly after Helen, Hacker, Kits and I got becalmed in the middle of the Mediterranean. I was handing over the steering wheel to Kits, when the thing just stopped. Kits and I swam to shore, found a taxi-driver who did not mind getting his seats wet, found the man who had sold me the boat (it took some time, he was having lunch and couldn't be rushed), leapt aboard his little dinghy, and off we went to the rescue. The ladies were calm enough, when we got to them, considering their becalmed state, but a certain frostiness was discernible, even in the great heat, when my man clipped the key on to the dead man's handle, turned it in the lock and the engine immediately sprang to life.

Of course, I knew all about the dead man's handle. The fellow had instructed me carefully on its use when I had bought the boat. The key had come out when I was handing over to Kits, and the engine had cut out to prevent the boat going round in circles. All you had to do to start it again was what your man had just done. I knew that. I had just forgotten it, okay? Am I supposed to remember everything?

When I mentioned on the air that Helen was pregnant with Mark, the listeners had sent me about forty pairs of bootees, so, when in 1972, we knew she was expecting Katherine, I kept the happy news to myself.

Things just got better and better. Because of 'The Fight on Flab', Playtex asked me to promote their Living Bra, along with a seven-minute disc of exercises. For a brief, shining hour, I was king of the nation's corset departments. I had compered *Miss United Kingdom* and *Girls Galore!* What more could life have to offer?

Mark White had another shot in his locker. Would I like to take over the early-morning ('breakfast') show on BBC Radio 2? It was a shock. I was comfortable in the afternoon, across both networks, with an established, growing audience. Now I was being asked to get up at all hours of the morning, and fling myself against the might of the country's most popular radio presenter, Tony Blackburn, on Radio 1.

Once again, the possibility of failure never occurred to me, and, anyway, Mark was the new Head of Radio 2 Music. If I was going to follow anybody, it was him. Carrying 'Fight the Flab' with me, I took to the morning air – and I have been there ever since, apart from eight years before the mast at the Shepherd's Bush Empire with *Wogan*, bless it.

I was not to everybody's taste, though, over the wheatybangs. John Dunn had been the previous incumbent. Soft-spoken, urbane, with impeccable diction and manners, he was a perfect English gent; who was this Irish gobdaw, with his ridiculous exercises, upsetting the British Breakfast? There was a letter to the *Sun*:

> *Almost every morning Terry Wogan is 'thrilled skinny' with our company, and hopes to find us 'bright-eyed and bushy-tailed'. Every time I hear these phrases, my nerves are set on edge …*

And I am still at it. I hope W.H.P. of Barnsley, Yorks, discovered in the intervening years how to switch over to another station.

Tony Blackburn and I started a radio quiz-game, *Pop Score*, that was to run for aeons, with Pete Murray as the chairman, and then, in October, came my first television series, *Lunchtime with Wogan*, for ATV.

It was live from its studios at Elstree, and featured music and song from Carl Wayne and Penny Lane. Everything else was down to me and an Old English sheepdog. If I had not had such character-forming experiences on early Irish television, I would have run a mile. Perhaps I should have … Nancy Banks-Smith, in the *Guardian*:

> *The built-in hazard of such a show is not that someone in the audience may drop off, but that they may drop dead. Wogan has an Old English sheepdog which is discriminating, and keeps trying to leave the stage …*

Mary Malone, in the *Daily Mirror*:

> *Wogan cods you along with that warm, hot-water bottle voice and glides through the audience with the smooth control of one who might have spent a lifetime as a male nurse …*

What a foul slur on the nursing profession. *Lunchtime with Wogan* was ahead of its time, as indeed were all daytime television shows of the early seventies. It would be at least fifteen years before the British public lost its sense of guilt about turning on the television in daylight.

# TEN

# WOGAN'S WINNERS

Our daughter, Katherine, was born in a Windsor nursing home at the end of August. She immediately became known as 'Missy', but that's as 'girlie' as she ever got. Competitive, impulsive, strong-minded, sentimental, feminine – she is a cross between her mother and me. Brave enough to set off for Madrid University when she was eighteen, her degree is in Hispanic studies, and she can bore a small crowd indefinitely on Cervantes. She has a wicked laugh and an independence of spirit that belies her reliance on her family. It is a constant joy to Helen and me how close she is to her brothers, and they to her. My children phone each other every day. We did something right ...

In December, Tony Blackburn once again won the *Reveille* Award for Top Radio 1 DJ and I won my first-ever award as Top Radio 2 DJ. Des O'Connor and Cilla Black presented the awards. Whatever happened to them? And, come to that, whatever happened to *Reveille*? If the photographs are anything to go by, it was probably stamped out because it frightened the horses. Everybody had hair down to their shoulders and sideburns to their chins; shirts with huge collars, suits with lapels a yard wide – what were we like!

This sartorial insanity went on well into the seventies; I know, because sometimes when it comes to contract negotiation time, the BBC ties me to a chair and forces me to watch re-runs of my *Blankety Blanks*; tight suits, bell-bottom trousers, those huge lapels, the shirts with the matching ties ... Why, in heaven's name, did nobody speak out? Where was Hardy Amies when we really needed him?

As a matter of fact, I interviewed Hardy Amies in the late eighties on *Wogan*. A man of some asperity, he offered me some advice as he left the stage: 'Your jacket's too tight,' he said.

The seventies passed happily, watching our children grow. We acquired an excitable Labrador called Duffy, I got a yellow E-type Jag that gave me more trouble than a speedboat outboard engine, and, in common with every middle-class young family household in the country, we got adopted by a Filipino nanny. Sophie smiled constantly, loved the children, and let the fried eggs go cold. She married and settled here, and I haven't seen her for nearly thirty years, but we still exchange Christmas cards.

As 1973 moved towards 1974, I seemed to be making more public appearances than the entire Royal Family combined. In July: Basildon, Lyme Regis, Slough, Portsmouth, Oxford, Leeds. I must have been cheap. Portsmouth I remember particularly. A huge crowd turned up, probably on the promise of free food and drink – and myself, Miss Portsmouth and the supermarket manager found ourselves atop a table, swaying perilously to and fro in the surging mass of humanity. I can still hear the manager, white with fear for himself and his plate-glass windows, shouting at me: 'That's the last time I have you to open anything!'

A kindly producer, John Bridges, asked me to chair a new radio version of *Animal, Vegetable or Mineral?* with panellists that included Willie Rushton, Brian Johnston and Anona Winn. Anona was a quiz-show legend, who famously always insisted on the stage lighting being just so. That's important, on radio. I expect she was worried about how she might look to the studio audience. She need not have bothered. We recorded *Animal, Vegetable or Mineral?* in the Playhouse Theatre, on the river, near Charing Cross, and the front two rows were usually made up of Lascars, brought in out of the cold by the Seamen's Mission.

Mention of the Royal Family reminds me that, about this time, Helen and I were invited to Buckingham Palace to meet them. It was not all that exclusive: we joined a long queue that wound its way through the doors, into the hall and up a huge staircase, and suddenly there they were! Helen went first, curtsying like a good 'un, and then it was my turn. I inclined a suitably loyal head, and the Queen favoured me with a word: 'Flab!' and laughed. Prince Philip joined in.

I smiled weakly and panicked. Helen had already got a drink and was moving into another room. I rushed towards her. 'Here!' said a regal voice. 'Don't forget about us!' In my terror, I had walked straight past the Prince of Wales and the Queen Mother.

Surprisingly, Her Majesty has kindly asked me to lunch and garden parties since then and, apart from kicking one of the corgis by accident under the table and causing the footmen to drop one of Her Majesty's Brussels sprouts, I have behaved impeccably.

## A THREAT TO LIFE AND LIMB

As we went through the gates of Buckingham Palace on that first visit, an Irish voice greeted me. The policeman on duty was from Dublin. That surprised, and pleased me.

Since I had arrived in Britain, the situation in Northern Ireland had got more and more grievous. The seventies in particular were not a great time to have an Irish accent in Britain, and it was reassuring to hear that Irish voice on guard at Buckingham Palace.

As I write, it looks as if peace has a real chance at last in Ulster. At times, atrocities perpetrated on Britain in the name of my country made it very difficult to open the microphone and address the British public in a cheery Irish voice. But throughout the tragedy, hatred and bloodshed that has been Northern Ireland over the last thirty years, I have never received a single word or letter of condemnation nor abuse.

I have a vague recollection of a bomb-threat at an outside broadcast, but that was probably a discerning listener.

The only other serious threat to my life and limb was about four years ago. A letter-bomb addressed to me was delivered to the Radio 2 offices at Western House, near Portland Place. Security police and bomb squad swung into action. The traffic was halted from Broadcasting House to Oxford Circus. Regent Street, Oxford Street, and, very quickly, most of London's West End, came to a shuddering halt. My producer, Paul Walters (otherwise known as 'Poorly'), bravely carried the bomb from the offices to the BBC post room, where it could be investigated and defused. He was subsequently rewarded for his bravery by having his knuckles rapped for 'foolhardy behaviour'. Good old BBC …

The bomb was defused, panic subsided, and the traffic returned to as near normal as it ever gets in the West End. The fuss went completely over my head. This was nothing to do with my natural insouciance nor pluck: I was away on holiday. I still do not know whether to be disgruntled or relieved that a person who hates me enough to blow me to Kingdom Come is not a regular

Radio 2 listener who knows when I am on holiday.

Even allowing for the good nature and tolerance of the British, it is surprising that I have not been the butt of anti-Irish hatred. I suppose that I have been in a privileged position, for I know well that many Irish people in Britain have suffered their share of discrimination and abuse because of terrorist outrage.

The vast majority of Irish men and women in Britain were neither supportive nor sympathetic to the IRA. Our feelings were of sorrow and shame at what was being done in the name of Ireland and the Irish. Perhaps one of the nicest things ever said to me was at an outside broadcast in Wales with the BBC Concert Orchestra. As I stood by the side of the stage, a man approached me and said, 'I've always wanted to meet you, and thank you for what you have done for the Irish in Britain during the Troubles.'

It was affecting, and made me very proud, but, on reflection, what did I do? Just my job.

## A PROPER JOB?

It is just a job, too – although, not a *proper* one. I wouldn't still be getting up at 5.30 every morning to go to a 'proper' job. If I was still a banker, they would have put me out to grass years ago. I love my job, the unpredictability, the eccentricity, the fun of it. My radio show is much different now than it was in my first incarnation in the seventies, but even then, from the start, I was shamelessly using my listeners' ingenuity and creativity, along with my own fantasies. Take this, from my first published oeuvre, *Banjaxed*:

> As the first rays of the morning sun glance off All Souls Church, and strike the bastions of the BBC a resounding blow, a lonely figure, garlanded in thyme and marjoram, and simply but disgustingly clad in string vest, long khaki shorts and scuffed tennis-shoes, lifts his scrawny arms to the sky, and calls upon Auris, the God of Broadcasting, the Ear In The Sky, to aid his minions in another attempt at broadcasting ...
>
> Later, the roof will come alive with gay striped awnings and the popping of champagne corks as merry chattering secretaries and clerks while away the day by the glittering swimming pool.

*There is laughter and high-spirited shouting from the tennis courts, and the air is heavy with the scents of jasmine and bougainvillaea. The Managing Director (Radio) whistles tunelessly as he tends the DG's vegetable patch, and the Head of Outside Broadcasts polishes the window with a will …*

The things that went on, on that roof: ageing producers regularly hurled from the parapet, to ease the Block On Promotion, boiling Nolan Sisters records poured on the heads of the incensed listeners below. And, most famously of all, the Dance of the BBC Virgins. This, the most lavish and sensual of all BBC rituals, never actually took place, because, as I had to point out to the listeners, nobody even turned up.

It is a testament to how deeply people can become involved in your fantasy on radio, that a rather stern middle-aged woman stopped me in the corridors of the BBC, and reprimanded me: 'There *are* virgins in the BBC, Mr Wogan. And I am one of them!' She then turned heel in her sensible shoes and stormed off.

## WOGAN'S WINNER

I had inherited a 'Racing Bulletin' with the breakfast show on Radio 2, masterminded by Tony Fairbairn of the Racing Information Bureau. When I took over, I wanted to make the thing more personal, more integrated into the programme, so we devised the idea of a daily tip, to be called 'Wogan's Winner'.

I must have taken more abuse, good-natured and otherwise, over that damned tip than anything else I have done, before or since. I know nothing about racing; horses frighten me, and the only time I go racing is when invited to Ascot by my friends the Clancy family – and only then for social reasons.

The nags I back rarely trouble the judge, and so it was with 'Wogan's Winner'. The bookies quickly copped on – a loyal listener sent me a notice pinned up on the board of his local turf accountant, which bore the legend: 'We lay 66 to 1 Wogan's Winner' …

In very short order, I was being abused in the street: 'You couldn't tip rubbish!', 'Ere, Tel, 'ow much are the bookies payin' you, then?' – and worse, much worse. The whole rotten business was further exacerbated by the World Council of Churches' 'Report on Gambling', which roundly condemned tipsters in general, but specifically exonerated me, as my tips constituted a positive disincentive to gambling. Sometimes, you don't know whether to laugh or cry. The listener was not slow, as ever, to join in the general barrage of contumely: 'Anon' burst into verse:

> I'll tell you a tale of the Beeb, lads,
> Where they play all the latest hits,
> And the harsh rending sound
> You can hear from the ground
> Is the DG performing the splits.
> Ah! But what is that terrible smell, lads,
> From that shed almost hidden from view?
> Hang your heads in disgrace
> For this is the place
> Where they melt Wogan's Winners for glue!

It all had to end in tears; I was persuaded to take an interest, a fetlock I think it was, in a two-year-old horse training at Newmarket. They called the unfortunate dumb animal 'Wogan's Wager', enough to stunt anything's growth. Which it did – the poor thing never grew bigger by a finger, not to mind a hand, from the time it was two.

'Wogan's Wager' had a couple of runs, hardly troubling even the starter, before I went to see him race, 'neath the ancient walls of Chester. He took up a position well to the back of the field, loped along easily, and finished unflustered, a good fifty yards behind the rest. It would not have been so bad if the race commentator had not compounded the felony by roaring over the public address: 'And last, is "Wagan's Woger"!' The jockey leapt lightly from his saddle, and said, 'He'll win a race yet, gentlemen.' And he did. Shortly after I sold my interest in him, he won three times, at 25-1, 100-8 and 3-1. Lucky Wogan, the Bookies' Friend ...

Painful as it was, my tenuous situation with racing gave me an entrée into racing's inner sanctums, and whenever Ma and Da visited me, it was my great pleasure to take Michael T. to Windsor, Newbury or Ascot, all not too far away. He loved his racing and knew his stuff, but, at race meetings, he was completely at sea. Bookies' offices he understood, but the hurly-burly of the race-course itself, the shouted odds, the bustling of the on-course turf accountants, confused him.

He always seemed to enjoy himself, but whether he was pretending, to keep a well-meaning son happy, I will never know. I think, like me, in the end he enjoyed the people more than the punting. With a couple of glasses of the right stuff lapping against the old back teeth, he became the 'Kissing Bandit'. He kissed everyone and everything that moved. Those that were lucky enough to escape, he engaged in earnest conversation.

I remember an occasion at Windsor, where he trapped an unwary Chinese gentleman and questioned him closely on the Communist Government, and, specifically, their great leader, Mao. Since the gentleman was a member of the Hong Kong Jockey Club, and certainly would not risk the mainland, and since my father insisted on pronouncing 'Mao' as 'Mayo', you can picture the spectacular lack of meeting of minds. I did not intervene, for fear of the Kissing Bandit turning his attentions to some unsuspecting dowager.

## ON THE ROAD

In 1974, I began my first chat-show, for Jock Gallagher, in charge of Radio Production at BBC Birmingham. Every Thursday I would hit the road for Pebble Mill, chat to Jock, the producer and the researcher about the guests, have forty winks on a little camp bed, then present myself in front of an audience of about three hundred, and introduce my guests to them, and the Radio 4 listeners.

It was my first real interview programme, and I hope that it went as well as I thought it did. It got well reviewed, but then, the guest-list was not too shabby: Norman Hartnell, Rolf Harris one week, Tommy Steele, Lord Lichfield the next; Lord Soper, Joe Loss, Patrick Moore, Mary Quant, Lady Barbirolli, Roy Plomley, Ronald Harwood, Richard Gordon. A broad church. Eclectic, even. Then I would pop into my little car and belt down the motorway for home. In bed by midnight and up again at 5.30 a.m., for the morning radio show, off to Caerphilly, Sittingbourne, Leicester, Cheltenham.

Home to a noisy, young family and a wife who always smiled, no matter how tired she was.

That was the year, too, when Abba won the *Eurovision* at Brighton, with 'Waterloo', the best-ever Eurosong. Britain's representative was Olivia Newton-John, who came fourth. 'Finished,' I pronounced. '*That* tolls the knell for Livvy. She'll have lost cred with the British pop-buying public.' She went on, a year later, to take Hollywood by storm with John Travolta in *Grease*, and become an international superstar. I can pick 'em!

I interviewed Abba for the radio, just after their win. Or at least I tried. There they were, Björn, Benny, Agnetha and Frida, on the threshold of greatness, in our Radio 2 caravan, when the lights went out. Stewart Morris, the TV director, his job over, and eager to be at the food and drink, had instructed that all the plugs be pulled. We never got the power back and I said goodbye to Abba in the dark. Another landmark missed. And I still speak to Stewart Morris ...

We were happy as Larry among the river folk, and had made friends there that are still among our closest and best today, but we needed a bit more room. The house did not have a proper hall, and with three children, very little room to accommodate guests such as family or friends from Ireland. We had plans made for an extension, but the great and good Michael Clancy discouraged us. From his building experience, he knew that with a young family, the hassle, the mud, the sheer chaos that building an extension would bring was not worth it. 'Buy a bigger house,' was Michael's shrewd advice.

We started looking and almost immediately were told by friends of a house that was about to come on the market. We knew the house – the owners were friends, we had had dinner there. It was perfect for us. I bought it. I had two large houses on my hands for some months, before our house by the river found a buyer.

The British press still thinks I live in Bray, on the riverside. So do the tourists and sightseers who plough up and down the Thames all summer, with the guides pointing out the residences of the famous: 'There's Terry Wogan's house,' they still shout. 'And look! There's Terry himself in the garden! Oh – he's gone inside – You've just missed him.'

*Wogan's World* (the Birmingham talk-show), *Pop Score, Animal Vegetable or Mineral?, The Year in Question, Come Dancing*, a TV pop quiz called *Disco*, the *Eurovision* and the daily radio show. There were television pilots, try-outs to see if the show was a goer or a goner. *Cry Wolf*? What was that? And *Crunch*? I have a vague recollection of *Crunch* as a sort of *Gladiators*, well ahead of its time. Ulrika had not even been born, for goodness sake.

## EN FAMILLE

In October, we moved into our new home, on a hill overlooking the Thames Valley with a view across to another, much grander house, on another hill, at Windsor. I often stand on my terrace and wave at our distant neighbours. I love this house, its large rooms, its view, its gardens so lovingly tended by Helen, its fields, hedges, trees. It is a wonderful house to come home to, full of happy memories of our children growing up. And the best thing of all, it is a place they still want to come home to, a place of warmth, comfort and love. And their mother's cooking, of course …

Michael T. Wogan had long since retired, and was running his old firm's pension fund. He gardened, he fished, he cooked his cheese and tomato on toast. On the occasions when we visited Rose and himself, Dad looked fit, slimmer than when he was working.

Unfortunately, the rheumatoid arthritis that had begun for my mother some years before, showed no sign of remission. It was painful to see such a formerly active woman, a person so full of impatient energy, slowed and diminished by pain. Her affliction waxed ever more fiercely through her body for the remainder of her life.

Because of my mother's suffering, I became involved with Arthritis Care. I found that it affected one in ten of the population, and two-thirds more women than men. Children are born with arthritis, and one of the first treatment centres was near my home, at the Canadian Red Cross Hospital, Cliveden.

My mother was treated there, when she stayed with us, and I often went to visit the children there. It is not easy to laugh and joke in the face of such pain, such bravery, particularly when the sufferers are so young; it's the unfairness of it. The problem with raising money for arthritis research and treatment, is that it is not an emotive disease. It does not strike fear, it is not seen as a killer, like cancer or heart disease. And yet, it does kill. Slowly, painfully, by a process of attrition, it killed my mother ...

It was always good to see them both on those trips back to Ireland. One day, as we were leaving, I kissed my father goodbye. 'Son,' he said, 'you haven't done that for years.' I kissed him every time I saw him after that, and have always regretted the thoughtless years that I and he missed. My sons and I always kiss whenever and wherever we meet, and it always lifts my heart.

Auntie May, my inspirational Auntie May, without whose books I could never have got to here, had passed away, smoked her life away. Nellie and Kitty and May had moved from Drumcondra to a smaller house in Whitehall, and now there were just Nellie and Kitty. Nellie always sat legs akimbo, and her elasticated knickers became a source of curiosity and joy to my children, just as they would shy away from Auntie Kitty's embraces because of her moustache. Nellie always looking for a fight, Kitty drifting dreamily through life.

When Mum and Dad would come to visit us in Britain, my father would walk around the 'new' house with a sort of wonderment: 'God, son, I don't know ...' He could never quite believe that I had got so far, and done so much. 'Brian's much funnier than Terry, you know,' he would say to our friends.

My success was a mystery to my dad, just as my success on the radio was a mystery to those who ran the BBC. They knew I was successful, from the audience figures, from the awards, from the public appearances, they just didn't know why ... But, then, nobody knows anything in our business, which is what my friend Sir John Birt could never quite accept.

## FOCUS GROUPS

An engineer by training, Sir John never grasped the essential imponderability of our game. He thought the inexactitude, the utter unpredictability of public taste could be ironed out by reason, procedures, good management – and focus groups, the constant referral to the public. What do they think? What do they want? Are we serving them? Laudable, but a waste of time.

If you put a group of people in a theatre and ask them to

criticize, that is what they will do. They won't just sit there and let it wash over them, as if they were watching at home. They will nag and niggle, pick little holes, because they are being paid to do so. They can only assess who and what they have just seen – and that subjectively. All you get is a series of subjective opinions that can never, logically, be brought into an objective whole.

And what can they tell of the future? Focus groups can never produce a new idea. All they can tell is whether they liked what they have seen. Which, famously, has led to the endless re-working of the same ideas: gardening, cooking, makeovers, documentaries, from driving schools to cruise ships. If a personality is popular with the focus groups, they are immediately signed up for enormous amounts of money, and stuck on every conceivable programme until the BBC gets its money's worth.

The reliance on the focus groups is like a government relying on a referendum every time it has a tough decision to take. It is an abrogation of responsibility, and for a television company it is a declaration of loss of confidence, and a loss of faith in the creative abilities of its production staff. The decline in BBC 1 Television is directly attributable to fear, and the focus group.

## OLYMPIAN DAYS

Harold Davison, my agent, was constantly trying to bring me to the attention of Bill Cotton, who was the Head of BBC Light Entertainment. Bill did not want to know, a fact he admitted rue-fully in public a couple of years later. And why would he? Nobody knows anything, even someone of the experience and showbiz know-how of Bill Cotton. Close your eyes, take a swing at it and hope for the best.

Jimmy Gilbert, Bill's second in command, thought it was worth a swing with me. He had seen me compere *A Song for Europe*, when the public vote for the UK's entry into the *Eurovision*, and he thought he saw something. He got on to Alan Boyd, his top game-show man, and instructed him to find something that even I could do …

Meanwhile, due to the prompting of Cliff Morgan, another who had always had an over-rated opinion of me, Bob Burrowes, Head of

Radio Sport, asked me to front the Montreal Olympics. I had gone to Heaven; but, first, Montreal.

I travelled there steerage, with the consolation of being in the company of the great and good Mary Peters, but came back, after a brief view of the extravagant arrangements that nearly bankrupted the city, first class, thanks to an upgrade. I have been lucky enough to fly first class a couple of times since then, but that first experience of luxury, of first-class lounges, of stewards carving beef on the aisle in front of you, has stayed with me, and no plane journey has ever been quite as exciting.

I passed up my morning show for a couple of weeks, and presented the 1976 Olympic Games from 10 p.m. to 2.30 a.m., from a basement in Broadcasting House. I loved every moment of it, from the Prone Bores to the Coxless Pairs, from a boxing commentator, forlorn and locked in a darkened stadium, to the cycling commentator who scoffed at the slow pace of a competitor, only to find that the chap had broken the world record.

I was equally privileged to present the 1984 Games from Los Angeles. I brought the family along, and every afternoon, after I had headed off to do my bit, Helen and the children would go to Disneyland, Knott's Berry Farm, Seven Pillars of Something, and every other theme park and attraction American ingenuity had to offer.

My kids did every drop, fall and ride on the West Coast, and every evening we would all have dinner together in a different Los Angeles restaurant. The children and I thought we had gone to paradise. Helen loved it because we did. We all went to the Coliseum for the spectacular Opening Ceremony, we saw the phenomenal Carl Lewis begin his extraordinary Olympic medal-winning career, we saw Seb Coe win his gold for Britain. Afterwards we all went to Aspen, Colorado, where a horse ran off with my wife, but brought her back in time for tea.

Ah, those Olympian days; I had a wonderful time in Barcelona in 1992, particularly as my friend David Hatch, then Managing Director of BBC Radio, was there with his late wife, Ann. In the evenings we would do the town, from little Catalan restaurants off Las Ramblas to the ones on the beach. We ran the gamut from *caracoles* to *chipirónes*, large snails in garlic to little octopuses in batter, and always a Cointreau *con hielo*. David loved the way they left the bottle with you.

# RUNAWAY SUCCESSES?

After Barcelona, Pat Ewing, who had always requested my services for the Olympics, left the BBC. She had been in charge of the new network, Radio 5, but the powers-that-be decided they wanted a more serious, news-oriented station. It became Radio 5 Live, under another excellent person, Jenny Abramsky, and was shortly pronounced a runaway success.

It actually was no more successful than the old Radio 5, but people, particularly the news-obsessed, believe what they want to believe ... And you can always fiddle the figures: 'All right, so we haven't got that many listeners, but what about our reach? And we don't want to be seen to be super-serving a middle-class minority, do we?' Ah, the media-speak gobbledegook that the BBC has swallowed whole, over the past few years.

I was enjoying a diet of quiz-shows on radio and television. Slightly disillusioning when you are given the answers, before anybody has asked a question – but, apparently, it is a tradition as old as broadcasting itself. Nobody wants to look a complete eejit, but I remember *The Year in Question* for Radio 4, when Lady Isobel Barnett wanted *all* the answers before she started.

*Celebrity Squares* with Bob Monkhouse provided all the 'celebs' with 'funnies' for every question, and the fine old tradition continues, from the smart-asses of *Have I Got News for You* to the dunces of Dictionary Corner on *Countdown*. Nobody, it seems, is prepared to go in front of a television camera if they are going to be made to look a fool – apart from the public, of course, who are not in on the gag.

It is a lack of nerve and self-confidence on the part of performers, who, anyway, are bears of very little brain, but it is a constant source of amazement to me that members of the public continue to allow themselves to be skewered by television interviewers and documentary producers. No matter what you say or do in front of a camera, you are at the whim, agenda and mercy of the producer and his editor. He can give whatever spin his bias dictates to the words and the action.

If I had a word of advice for anyone outside the game, when faced with the alluring prospect of fifteen minutes of fame, it would be: no matter how charming the researcher, how engaging the interviewer, how reassuring the producer, don't do it. They have a programme to make, and if they have to leave you bleeding on the floor to make it, they will.

I even got paid the compliment of being asked to be a panellist on Radio 4's *Any Questions?* a few times. Now, there is a proper live radio programme, where you have no sight of the questions beforehand, and you are actually given credit for having a smidgen of wit and intelligence of your own. You might even have read a newspaper …

The really difficult part of *Any Questions?* was dinner. This was always taken before the show, in a decent restaurant, close to the hall from which the programme was broadcast. It is not all that easy to relax and enjoy a delicious four-course meal, with attendant wines, port and cigars, if you know that you are shortly to be bombarded with questions on issues of the day, live on the radio, in front of an audience gathered from every right-wing corner of the shires.

I even did *Going for a Song*, with the irreplaceable Arthur Negus, at Stratfield Saye, the Duke of Wellington's country seat. Knowing that the Iron Duke had been born in Dublin, I chanced my arm on the provenance of a piece of old Dublin crystal, and won a Victorian glass rolling pin.

Socially, it was a madcap whirl: Royal Ascot, Henley, Gleneagles for the golf, dinner with the Director-General and later my friend Jay at the Windsor Dining Club, where the port had wings and the members smoked white clay pipes. I was going native!

And I, who had never lifted a cricket bat in anger in my life, even staged a charity cricket match on behalf of Taplow Cricket Club. Denis Compton played, and John Edrich, Tony Blackburn, Willie Rushton, and Brian Johnston. My non-cricket playing became even more incongruous a few years later, when I was installed as President of the Lord's Taverners, a marvellous conglomeration of cricket-loving showbiz folk, which had been founded in the Tavern, at Lords.

It did not seem to occur to anybody that a non-cricket-playing Irishman might not be the happiest of choices to lead such a band, but I was proud to serve for two terms, and prouder still that during my incumbency, the Tavs broke through the million-pound barrier for the first time. They have sustained that mighty fund-raising effort ever since, under Presidents such as Ronnie Corbett, David Frost, Tim Rice and Nicholas Parsons.

Mention of Nicholas reminds me of a Taverners tour to Monaco. We brought the sacred turf of Yorkshire in the back of a lorry, and laid it on the football pitch. The Monégasques were no patsies, and featured plenty of athletic fellows in hiding from their native tax authorities. There were at least a couple of Australian ex-Test players. The Tavs, however, feared no one. We had Jeffrey Archer, Nicholas Parsons, Omar Sharif – old Cairo Fred himself. He had played cricket at school in Alexandria and impressed us all with his eagerness, and crisp turn-out.

It was the worst of luck that a ball, coming out of the sun, caught Omar straight between the eyes, and he took no further part in the game. He came to the dinner afterwards in the best of spirits. He wanted me to come to the casino with him, but fearing for my home and mortgage, I timidly excused myself.

The following morning, he looked a little the worse for wear. I enquired after his health, thinking it might be delayed reaction from being laid flat the day before:

'No,' he drawled languidly, 'it's the same every night. I get back to the hotel from the Casino, and there they are, waiting for me, the women …'

'How awful for you,' I sympathized.

He shrugged his shoulders in the French manner, and the liquid brown eyes glazed over: 'What can you do?'

He was similarly philosophical when we next met, at the most famous *Wogan* TV show of them all, the night George Best was footless. Omar Sharif was his fellow-guest, and afterward I felt I had to apologize to Omar for the shambles, and hoped that he had not been too embarrassed. This time the limpid brown pools sparkled. 'Embarrassed? My dear fellow, all my friends behave like that …'

That night in Monaco, at the Hôtel de Paris, the Lord's Taverners – Willie Rushton, Richard Stilgoe, Anita Harris and Nicholas Parsons – staged a cabaret for our Monégasque friends. Every Taverner shared a table with his largely French-speaking hosts. All went swimmingly, the *entente cordiale* at its brightest and best, until

Nicholas shimmied on stage. He left the room for dead with a cod-French act. Picture, if you will, an upper-class Englishman going into an Irish pub, and doing a stage-Irish act. At least in an Irish pub, the atmosphere would have been broken by flying fists. In Monaco, the entire Hôtel de Paris frosted over.

## TOP OF THE POPS!

From Monaco, to Castlebar, Co. Mayo, and the International Song Festival. From all over the world they flocked to Castlebar, including Acker Bilk, who was doing the cabaret, and me presenting the thing. Acker and I flew into Castlebar from Dublin in a small plane. It needed to be small, the runway was about 100 yards long, with a brick wall at the end.

Those who poke fun so easily at the *Eurovision* have never attended the Castlebar International Song Festival. This was staged in a large corrugated iron shed, and all I really remember with any clarity is standing outside in the rain, while the promoter counted out my money in dirty pound notes from an old biscuit tin.

Along with 'Dead for Bread' and 'Valentine's Goodbye' from Faust, a great bathroom favourite with my dad had been 'The Floral Dance', the baritone's revenge. And, for reasons lost in the mists of time, an outfit called the Brighouse and Rastrick Brass Band issued an instrumental version of the old boiler. I could scarce forbear to sing along, whenever I played it.

It became a great hit with God only knows what section of the listening public, selling well over a million copies. But I began to receive hundreds of disgruntled letters from the barking multitudes, complaining that they had only bought the record because they thought I was singing on it.

A man called Mike Redway appeared from behind the arras, and, hey presto, we did a vocal version, my bird (as they say in Cornwall). It went to Number 15 in the Top Twenty, and I did two appearances on *Top of the Pops*. Me, the light blue suit with the flared trousers and the big lapels, sideboards and all. On the second appearance, I brought on some flowers and threw them gracefully to the crowd as I sang. They hurled them back, and I knew that my days as a pop idol were numbered. The loyal listener rallied to my side:

*I thought I heard the curious tone,*
*Of Wogan on the gramophone,*
*Grunting here and groaning there,*
*Devoid of timing, tone and flair,*
*Trying to make the most of his chance,*
*With his attempt at the 'Floral Dance'.*

I am supposed to have no feelings, of course. Then one bright morning in 1978, Eamonn Andrews burst into my studio at nine o'clock with the Big Red Book, and I realized that Helen had been deceiving me for months, and I had never noticed a thing. Up to that moment, I had thought of myself as sensitive, aware of nuance and any deviation in the pattern of behaviour of my nearest and dearest. *This Is Your Life* helped me to realize that I had all the sensitivity of a lavatory seat.

They dragged me out of the studio, and I continued to speak to my radio audience from the BBC Radio cab, as Eamonn, myself and blessed Derek Mills, who had connived at it all behind my back, drove to the TV studios on Euston Road. They were all there, of course – friends from Ireland, Laurie Holloway, Marion Montgomery, Val Doonican, Frank and Peggy Spencer from *Come Dancing*, Pete Murray, Tony Blackburn, an audience full of the friends we had made in Britain, and, most importantly, Helen, with Alan, Mark and Katherine. Brian and his wife, Pauline, were there, too, and with them, Rose and Michael.

It was a wonderful, emotional day; Eamonn and his team treated everybody with typical kindness and professionalism, and we all ended up with a late lunch at a trat in Charlotte Street. I sometimes regret that I was done by *This Is Your Life* so early in my career in British radio and television. Compared with what was to come, I had done very little. On the other hand, I am grateful that it happened while Rose and Michael were still alive. They were bemused, but, I think, proud, and Michael T. got to sing 'The Floral Dance' along with the Brighouse and Rastrick Brass Band.

# ELEVEN

# 'BRITAIN'S BEST-KNOWN'

Despite Bill Cotton's indifference, BBC TV's Head of Light Entertainment, Jimmy Gilbert, was keen to find a 'vehicle' for me. He commissioned producer Alan Boyd to dredge through the detritus of US TV game-shows, and come up with something.

Boyd, a mischievous Scot, with a genius for turning dross into what looked like gold, until you scraped off the surface, came up with *The Match Game*, a popular daytime show in the States, which featured minor celebrities and a host no one cared twopence about, who was remarkable only for his thin tubular microphone, which he waved about like a wand.

Boyd thought it was just right for me. He could make it work. After all, hadn't he turned Larry Grayson's limp-wristed camp style into a winner on *The Generation Game?* Nothing was impossible. A hitch here, a tuck there … Why not call it after the Australian TV version – *Blankety Blank?* We did a couple of pilot shows, which proved nothing – because, as cannot be said too often, nobody knows anything in this business until the red light comes on. So we gave it a go, Boydie, the BBC and me.

From the start, I loved it. At last, I was not trapped in a tuxedo, or behind a desk. The ridiculous microphone gave me something to do, with at least one hand. I could walk and talk where I liked, without looking for marks on the floor. The winning of various awards had given me confidence, as had shows like *A Song for Europe* and *Variety Club Awards*, but *Blankety Blank* was the first time I felt as easy in front of a TV camera as I always had before a radio mike.

It did not exactly set the woods on fire for the first series. Some of the early critiques might have shattered a more sensitive psyche: 'The concept of the game is negligible, the prizes insignificant, and yet almost as many people watch Wogan on *Blankety Blank* as listen to him in the morning. The sight of the lad himself in loose charge of one of the most unbelievably bad quiz-shows on television is more than flesh and blood can stand ...'

But *I* loved the insignificant prizes. They made the whole thing work on a different level. For me, it was the tackiness of the prizes that gave the show its distinctive flavour, that turned it into a tongue-in-cheek send-up of a game-show. A mug-tree, for goodness sake! A plastic bicycle, a star prize of a weekend in Reykjavik – and for all the contestants, winners and losers, a remarkably cheap combination of plastic and wood, that was the *Blankety Blank* Chequebook and Pen ... I have mine before me as I write, and dash away a manly tear at happy memories.

*Blankety Blank* was a watershed for me, the start of a decade of extraordinary success and acclaim: ten *TV Times* Awards in succession for Most Popular TV Personality, Variety Club Awards, Radio Industries Awards, Sony Awards.

Realizing that the day would come when the shades would fall from the British public's eyes, I asked to be excluded from the *TV Times* Awards after I had won my tenth in succession. They left me out of the running, someone else won for the first time in ten years, and the headlines read: 'Wogan Loses At Last!' What can you do? At the time I could do no wrong, as far as the public, and, yes, even the press, were concerned:

> Blankety Blank *is a genuinely horrible concept – yet it is a success and we have Wogan to blame for it. It would be worth a lot of money to know how he does it. He is not good-looking, but he looks as if he hopes to be, one day, and it is this ability to keep it going in the face of almost continuous small failure, which helps him to flourish ...*

After initial timidity, the stars began to rally around 'Blanks'. David Jason, Henry Cooper, Shirley Ann Field, Paul Daniels, Lorraine Chase, the very young Michael Barrymore, Lennie Bennett, Jack Douglas, Mike Yarwood. As the show became more and more successful, we were beating off the great and the good. But we always found a special place for three special people: Beryl Reid, Kenny Everett and Larry Grayson.

I don't know why Beryl took a smack to me; she could be difficult, temperamental, with others. With me, and on *Blankety Blank*, she was perfect. The public loved her on the show, as they loved Larry and Kenny. Beryl played it absent-mindedly, scatty, Larry with camp disdain, and Kenny? Well, Kenny bent my mike whenever I was foolish enough to get close to him.

The younger viewers particularly loved Everett's madcap ways, and he was very popular at that time, with his own eccentric, anarchic TV show. I guested on it, a couple of times. I hope he liked me as much as I liked him: he died far too young. His Requiem Mass at Farm Street Church was too sad for words. I miss him yet, and Larry, and Beryl ...

The star attraction of BBC TV's Christmas 1979 was *Blankety Blank*, and it did not let them down; it topped the season's ratings for that year. I can't remember how many seasons I did of the show, but it never lost its appeal for the viewers. I gave it up because other things were in the pipeline, and although Jimmy Moir, Head of Light Entertainment, did not agree at the time, it was the right decision. It was not a bad decision for Les Dawson, either, for he picked up the silly microphone and ran with it successfully for several subsequent seasons. In recent times, the BBC revived it yet again, with Lily Savage, but this time it seemed a bridge too far.

Les Dawson is another who has passed away too soon, another with whom I felt a special rapport. When the BBC asked me to take over *Blankety Blank* again, after Les's passing, I would not consider it. Just as there were tentative approaches for *This Is Your Life*, after Eamonn Andrews's death. I did not think it appropriate to follow in another Irishman's footsteps, not to mind whether I was good enough to do so. Michael Aspel took up the Red Book, and nobody could do it better. *This Is Your Life* has outlasted everything, including *Blankety Blank* and *Come Dancing*.

Not Jimmy Young, though. It is wonderful to hear him chuntering on like a two-year-old on Radio 2, every bit as bright and sharp as I remember him, thirty-three years ago, on Radio 1. In my first incarnation as a Radio 2 jock, I broadcast from 7.30 a.m. to 10 a.m., and Jimbo followed on with his eclectic mix of politics, medicine, law, gardening and groceries.

Somewhere in the late 1970s, the cheeky old blighter wheeled his mobile commode into my studio, and we immediately engaged in airy badinage. It went on for years – more like centuries for the discerning listener. The mutual recriminations and barely veiled insults, unscripted, unrehearsed, became the high spot of both our programmes. We made the cover of the *Radio Times*. Her Majesty the Queen expressed her delight. Features were written, pictures were taken. JY and I were the biggest thing on radio, eclipsing Noel Edmonds on Radio 1.

By now the BBC was claiming eight million listeners a morning for my show, but I have always known that those who live by the figures, die by them. Like awards, if you believe it when you are winning, you have got to believe it when you are on the slide. Better to be Kiplingesque, and treat them both the same.


## BEST-KEPT SECRETS

I am ignoring the same kind of attention at the moment in my current incarnation as Radio 2's breakfast buddy. A year or so ago, amid the muck and bullets of the Chris Evans/Zoë Ball Radio 1/Virgin rivalry, a keen-eyed journalist took a look at the overall listening figures, and, blow me down, found that the Old Geezer on Radio 2 had by far the biggest audience, at nearly 7 million. I was pleased, because nobody had told me. The BBC has never liked to encourage the hobbledehoys too much, feeling that it would give the simple-minded presenter ideas above his station.

Indeed, in the compartmentalized corporation that was Birt's Beeb, the success of my show, and that of Radio 2, was regarded as Something Best Left Unsaid, in case it would lead to a loss of confidence among the sensitive young souls of Radio 1. I still refer to Radio 2 on the air as 'The BBC's Best-Kept Secret', and 'The Silent Service', but I don't really mind. A gentlemanly reticence suits the cut of our cardigans, on the Old Geezers' Network.

So there I was, ten years on from crossing the Irish Sea, with the double: the most popular programmes on British radio and television. Obviously, one complemented the other, and radio was shrewd enough to exploit my visibility. We took the Radio 2 show everywhere: Scotland Yard's Black Museum, Lord Montagu's Beaulieu, the Channel Islands, the Isle of Man, Great Yarmouth, Bridlington, an oil rig on the North Sea. We even did the show from my home. My friend Parky turned up, Dr Miriam Stoppard, Gilbert O'Sullivan, Max Bygraves, Stephanie Turner, star of the biggest cop-show of the day, *Juliet Bravo*.

Derek Mills, my executive producer, always accompanied me on these trips, the most amenable of companions. The trouble about doing an outside broadcast at 7.30 in the morning is that it is a bit early for Joe Public, particularly when he is on his holidays. Nor did it add a single extra listener to the morning mix, in fact, it probably irritated the regulars who didn't like their old routine disturbed. I asked Derek Mills why we bothered with the outside broadcast. 'It gives me a chance to get rid of all those awful Radio 2 pens ...'

The one constant factor in those years of radio when the BBC kept changing my producer was Derek Mills. Geoff Mullin, Dennis O'Keefe, Paul Walters, Colin Martin, all served their time at the Wogan coalface. They are all still friends of mine, every one of them a producer in the very best traditions of BBC Radio: good-humoured, calm, competent, professional, and fond of a decent lunch.

Those were the days of pluggers' lunches; if all of the executive producers and producers of BBC Radios 1 and 2 did not have their own tables at Wheeler's, Kettners or Sheekey's, I would like to know why. These people never ate a meal at home; the saving on the family food budget was regarded as a legitimate perk. But not in these days of good husbandry: John Birt has taken a lot of stick, but he tightened up the slack. And there was a lot of it in the BBC of the seventies and eighties. Executive producers would turn up at ten, push the paper about for a couple of hours, then lunch and 'no point in going back to the office, it's five o'clock ...'

As I've said, the reason they kept switching producers on me, was the extraordinary idea that a producer and his presenter should not become too close – friendship might inhibit the producer's ability to correct or discipline the presenter. Barking. That is another thing that has changed for the better. If they tried to take Pauly Walters away from me now, there would be blood all over the turntables. Yes, we have still got turntables on Radio 2 – thank heaven, there is still a corner of popular radio where the auld dacencies prevail.

## LITERARY FLOURISHES

The year 1979 was a big year. I had been looked after by Harold Davison, and then MAM, for agency and management, but Harold was leaving for America to exclusively represent Engelbert Humperdinck. My personal guru in the office was Jo Wright, who had just married another very successful agent, Ralph Gurnett. Jo looked after a number of jocks, as well as me – Kenny Everett, Tony Blackburn, Ed Stewart, a couple more.

With Harold going, it struck me that I would be far better off with Jo as my personal manager than handing ten per cent of my hard-earned to MAM every week. So Jo and I set up business together in a little office in Queen's Gate Mews, Kensington. An excellent book-keeper, a friend of Jo's named Lynda Trapnell, joined us, and Jo Gurnett Personal Management (JGPM) was born. Kenny and Tony, to whom Jo was more of a surrogate mother than a manager, quickly joined the roster. We have been together now for twenty-one years, Jo and I, and it don't seem a day too long ...

JGPM is housed nowadays in a duck-egg blue, four-storey block on the New King's Road, and Jo and her team look after everybody from radio presenters to TV vets, from choreographers to scriptwriters. And Jo Gurnett is what she always has been: hard-working, efficient, honest, clever, and a tiger for her clients, the best liked, most respected agent and manager in the business. And my lifelong friend ...

My first book, *Banjaxed*, was published. It told of the Unspeakable Goings-On at the BBC: the DG's human sacrifices, the Dance of the BBC Virgins, the *Dallas* saga, and the demented outpourings of the listeners. It went straight to the top of *The Times*' Bestsellers List, and provoked the tart comment from Bob Monkhouse that 'Only Terry Wogan could get away with using his listeners as unpaid scriptwriters and then sell their letters back to them in a book ...' Fie, Bob.

The listeners had formed themselves into groups (or in beloved Birtspeak, 'tribes'). There were the IDIOTS (I Dream Incessantly Of Terry Society), the TWINKLETOES (Terry Wogan Is Not Kinky Like Everyone Thinks Or Everyone Says), but the most powerful grouping were the TWITS (Terry Wogan Is Tops Society). Such was the groundswell that Derek Mills had TWITS T-shirts made, bearing the simple legend and my kisser.

Opening a supermarket in Woking or a department store in Luton, I would be astonished to see small knots of people here and there among the surging masses, with my face on their chests. It is hard to credit that twenty-one years on, they are still at it, although with a different alias. Now, they are called TOGS – Terry's Old Geezers (and Gals). Now, they write to me by e-mail and fax, rather than letter.

The e-mails particularly come pouring in at the rate of five or six hundred a day, with sometimes as many as a couple of hundred while the programme is on the air. Pauly Walters ('Poorly', or 'Wally Paltry', call him what you will – and you do) gets in before the streets are aired to sort them all out, and, during the show, resembles nothing so much as a human dynamo, one foot in the studio, the other in the control room, surfing the net with one hand, making coffee with the other, and still finding time to banter playfully in that homely way of his ...

TOGS have become much bigger, better organized and far more frightening than the TWITS ever were. In 1995 I wrote the *Bumper Book of TOGS* to try to explain the phenomenon; to try, somehow, to encapsulate the growing monster, to curtail the horror: TOGS, I struggled to explain, could be recognized by their use of such arcane phrases as 'Is it me?', 'They don't know they're born', or 'I never saw chocolate until I was fourteen.'

They drove Reliant Robins, Mini Travellers with wood trim, or, in extreme cases, Volvos, all in the middle lane of the motorway, at a steady 60 m.p.h. (inside lane, 50, middle lane 60, outside lane 70). They had stickers on their rear windows that read: 'I Stop For No Particular Reason.' TOGS youth had been blighted by Thermogene vests and knitted swimsuits, and their hero was Ethelred the Unready, who was, in fact, ready all the time, but whose wife said he could not possibly go out in those shoes with those trousers and that shirt, and sent him upstairs to get changed.

It was while I was promoting this mighty tome in various bookshops and department stores up and down the country that I first got a whiff of the Winds of Change. In Glasgow it was at its most evident. Frankie Ayerst and Donna Mackenzie, two founder-TOGS, nodded briefly in my direction, and then spent the morning talking to each other, completely ignoring me. A cold hand of fear clutched at my vitals – they were cutting out the middle man! I was superfluous to needs!

The new movement grew like wildfire. Who needed Wogan? Why talk to me when they could talk to each other? In jigtime, a computer buff, Mick Sturbs (they all work under assumed names – Drew Peacock, Rudolph Hucker, Tes Tickle – what are they ashamed of?),ad built the TOGS website, featuring the TOGS chatroom. They pretend they don't know who I am, whenever I try to join in. They have a TOGS convention every year, to which I have to plead to be invited. Last year they took over the fine old university town of St Andrews and took the place apart, like sailors on shore leave, flaunting their TOGS sweatshirts (legend – Do I Come Here Often?). I would wash my hands of them only it's too late. They have already washed their hands of me …

### 'J.R. MEETS T.W.'

Along came *Dallas*, and played right into my hands. It was like a weekly *Eurovision Song Contest*. Over the top, full of ridiculous characters, deeply, deeply foolish; and just like the *Eurovision*, Posh Spice and Richard Whiteley, riveting to watch.

It was just as successful in the States, but then again, rather like the European viewers of the *Eurosong*, Americans watched *Dallas* from an entirely different viewpoint than we did. They thought it was a drama series of everyday Texan oil-billionaires;

HRH the Queen Mother, as ever with a kindly word. She told me she was a regular listener, particularly to 'Wogan's Winner'. Her Majesty the Queen, too, assured me of the royal ear, as she downs her first cuppa of the morning.

*Left* A rare picture of Jimmy Young standing unaided. Throughout the 70s and much of the 80s he would trundle into my radio studio in his mobile commode. My own fault – I was too nice to him …

*Below left* Rose and Michael with the family in Spain. Sadly, the last holiday we all spent together.

*Above right* A Christmas edition of *Blankety Blank* with guests Roy Kinnear, Beryl Reid and Patrick Moore in the back row, Sabina Franklyn, Freddie Starr and Ruth Madoc in front. I'd forgotten about Freddie Starr. They say the body has no memory of pain …

*Right* This bus was driven right across America by BBC engineers and parked in a dingy film-studio parking lot in Los Angeles, from where we covered the 1984 Olympic Games. It was the most fun I've ever had in broadcasting.

*Above* My very first chat show – a one-off with Larry Hagman, the infamous J.R.Ewing. *Dallas*-mania was in full cry, and Hagman loved every minute of it.

*Left* A fragrant nosegay from the Saturday night *Wogan* series. I don't know what became of the thrusting young politician pictured …

*Below left Wogan* in the 80s, and Madonna at her peak. It was recorded in Cannes, at the Film Festival, which is my only excuse for that shirt!

*Right* Griffin always managed to capture my essential apprehension. How well, too, he caught Dolly Parton's attributes …

*Left* One of the high points of my career: presenting the *Eurovision Song Contest* from the NEC Birmingham to a world-wide audience of 300 million or more, and with the lovely Ulrika for company ...

*Above* Back to the old sod. Filming *Wogan's Ireland* in the lovely village of Adare, in my home county of Limerick.

*Overleaf* With Gaby Roslin and Pudsey on *Children in Need*. I have been part of the great television and radio appeal since the very beginning. So far, we've raised £250 million and every penny goes to the children. It's the best thing the BBC does.

we thought it was a comedy. We were right. Who can forget Southfork? Home of the richest family in Texas, with a tiny, wind-blown swimming pool, in which nobody ever swam, except John Ross Ewing Junior, an extraordinary child who grew in fits and starts, but changed his head regularly. Nothing unusual there of course; the doyenne of the series, Miss Ellie Ewing, Mamma, changed her own head and body on at least a couple of occasions, as did another character, Digger Barnes.

Millionaires' Mansion, Southfork, had only one phone, in the hall, and walk-in wardrobes with wire coat-hangers. Weddings, christenings, parties were all held in the small drive, in front of the garage. All the family gathered for breakfast in the morning and dinner in the evening at tables overflowing with food. Nobody ever ate a thing. The biggest social event of the calendar was the Oil Barons' Ball, which was held in a tiny room, with only about twenty people present. I never saw, nor heard, a band.

The hero was J.R. Ewing, a womanizing, treacherous, amoral sonofabitch. Everybody loved him. There was his brother Bobby, a former Man From Atlantis, who was certainly wet; Sue Ellen, also damp, but from the drink, to which she had been driven by J.R. Purer than the driven snow was Pam, Bobby's wife, who looked and dressed like an upmarket Vegas hooker. There was a small chunky blonde, remembered only as the Poison Dwarf. (Years later, my friend, the famous solicitor Sir David Napley, told me that if he had known me at the time he would have warned me against such name-calling. The little biddy could have sued my socks off.) There was Clayton Farlow, whom I always expected to burst into 'There's a Bright Golden Haze on the Meadow', because he was played by Howard Keel.

Nothing on television now commands the attention as did *Dallas*. Remember 'Who shot J.R.?' The dirty dog got the works in his office in the dead of night, and for weeks the public talked of nothing else. There were T-shirts bearing the legend, posters, car-stickers, mugs. Speculation on the suspected assassination swept the planet. The attempt on President Reagan's life got less attention. In the end, the culprit turned out to be none other than Bing Crosby's daughter! Can you beat that?

Actually, the show's producers tried to, by abandoning a tired story-line that was losing viewers. This they did by the simple mind-boggling expedient of pretending that weeks of plot had simply been a dream of Bobby Ewing's, as he nodded off in the shower. And they got away with this bare-faced insult to the audience's intelligence, but not for long. The audience drifted, as the plot and characters of *Dallas* tumbled from silliness to stupidity. It passed away to be replaced by another Aaron Spelling blockbuster. *Dynasty*, though, heaven knows, silly enough, never had quite the charm, the enchanting utter foolishness that made *Dallas* so wonderfully watchable.

J.R. Ewing did not die; he turned up at Royal Ascot as his alter ego, Larry Hagman. Hagman was perfect casting, not only as an actor; he adored the role and gloried in the worldwide stardom it brought him. He rode the whirlwind with open delight, with an enthusiasm that only an extrovert American actor could have done. At Royal Ascot he threw away 100 dollar bills with his face on them, tipped his stetson, with its budgie feather band to all and sundry, and delighted my friend Michael Clancy by joining us all in the Clancy box in the grandstand.

The day before Larry Hagman – who knew of the important part my listeners had played in *Dallas*'s television success in Britain – had dropped in on my early-morning radio show. Some time before, a television producer named Frances Whittaker got the bright idea of bringing over Larry, and having a TV confrontation: 'J.R. meets T.W.'. It was my first-ever television talk-show, and I loved it. I could not have had a better guest than Hagman; he played the J.R. role to the hilt, slipping in and out of the character like the terrific pro he is.

Frances Whittaker, a belt-and-braces producer if ever there was one, thought she would cover any possible hiatus in the proceedings by adding a little comedy feature. This time the over-egged pudding worked: it was John Wells with an impersonation of Denis Thatcher. It was the very first time he had done his *Private Eye* bit on television, and it led to countless more television appearances, and his highly successful one-man show in the West End. John Wells became a friend, but then he was a friend to everyone who knew him, with the possible exception of the Thatchers …

Larry Hagman and Linda Gray, the gin-soaked Sue Ellen, subsequently joined me at the TV Theatre, Shepherd's Bush, for a Christmas edition of *Wogan*. They were funny, talkative and as perfect a chat-show pair as you could hope for, but it struck me at the time that their behaviour off-camera seemed to mirror their roles in *Dallas*. Larry was the dominant one; Linda followed meekly in his wake. Unlike the bullying J.R., he merely suggested – but she followed.

Before the show, Larry told Linda what to say and what to do. It made me wonder if soap-opera characters are created by the scriptwriters, or whether the scriptwriters are reflecting the actors' real characters. It must be said that a passing acquaintance with some of the casts of *EastEnders* and *Coronation Street* inclines me to the latter theory.

## FAMOUS FIVE

Michael Parkinson was well into his first incarnation as a chat-show host at this time. A couple of years later, he upped sticks and joined David Frost, Robert Kee, Angela Rippon and Anna Ford as the Famous Five, who were to revolutionize Breakfast TV.

The Five foundered, on the twin peaks of Frank Bough's cardigan, and Selina Scott's drowsy sex appeal, the two of them cobbled together by the BBC in the forlorn hope of combating the Five Big Ones. To everyone's surprise, and, most of all the BBC's, the Cardigan and the Blonde took them apart, although, I have to say, with the greatest respect to Frank's charm and professionalism, it was the languid Selina who did the damage.

And damage it was, to some of the Famous Five. It did not take a feather out of David Frost of course – the man's a bouncy castle – and Robert Kee went back to 'serious' journalism, but it slowed down Anna, Angela and Michael. Anna got married and had a young family to think about, but Angela and Michael disappeared for years into the opaque recesses of daytime television quizzes and regional magazine programmes.

It is a strange business that can cast aside its major stars without a backward glance. The same thing would have happened to me after the BBC's appalling mishandling of the end of *Wogan* chat-shows, had it not been for David Hatch's good offices. Thanks to him, I was able to go back to my Radio 2 morning show, re-establish my credentials, and renew acquaintanceship with my audience.

It is good to see Angela back on network shows again, and, of course, Michael Parkinson at long last is being re-appreciated for his abilities as an interviewer and presenter. How come he had to spend fifteen years in television's backwaters before some bright spark thought to revive him?

According to Anna Ford, she and Angela Rippon thought that they had been let down by the others when the Famous Five broke up, and when at Christmas, David Frost sent Anna a chrysanthemum in a pot, she threw it out the back door. There, in the bare ground of her backyard, the plant grew and flourished, a fitting metaphor for Sir David Frost himself.

In 1981, Parky had me on his chat-show, along with Andy Williams and Jimmy Young. Maybe Jimmy is only a figment of my imagination, because we dogged each other's footsteps in those days. Anyway, as the interview came to a close, Michael asked, 'So where do you go from here?' I said something along the lines of 'You make it sound like I've reached the peak. I feel I've only just begun to climb.'

I have always felt like that – I still do. I can't believe that Helen and I are thirty years living in Britain – I still feel as if I have only just arrived. I would still like to try something new and interesting on television; but perhaps when you are no longer new nor interesting yourself, that is wishful thinking.

Russell Harty invited me on his chat-show as a guest, and at one point I reached out and touched his arm. I didn't know it, but Russell hated to be touched. He leapt out of his chair like a scalded cat, and I had to chase him round the set to get him to sit down again. It was live.

Russell had nerve – well, more reckless bravado, really, because he was a hopeless interviewer. Which is what made his shows viewable. As a guest, you never knew what he was going to ask. His eyes ablaze with blind panic, a light sweat on his upper lip, he was a terrifying interviewer, because you knew that he was going to say the first thing that came into his head. After hours of my talking to his researcher beforehand, Russell Harty's first question was: 'That's a nice tie, where did you get it?'

One of the main tasks of the chat-show host is to calm the guests, to instil confidence, so that they may give their best. When Russell was host, you felt you had to calm him lest he take fright and run off stage. His natural successor today is Richard Whiteley, old Twice-Nightly, The Man Who Dresses Like A Deckchair. Whiteley has brought bumbling incompetence and dreadful comic timing to a fine art on Countdown, and the public and his fellow-presenters love him dearly for it. The strange coincidence is that Russell Harty was one of Richard Whiteley's schoolteachers. Spooky or what?

I guested on Des O'Connor's show, too, and sang something silly with Pete Murray and Tony Blackburn on Val Doonican's musical extravaganza. I began writing regularly for Woman magazine; it was a full life.

## GOODBYE – AND A LAST LOOK

We put a swimming pool in the back garden, and all the children became good swimmers – Mark, the Maidenhead and District champion. We took Rose and Michael with us on holidays with the children, first to Lagos on the Algarve, and the next year to a friend's villa near Marbella. Rose and Michael, who had never travelled any further on their holidays than the Isle of Man, loved it all, from Portuguese sardines to Spanish tapas.

Dad enjoyed Portugal more than Spain. He was a constant source of amusement to my children, just as I am today, as I grow more and more like him. But he was weakening. The pills he had taken for some years to appease his angina were less and less effective. He was more ill with every year.

In October 1980, Michael Thomas Wogan, the kindest, gentlest, most loving of fathers, died, as he had lived, quietly and without much fuss. He is buried with a view of the sea, which would have pleased the fisherman in him, but it was the evening that they brought his remains to the church for the blessing that would have pleased him most. His coffin had a police motorcycle escort. How he would have loved it, sweeping majestically through red lights, and over roundabouts and crossroads without a sideways glance. Other traffic pulling to the side of the road, as Michael Wogan's hearse overtook and roared by. He never knew how to overtake; I only hope he was watching the spectacle from above.

Hundreds were at the church; funerals have more significance in Ireland than weddings or christenings. It is more important to pay your respects, to say goodbye to a spirit passing on ... On the way to the burial ground, my mother insisted that the hearse be driven past the house on Glasnevin Avenue where she and Michael had lived for twenty-five years. She wanted him to have a last look ...

## AWARDS AND ACCOLADES

The awards continued to roll in: the Pye Society of Authors Radio Award, Variety Club, Radio Industries Club. Throughout the eighties, there was a constant stream: Tie Man of the Year, Best-Dressed Man of the Year, Man of the Year, *TV Times* Most Popular TV Star of the Decade, *Daily Mail* Most Popular Radio Star of the Past 25 Years, the *Express*, the *Mirror* and the *Sun* Popularity Polls.

It must have been galling for other presenters, because no matter how much we demur, awards – any kind of award – be it from your peers or your public, are important, if only to the self-esteem. In an insecure business, full to the bursting with fragile egos, an award helps to keep your feet off the ground.

By the end of the decade, *Tatler* magazine was calling me 'Britain's Best-Known Face'. Another poll had me running third to Her Majesty the Queen and Prince Charles. I always felt that when I topped the polls for 'Most-Loved' and 'Most-Hated', I would disappear by spontaneous combustion. I disappeared anyway. When you are winning polls and awards, always in the public eye, it is self-perpetuating; once you drop from sight, you are out of mind. I won the odd award in the nineties, but they were a kind of consolation prize, for long service, diligence or, more usually, for still being there.

It was implied by a distinguished BBC mandarin that, were I willing to change my nationality, from Irish to British, greater honours might come my way, but I thought such a change might display a certain lack of dignity, an unseemly, turncoat craving for a gong. Anyway, I am entitled to dual nationality, or at least an Irish and a British passport, having been born in Ireland before 1948, when Ireland declared herself a Republic; and the passports are all the same colour these days, thanks to the boys in Brussels. So, much as I would have been honoured by it, I thought I would say goodbye to the ultimate accolade – an OBE/CBE/Gong.

## CHILDREN IN NEED

Mark Patterson had been a director and a producer on the now-legendary nightly TV news magazine, *Nationwide*, but I first met him when he was producing the annual BBC charity appeal, on behalf of children. It was something the BBC had been doing since the twenties – Stuart Hibberd did the first on radio. With ten minutes on BBC 1 television, five minutes first on the Home Service, and then Radio 4, it raised thousands of pounds.

For a couple of years Mark asked me to present the TV appeal, and then in 1980, an idea that had been festering in his keen brain came to fruition: a charity telethon! American television had been doing them for years, why not the BBC? Wise Bill Cotton, the most acute barometer of public taste and popularity there ever has been in British television, gave it the green light.

The first-ever *Children in Need* television marathon fell on to the screen on a wing and a prayer on Friday 21 November, 1980, and I have been privileged and proud to help present it, ever since. That first night was complicated by the programme being staged as an outside broadcast, rather than more simply on one of the big sound stages of Television Centre. Probably some inter-departmental scuffle – very BBC.

Even more BBC was that much of the Corporation did not

want anything to do with it. Some local radio stations felt that their independence was being compromised, and most of the network shows that were being transmitted that night regarded *Children in Need* as a downright intrusion.

The appeal was transmitted from the ballroom of what was then the Cunard Hotel, Hammersmith. It was presented by Esther Rantzen, Sue Lawley and me, in intermittent bursts, in between the programmes. Throughout its duration, the main light-entertainment show of the evening, *It Ain't Half Hot, Mum*, carried no information on the appeal, not even a scroll along the bottom of the screen to hold the public's interest with phone numbers nor running totals. The producer felt that it would detract from his show – a view shared by every other producer.

The *Children in Need* appeal was nothing more than a running interruption that night, although later on in the evening, many BBC stars rallied round for face-checks and the odd contribution. I asked Sir Robin Day to regale us with some well-chosen staves but, as usual, time ran out and I had to interrupt him. Good cause or not, he did not take it well. Still, he gave his time willingly and for free, because he thought the cause worthwhile. It would be quite a few years before everybody at the BBC was similarly convinced.

Remarkably, on that first momentous night, the *Children in Need* appeal raised a million pounds in contributions from the viewers and listeners. This, with the minimum support from regional or local BBC television and radio; and, if it comes to that, less than a hundred per cent from BBC national TV and Radio. A million pounds from a standing start, with no easy way to make contributions through banks, post office counters, nor credit cards, and with a minimum of pre-publicity from a cautious BBC.

A million pounds in 1980 is not too far removed from ten million pounds twenty years later; and in November 1999, we raised 11.6 million pounds on the night. But that is not much of a difference, considering the whole evening's transmission is now given over to the appeal, and that it runs for at least two more hours. Also it now has a one-million pound contribution from

Radio 2 listeners, and a tremendous input from every BBC region and local radio station.

Pudsey Bear is now the best-known charity icon in Britain, and the appeal has long since won the hearts and minds of the British public. So, why are we not doing better on the night twenty years on? Oh, I know that by the time all the pledges are in, the grand total doubles to twenty million pounds or more, but why have we just kept pace with inflation, on the night?

The BBC is a broad church, and many a dissident voice has been heard from the pews on the subject of *Children in Need*. Should the BBC be doing it at all? Is it a good thing? If we are taking a licence fee should we also be taking money for charity? Why don't we do it for pensioners? Throughout the years the begrudgers have whinged, and producers, heads of department and controllers of programmes have bewailed the unwelcome interference in their plans and schedules. Never mind that it has become the people's charity, and the one truly cohesive event within a BBC in dire need of unity of purpose.

It was five years before Michael Grade knocked heads together, and built the evening's schedule around the appeal. From then on, the grand total rose every year, and that Friday in the third week of November grew and grew in the hearts of the British public.

It never fails to astonish, how, every year, the public, without any prompting or persuasion, and precious little advertising from the BBC, spontaneously begin thousands of fund-raising drives in homes, parish halls and schools. From bazaar to bizarre, anything goes, as long as it is for the children. People ask me if the huge amounts pledged by companies and individuals are honoured. They are not only honoured, but improved upon. How else would the big night's total be, literally, doubled every year?

The press has largely ignored *Children in Need* and the critics have been sniffy. By and large it has been a show that only the public have liked. The stars have turned out in their hundreds, from the States and Europe as well as Britain, all of them prepared to do anything, however ridiculous, just to help. It would be impossible to list them all, even if I remembered each show clearly.

I know in the eighties the then Prime Minister, Margaret Thatcher, turned up, because I have a photo to prove it, but everybody that is invited turns up. The odd arm has to be twisted – usually within the BBC itself. For, as I have said, it is within the BBC that little pockets of apathy may be detected. In certain areas, not a million miles from the sixth floor of the Television Centre (Where All Power Resides), there is little enthusiasm for *Children in Need*. It is not trendy, it is not pacy, it is not in your face. Why can't it be more like *Comic Relief*?

Never mind that *Children in Need* gets as good, if not better, viewing figures than Red Nose Day, certain executives would rather bask in the reflected glory of Richard Curtis – and then, there is lunch at the Groucho, with Lenny, Angus, Paul or Chris. C'mon, *Children in Need* is just not sexy, is it?

*Comic Relief* is a wonderful achievement, brilliantly driven by Richard Curtis, and with an enviable cast of the brightest and best in British television and the theatre. It raises phenomenal amounts of money and entertains while doing so. So does *Children in Need*, in its own time-honoured way.

A little more appreciation from the top of the executive ladder might well instil a greater enthusiasm from those who can help, a couple of rungs down. Publicity might be stepped up, more air time granted for trails and films, certain listings magazines might be persuaded to rally round. And, you never know, it might make a difference on the night.

Support for *Children in Need* has never been lacking from higher up; Chairmen and Director-Generals have rallied round splendidly: Sir Michael Checkland, Sir John Birt and, I have no doubt, Greg Dyke. Marmaduke Hussey was a great enthusiast for the cause, willing to take part in any publicity, and Sir Christopher Bland has been no less cooperative.

No, it is a step or two down that the problems occur for the reasons given, but also because the executives in question were not around when *Children in Need* got going. *Comic Relief* is much more their baby, their era. Although it raises less money and gets a smaller viewership, it reaches a younger audience than *Children in Need*. And that appears to be the most important consideration.

In 1999, it was decreed that *Children in Need* should try to win over a younger audience. Apparently, it was not reaching the 'young male' ... Why it should wish to reach disinterested young males when it was more than satisfying its target audience of the very young and their parents and grandparents remains a mystery. Such views have, however, changed the programme over the years. It is much quicker, slicker, pop-orientated, but not *better*. It raises less money on the night, gets no bigger an audience. In my opinion, it has lost the warmth and spontaneity that made it so successful. The cock-ups, the pratfalls, the breakdowns, the technical disasters, the sheer unpredictability of it all are what people remember most affectionately about *Children in Need*, not the latest pop group miming to their current rave.

Patrick Moore and Roy Kinnear roaring in on a motorbike like a couple of First World War air-aces, that is what people remember. TV chefs getting their kit off *à la* 'Full Monty', Peter Snow dressed as Tarzan, Joanna Lumley down to her suspender belt (God, how I remember that ...), Roy Castle setting the whole country tap-dancing, microphones going down as the show opened, lights going off as I handed over to Plymouth, people addressing the nation and not a sound coming out, others struck dumb in the dark. Opening the show from the top of a huge staircase and only then realizing that the camera was too far away for me to read the Autocue. Building the biggest bear in the world, with all the regions contributing, and finding the thing looked more like a mile-high lump of coal. Filling the gaps, winging it – live and real. That is the way I like it, even if the 'young male' does not.

Over the years I have been lucky in my co-presenters, too: Esther Rantzen, Joanna, the charming Sue Cook, the effervescent Gaby Roslin. It sounds showbizzy and smarmy, but I can't help it: everyone a sweetheart, a love ...

## CHAIRMEN AND DIRECTOR-GENERALS

I have known my share of Chairmen and Director-Generals of the BBC – and, over the long years, even got close to a few. In the seventies, Lady Curran rang me one morning to play a request for Sir Charles, the DG at the time, on his birthday. She had taken the opportunity to ring me while he was in the shower.

Sir Michael Checkland and I saw many a rugby match together. I remember him being late for lunch one International Saturday at Twickenham. Michael – an accountant by profession – had driven himself to the game, rather than spend the BBC's money on a driver.

Sir Ian Trethowan would repair to his room, turn on the telly and lock the door whenever there was decent racing on the box.

Alasdair Milne called everybody 'boy', and poured you a single malt, if you were very good. Then you had to listen to a lecture on the correct pronunciation of 'Glenmorangie'. The story is told that Alasdair took one of his senior executives shooting, and, after a weekend of eating, drinking and knocking seven bells out of our feathered friends, turned to his replete companion on the way back to London in the car, and said, 'By the way, boy – you're fired.'

Sir John Birt, now his Lordship, took me to the ballet. Probably the most controversial DG of them all, I always found him warm, but shy. And in the way of many shy people whom I have known, possessed of blazing determination and single-mindedness. Professor Laurie Taylor, a great friend of John's, tells a tale that sums him up: 'One Wednesday, John rang me up: "D.H. Lawrence, right or wrong?" he asked tersely. And I knew,' says Laurie, 'that when we met on the weekend, I had better have the answers.'

That was John Birt during his time with the BBC: analyse, diagnose, categorize, organize. John Birt was known as Bert Birt to my radio listeners, and his sidekick was Phyllis – actually a decent man called Bob Phillis, who was his deputy. According to my crowd, Bert and Phillis wore matching shell-suits, as they went about their early-morning jog around Broadcasting House. It was said that they used to run a homely pub in Fitzrovia, specializing in real ales and hearty ploughman's lunches, before being promoted beyond their abilities to run the BBC.

The Radio Doctor was the first Chairman I came across, but I knew him even less than I did Sir Michael Swann, the next man. George Howard of Castle Howard was a patrician, a throwback to more spacious days. I joined him for dinner once at Harrogate during the *Eurovision Song Contest*. He fell asleep, somewhere in between the main course and the pudding. He had no idea about radio or television, not to mind anybody on them, but his son knew a thing or two about pop music, or so he thought. George insisted that the Controller of Programmes, Radio 1, explain his music policy to the lad. It was the way things were then, a bit baronial. It was a wonder to me that George did not demand *droit du seigneur* whenever a member of staff got married.

Stuart Young was charming, approachable, unstuffy, a Chairman for the latter half of the twentieth century. We played golf at Turnberry together when he came up for the *Pro-Celebrity* series. He liked to see programmes being made, he was interested, involved. He might have been one of the great Chairmen, but he died, suddenly and far too early in an active life.

He was followed by someone who did become one of the great Chairmen, Marmaduke 'Duke' Hussey, now Lord Hussey. 'Duke', or 'Dukey' as he preferred, was every inch the patrician that George Howard was, but he had the common touch, and he loved his people and the BBC, his sacred trust. He had hardly come into office before he called me in to see him: 'Princess Anne told me you were the man to talk to, if I wanted to know anything about the BBC!' he bellowed.

Dukey does not speak softly, what you see is what you get – no subterfuge, no artifice. He lost a leg in the Italian campaign of the Second World War, and dragged himself the length of Italy, without it. He has never been without pain since. Nor has he ever complained. I don't know where Princess Anne got the idea that I knew something about the Beeb, but I told Dukey to be nice to the commissionaires and tea-ladies, the most important people in the building – get on the wrong side of them and you were dead.

Early in Dukey's reign, a masochist tendency gained favour in the BBC, and it was decided to produce a yearly exercise in self-flagellation entitled 'It's Your BBC', or some such. The idea was that some hours of a weekend's viewing should be given over to the indecent exposure of everything the Corporation had to offer. Throw wide the shutters! Blow away the cobwebs! Fling open the books! Loony, of course, and doomed.

At a lunch, I asked Michael Checkland why in heaven's name he was allowing it, but he obviously thought it was a great idea; so, puzzlingly, did Bill Cotton, whose nose for trouble was normally so acute. Obviously, it had come down on tablets of stone from somewhere high up: the BBC, public service broadcaster incarnate, must expose all to the public! I advised Dukey against it, but he appeared anyway, and took a hammering for presenting the thing, as the BBC's main front man.

Despite the dogs' abuse, and the patent foolishness of the enterprise, the BBC could not just drop the idea, so the thing dragged its slow length along for a couple of years, before it was allowed to fade away and die. I suppose its occasional outbursts of raving naivety is one of the things that is endearing about the BBC. Yet Dukey, in time, wormed his way into the heart of my listener. From the *Bumper Book of TOGs*, a telling tome produced against all the odds, in 1995:

> '*A Thousand Years, Chairman!*
> *Floreat! Floreat!*'
> The shouts and cheers ring out from the serried ranks of bowler-hatted middle management, as the Great Coach of the BBC, drawn by its four proud, prancing, jet-black stallions, snorts and steams to a halt outside the mighty portals of Broadcasting House. A servile ostler scampers forward with the steps as the coach-door opens. A Byronic, patrician figure steps down. Even as he does, the bowler-hatted ranks prostrate themselves, kow-towing in the time-honoured fashion. The tall silver-haired figure with its great purple cloak, strides silently to the doors. A eunuch in the Director-General's Court sidles up to whisper in the Great Man's ear: '*Remember, Dukey: you, too, are human ...*'
> The Chairman has arrived.
> Another day at the BBC has begun ...

Dukey took it all, and more, in good part, as indeed does the relatively new kid on the block, Sir Christopher Bland, greeted by all with the simple, honest slogan, 'Bland is Grand'! As Dukey did, Sir Christopher drops in to see the workers of the coalface every so often of a morn, and shares a dish of Rosie Lee with the lads. There is some rough manly banter, jostling, and a heavy cuff or two to the mazzard, and then Sir Christopher makes his way to his lavish apartments, leaving behind his yeoman broadcasters, flushed, but invigorated.

# TWELVE

# THAT'LL DO

In 1981, Michael Grade, then running London Weekend Television, came to me with a proposition: 'Here's a hatful of money, come over to the other side of the river.' I liked the idea – I like Michael – but I eventually gave it the elbow; my radio show was the biggest in the land, *Blankety Blank* was still going like a train, and I knew that Bill Cotton had big plans for me.

Now, when Melvyn Bragg deigns to talk to me, he is at pains to point out what a mistake I made – had I jumped aboard the LWT gravy train then, I would have made millions, along with himself and the rest of the gang, among them Sir Christopher and Greg Dyke. John Birt was also one of the boys, but he jumped ship before they struck the mother-lode. Recently, I heard him say: 'People ask me if I ever regret turning my back on millions, for years of insult and abuse at the BBC.' A look of real sorrow crossed the impassive face: 'Well, whadda you think?'

Michael Grade wanted me to present the *Six O'Clock Show* for London viewers, and a network talk-show on a Saturday evening. The producer of the *Six O'Clock Show* was Greg Dyke. Not too long afterwards, Michael left London Weekend, also missing Bland's Bonanza, seeking fame and fortune in the Hollywood Hills. I met him there a few years later, in 1984, when he had become a little disenchanted with the Boulevard of Dreams, and Bill Cotton was in the process of luring him to the BBC, to become Director of Programmes.

A three-nights-a-week talk-show was in the air by then, and since I was in Los Angeles for the Olympic Games, and Bill Cotton ditto, we agreed to meet in Bill's hotel suite for a little Hollywood plotting. It was a block or two from my own hotel and a lovely sunny day, so I took to the pavements. By the time I got to Bill's hotel my shirt was sticking to my back and honest sweat was running off me in rivulets. Michael Grade looked at me in astonishment: 'What have you been doing?' 'I walked here,' I gasped. He shook his head. ' In Hollywood, Terry,' he explained gently, ' you pay somebody to walk *for* you ...'

## THE MISTS OF TIME

In August 1981, Helen and I took the kids to the States for a holiday: San Francisco, down the Pacific Highway to Pebble Beach, across the mountains to Yosemite National Park, then into Nevada to Lake Tahoe, back to San Francisco and home.

When we had visited Florida and Walt Disney World, a couple of years previously, Katherine had been a bit too young to take it all in, but this time she was old enough to enjoy it as much as her brothers. She particularly liked Yosemite, with its huge spaces, wildlife and cow-pony-trekking.

The latter activity certainly left an impression on her mother and me, for several days ... It was Katherine's birthday while we were at Yosemite, and the rest of us pretended we had forgotten all about it – no cards, no presents, no fuss. She did not say anything, but got quieter and quieter as the day went on. The boys were bursting to tell her, and her sad little face was breaking my heart, but we all kept the secret.

That night, we had dinner on the terrace of the Ahwahnee Lodge, with deer keeping their distance in the park, and raccoons boldly coming up to the table for scraps. Katherine grew more silent. Then, through the doors came the waiters, carrying gifts, cards and a huge birthday cake, and singing 'Happy Birthday to You', as if they were auditioning for the third touring company of *The Music Man*, which indeed they probably had. Katherine's face was a picture: shock, then laughter, then tears of happiness and relief. Her family had not forgotten.

For the purposes of this book, I have had to dredge what remains of my brain in a futile attempt to remember any of the supposedly important happenings in my radio and television career, yet that evening in Yosemite, and my daughter's laughter and tears, is etched forever in my memory.

I have only the haziest recollection of a show entitled *You Must Be Joking*, which went out at peak time on Saturday nights on BBC 1. It was a Japanese idea and involved showing two teams (say, policewomen against firemen), bits of film of activities that were far-fetched in the extreme. Some were true, some were false – the teams had to decide. I remember virtually nothing about it, perhaps because it disappeared without trace, after what can only be described as a 'brief run'.

Chris Greenwood, who has been a researcher and producer of TV chat-shows both here and in Australia since before Michael Parkinson was born, tells me we did one together in 1982, on Tuesday nights on BBC 1. Again it appears to have had a mercifully short life-span, although I do remember Bruce Forsyth, who was having a hard time from the press at the time, telling me not to expect my own career to continue on an ever-rising curve.

Through the mists of time, I see David Frost, too. I don't remember the interview, but I do have a clear memory of meeting the great man for lunch about that time, at Les Ambassadeurs, an impossibly ritzy joint on Park Lane.

As I entered, I could hear David's voice. He was all over somebody in the foyer: laughing, joshing, hugging. After some more moments of extreme good fellowship and bubbling *bonhomie*, David joined me, and we went to the table together. The man who had been the object of Mr Frost's warm affection sat down at a table across the room. 'Who's that?' I enquired. 'I dunno,' said David Frost.

In a 1982 diary, I see that on one show I interviewed Randy Edelman, Robert Carrier, Jeffrey Archer and Beryl Reid. So, it was a proper talk-show. I also remember having a co-host for the first couple of programmes – well, a hostess actually. It was Paula Yates – bouncy, bubbly and way ahead of her time. Too hot for the BBC to handle.

Somewhere around this time of frantic, short-lived endeavour was a live Saturday BBC 1 show, *What's on Wogan?*, over which time, mercifully, has drawn a veil. It was produced by Alan Boyd, just before he took off for the other side of the Thames. He wanted to take me with him, for a new exciting 'people' show, *Game for a Laugh*, but, again, I thought my prospects were better at the BBC. *Game for a Laugh* made stars of Henry Kelly, Matthew Kelly and Sarah Kennedy, and Alan Boyd went on to run various television networks.

Amid the dross, the odd gem glittered: I linked the Royal Wedding of Prince Charles and Lady Diana Spencer for BBC Radio from outside the gates of Buckingham Palace from early morning, as the crowds gathered on the Mall, till the happy couple waved their farewells from the balcony, and the millions that had thronged the route, made their contented way home.

What a day: chatting to an excited crowd, describing the scene, working alongside legends such as Wynford Vaughan-Thomas and Richard Burton. The pomp, the panoply, the majesty of it all – that I can't forget. And I have one quirky memory: Dame Kiri Te Kanawa had sung, magnificently at the Abbey, and as I made my way up Green Park, back to Broadcasting House, she suddenly appeared, glass in hand, on a penthouse balcony above. She was unmistakable, still wearing the outrageous rainbow outfit and hat that had almost made as big an impact as her voice. She waved at me. It made a great day even better.

Patricia Houlihan, a green-eyed producer of Irish descent, had a good idea: why don't we do a *Wogan's Guide to the BBC* documentary? Not the usual well-meaning stuff, heavy with Reithian overtones and public-service stuff, but a light-hearted look at the old Corpo. The programme worked with the public and the critics. They liked the little-known fact that BBC Television Centre was built in a circle so that the rumours could circulate faster.

Esther Rantzen said that working for the BBC was a bit like sex. Her husband, Desmond Wilcox, disagreed, 'I had seventeen years of it,' he whinged, 'and it wasn't at all like sex'. Different strokes …

News announcer James Alexander Gordon described the ghost that haunted the bedrooms of the old Langham Hotel, where the overnight announcers made their weary trundle beds: 'A fluorescent shape with very sallow features, sunken eyes and a long cape.' It was obviously the Head of Light Entertainment, but Gordon's response was in the finest traditions of the BBC. He civilly asked the thing its name, and, on receiving no response, threw his false leg at it.

That queen among television critics, Nancy Banks-Smith,

found 'the twang', as we snapped Auntie Beeb's garters, 'irresistible'...

It is strange, but, with the passage of years, the BBC has taken itself increasingly seriously, and in this new century is much more given to introversion and navel-gazing than it ever was eighteen years ago. Patricia Houlihan would never have been given the necessary cooperation to make *Wogan's Guide to the BBC* in the Birt years. Mind you, there were so many different departments, structures, systems and procedures created in those seven years, that it would have been like searching the catacombs.

Around this time, the respected radio critic, Gillian Reynolds, expressed the opinion that I was all over the radio networks like a rash. She spoke sooth; the *Wake up to Wogan* show on Radio 2, *The Year in Question* and *Any Questions?* for Radio 4. I had even read the Morning Story ...

## DON'T GIVE UP THE DAY JOB

Then came another series for Radio 4, the brainchild of a producer, Helen Fry. I had produced another literary triumph, *The Day Job*, based yet again on the wit and wisdom of my listeners, that had gone well without ever troubling the Booker Prize judges. Helen's idea was to send me out into the wide world in a variety of daily tasks, and call the series *The Day Job*.

Being the Carol Vorderman/Carol Smillie of my day, anything I wanted to do was hunky-dory with the BBC, so I spent several months in a variety of uniforms and guises. I was a hotel barman, an AA patrolman, a bookie at the ring in Newbury, but, most memorable of all, an air-steward on Concorde.

It was time-consuming, because all the 'day jobs' required training. I had to do them for real, with a concealed tape recorder. It is surprising how unrecognized you are by the public, when in a different context. I took dogs' abuse as a barman and a bookie, and, given my ineptitude with things mechanical, you can imagine what the stranded motorist thought of me as an AA man.

'Steward on Concorde' was the gem in the diadem. After a week of learning how to shovel a canapé, and pour Champagne with one hand while balancing a tray in the other, I took the coats at the door of a Concorde flight to Washington. You rarely see an overweight steward, and I am not surprised. I was up and down that plane like a bee's wing, all over the Atlantic:

'Man in row four wants a Martini.'

'What? Vermouth?'

'I'll ask him.'

Back up the plane. Back to the galley. 'Yes.'

'Yes what?'

'Vermouth.'

'Vodka or gin?'

Back to your man. Back down again. 'He's not sure, he thinks he'd prefer brandy.'

'Brandy! Is he barking?'

'I don't think he knows what a Martini is – he looks a bit panicked.'

'For heaven's sake ask him if he wants the brandy and the vermouth in separate glasses.'

Up the aisle again. Back down to the galley.

'Well?'

'He's asleep ...'

Not a drop of Champagne, not a sliver of foie gras passed my lips. It was Concorde starvation at the speed of sound.

## TRAPPINGS OF FAME

Our good friends the Young family were related to a famous Barbadian family, the Goddards, and had the use of the Goddard family house on St James's Beach, Barbados. They invited us to join them after Christmas. As we landed, the first drops of rain splattered on the sun-dried earth. We have always been followed by our own private raincloud and it didn't let us down. Everywhere we go, be it Europe, the Far East, the West Indies, the natives commiserate: 'It's the first rain we've had for five years ...'

We ate flying-fish pie, drank a lot of rum, the children learnt to water-ski. I didn't. The boat-engine just was not powerful enough to haul my great bulk up out of the water, but I didn't have the common sense to let go of the rope. My legs grew further and further apart, as we hurtled through the blue Caribbean. They might have separated altogether, if the boat had not slowed down. The insides of my thighs were black and blue for the remainder of the holiday.

My enduring memory of our Bajan odyssey was the journey outwards. My friend Brian Young and I were sitting together in Club, when a familiar flop of flaxen hair and a well-tailored suit emerged from First Class. It was Michael Heseltine and he made a beeline for us. Well, not me – he ignored me completely, and, reaching over, took Brian warmly by the hand. 'Mr Young!' he said, 'we've never had the pleasure, but I'm delighted to meet you, your political interviews are first class. I know Margaret is a particular fan …'

At this point, Brian disengaged his hand. 'You've got the wrong Young, I'm afraid.' 'You're not Jimmy?' 'No.' The noble head jerked convulsively, and then without a word of apology or explanation, the great man disappeared behind the First-Class curtain, never to re-emerge. He had obviously taken a look at the passenger list, seen Wogan and Young together, and leapt to the obvious and pitifully wrong conclusion. Ever since, I have never been entirely confident of old Goldilocks's judgement.

The Variety Club gave a lunch for Helen and me, which was televised. They all turned up for me, which was gratifying and touching. Bob Monkhouse spoke, and Peter Alliss. Kenny Everett was there, and Larry and Beryl, Patrick Moore, Vincent Price, Jimmy, Gloria, David Frost, Les Dawson, Jimmy Tarbuck, Derek Nimmo, Clement Freud, Danny La Rue.

I don't know what kind of a television programme it made, because I am saving the tape for viewing in my declining years, but it was a lovely lunch.

I continued to present the *Variety Club Awards*, with the voice-over introductions down in the deep brown tones of my Radio 2 early-morning mucker, Ray Moore. From the desolate remoteness of the graveyard shift, Ray had won the hearts and minds of the listeners, and his tragic death was a sad blow to millions, as well as those who knew and loved him and Alma.

I was honoured to speak at his memorial service in All Souls, the Nash church in Langham Place, just by the BBC. I said that I regretted that Ray had not been appreciated as much in life as in death. He was the best of men, good-humoured, witty. Relaxed and urbane to the listener, yet nervous to the observer. He perspired freely during his programme, surrounded by a cloud of Senior Service smoke, and I never intruded into his studio, because I knew that it made him uncomfortable. He was extraordinary – tense as a coiled spring, yet sounding as if he were about to fall off a log.

Ray Moore hated appearing in front of the camera. He was a sound-man, a voice – a voice of comfort and joy, on many a dark morning. Sarah Kennedy now occupies Ray's seat – funny, talkative, creating a warm and quirky world for the insomniac and the early riser – which is the secret of it all.

The trappings of fame came thick and fast: I stood for two hours in an upstairs room in Madame Tussaud's, while they photographed me from every conceivable angle. Then they moulded my image in wax; I gave them a spare suit, shirt, tie, socks and shoes, and it looked nothing like me. That was the *Blankety Blank* dummy, complete with microphone.

About eight years later, the good Madame's wax-modellers essayed another attempt, this time a 'Wogan' dummy. It looked no more like me than the first effort. As Burns put it, it might have helped the world along if God had given us the gift of seeing ourselves as others see us, but sorry, Madame Tussaud, I could not see it.

Madame's is, I understand, Britain's second most popular tourist attraction, and I can vouch for the teeming multitudes that queue up there; I pass them every morning, rain or shine. I wonder how many are queuing up for the second time?

I have never seen a dummy in Tussaud's that looks remotely like the person it is supposed to represent. If I were Her Majesty the Queen, I think I would sue them, for the Royal Tableau. The entire Royal Family look like refugees, their regal finery straight out of Oxfam's window. The only waxworks that look real are those we have never seen in real life, films, television or photographs. Queen Elizabeth I, for instance, and various stranglers. And if you think these are the rantings of an embittered man, whose waxen image now graces a shelf in the back room of dear old Madame's, you may be right. Still, as they say in Ireland, I saw the two days ...

The RAC asked me to drive in the London-to-Brighton Rally, and provided me with a 1904 Thorneycroft with which to make the run. I had a couple of lessons with the veteran, acquiring an easy mastery of the gears, clutch, steering wheel and carburettor. It was a family expedition and we stayed the night in London before assembling, wrapped up like eskimos, in Hyde Park.

The start was deceptively smooth, and off we bowled in the old beauty, a little frozen around the gills in the open-topped roadster, but quietly confident of barrelling into Brighton before lunch. The first unscheduled stop was at Streatham, as we were making more steam than the *Royal Scot*. The engineer, who had been perched merrily on the running-board, damped down the fires.

We set off again, this time getting as far as Horley, in Surrey, before the old girl began to bubble up nicely again. And so the long day wore on. The Royal Automobile Club's official-entry car must have been made on a Friday around knocking-off time in Thorneycroft's garage, because it was the lemon of the rally.

I must say that the children bore it all with remarkable cheerfulness, but I could see that the adventure had palled for Helen, as it had for me, long before we limped into a dusky Brighton, with the engineer leaning perilously over the engine, his finger jammed into the carburettor.

There can be few things more discouraging in life than coming last in the London-to-Brighton veterans' rally. It is particularly galling when you are only halfway to the seaside, to be waved at by other old crocks who have been there, had their lunch, and are on their accursed way home. By the time we got there, there was not as much as a cold chipolata left, so we accepted the offer of a lift back.

Cold, hungry, disillusioned, we clambered into the back of a four-wheel drive vehicle of reliable, modern manufacture. I was just nodding off, when we hit another car. The thing on the front of ours for pushing cattle out of the way did most of the damage, and it was some time before the unfortunate owner of the other car, which had folded up like a cardboard box, could be sedated. It must have been midnight before we got home, but Helen being Helen insisted on cooking a meal for the man who had nearly killed us.

## HIGH DAYS AND HOLIDAYS

The children were growing up; we looked at a couple of Catholic boarding schools for Alan. I don't know why we bothered. We knew that we could not bear to be parted from our children, and Alan in particular was a bigger home-boy than even his father, who, you will remember, never left the comforts of home until the day he married.

Alan stayed happily at his day-school in Maidenhead, as did Mark, less happily. Blaming yourself is an old parents' trick, but perhaps Mark's schooldays would have been happier if he had not had to follow so closely in his brother's footsteps. Katherine eventually finished her schooling in Reading. It was a chore for Helen getting them all off every morning, driving to Maidenhead and then on to Reading, but a delight for me to pick them up every afternoon, even if Katherine insisted that I park the Rolls around the corner from the school, to avoid embarrassing her in front of her friends.

As I write, none of my children has, as yet, produced any grandchildren. Most of my contemporaries are now proud to call themselves Granny or Granddad, and look at me pityingly. I am in no hurry. I had the great privilege and joy of seeing my children grow up, and spending time with them every day, helping with homework, telling stories, playing football or tennis, swimming. Other fathers, in more conventional jobs, are not so lucky. Maybe that is why they so enjoy grandfatherhood – they can afford to give the time to their grandchildren that they were unable to give to their children.

Derek and Mina Russell, two firm friends, invited us to join them for a holiday at their villa on the south-east coast of Spain, south of a town called Torrevieja, on a golf course called Villamartin. We liked it so much, we bought a house on a promontory nearby, Caboroig. It had a pool, a garden, and looked out over the sea. The Wogan family had thirteen extraordinarily happy years there. We all learned Spanish, to a greater or lesser extent. Katherine's degree is in Hispanic studies and Alan taught in the regional capital of Murcia for six months.

As the children grew, they spent more time in pubs and clubs, and less on the beach and in the pool. Then, as they grew still older, they outgrew the all-night rave, and began to go less and less. Helen and I invited friends down, played golf, ate and drank too much. But slowly, inexorably, the excesses of Spanish development began to wear us down. Torrevieja grew faster than any town in Spain. The road from Alicante to the town became a nightmare of jerry-building sites – new slums in the sun. The golf courses were overwhelmed with people. We put the house on the market, said goodbye to our housekeeper, Josepha, queen of the paella, and looked elsewhere.

Some months after we bought in Caboroig, Michael and Kathleen Clancy bought their villa on the golf course, Villamartin. Kathleen is still there, entertaining her family and her numerous grandchildren. Michael died suddenly and far too young, no more than a year after buying their place in the sun. The Clancys had a place in the rain as well, at Lahinch, in their native Clare, on the Atlantic seaboard of Ireland. And so many happy times did we spend together there.

There are two golf courses at Lahinch, and the Clancy homestead overlooked both of them. To tell the truth, if you did not play golf in Lahinch, there was not a great deal of anything else going on. Certainly, of a weekend, people would batter the floor, the banjo, the bodhran and each other in the pubs, but in general, Lahinch was quiet. Still is.

To put it at its best, the weather is changeable there. All four seasons in about ten minutes, particularly if you are stuck out in the middle of the golf course. There is one sovereign way of telling what the weather is going to be like: the goats. If they are out, quietly cropping the fairways, there is a slim chance of avoiding severe exposure and hypothermia. If they are sheltering in the lee of the club-house, only Ranulph Twisleton-Wykeham-Fiennes would be eejit enough to venture abroad.

Hospitality at the Clancys' was far-famed. Breakfasts of rashers, eggs, sausages, black pudding, white pudding, farls of oaten bread, rafts of marmalade and bucketfuls of tea were nothing, of a morning. I remember striding along a fairway, into a gale strong enough to blow a tinker off his missus, and shouting to Michael: 'That breakfast is weighing heavily on my golf swing.' He turned to me and roared, sagely: 'Lahinch is no place to be playing hungry golf.'

Kathleen and Michael were the perfect hosts, in Lahinch, Spain, their beautiful home in Denham, Bucks, their box at Ascot, and the hundred and one holidays to which they invited their friends. Michael had the gift of cohesion. He brought people together, made his friends each others' friends. And we are all still together, thirteen years after he so suddenly left us. The gift of friendship and love is the best of all legacies to leave behind.

Michael Clancy belonged to that blessed band of Irish men and women who grew up in Ireland's hungry years, and, without a farm to inherit or a job to go to, took the mail-boat from Dun Laoghaire to Holyhead. They dug, built and toiled as generations of immigrant Irish had before them. Most of them drank as hard as they worked, and lost sight of their dreams. Some of them, like Michael Clancy, were of a different breed: determined, ambitious, intelligent. They built huge, successful businesses from standing starts as labourers, hod-carriers, lorry-drivers. Their names are everywhere: McNicholas, Murphy, Henry, McInerney, Kennedy, Clancy, hundreds more all over Britain.

They make me proud, these homespun, home-made Irish-men. Nowadays, the labourers are going in the opposite direction, from Holyhead to Dun Laoghaire, as the Irish *Wirtschaftswunder* – economic miracle – continues to boom.

The Irish coming to Britain now, are graduates, investment bankers, lawyers, website wizards, products of an educational system second to none in the world. The boys who came over in the forties and fifties knew their three R's, too, thanks to the Christian Brothers. They had trouble with their Th's, but they could count.

Most of them, the ones whose names you see on building sites, roadworks and the sides of lorries, had two jobs. My friend

Chris Henry laboured by day and worked as a bouncer by night. He only bounced other Irishmen, of course, in various Irish dancehalls and clubs around London. That is the thing about the Irish – they only fight among themselves. You will never find a gang of Irishmen picking on another group because of their colour or race. They would rather knock lumps out of each other. It is the story of the four green fields.

Chris's muscular work was noted by a passing Italian restaurateur, who asked him to mind the doors of his trattoria. After weeks of free pasta, and not the slightest sign of trouble, Chris felt that the eyes of the owner were upon him, and that he ought to be doing something for his lasagne verde. He went to a pub in Kilburn and recruited a couple of his fellow-navvies. 'Lads,' he said, 'I want you to come up to the trat on Saturday night and make a bit of trouble. Nothin' much – a shouting match – and I'll throw ye out, and old Antonio will think he's getting his money's worth. There's a few pints in it for you.'

The lads readily agreed. Unfortunately, by the time they arrived at the trattoria, they had already had the few pints, and a few more besides. The pretend argument turned into a real fight – bottles flew, tables and chairs were smashed, and Chris Henry had to end the mêlée by throwing his two pals out, through the plate-glass window. He did not get to keep the job, but until the day he sadly passed away, he popped in regularly for his lasagne verde.

Chris Henry had a wonderful way with the English language: for instance, he knew a friend who had a 'pandemonium' in Florida. Taking a seat next to Helen in a plane, he asked: 'What's that you're reading?'

'Oh, it's a Maeve Binchy.'

'Oh,' says Chris, 'is that fact or friction?'

He knocked the French language about a bit as well: he loved his white wine, especially 'Pussy Fussy'. His favourite saying, in moments of quiet contemplation, was: 'And he walloped it into Mary while the mother was out for turf …' The Irish are full of little non-sequiturs like that: 'Aha,' said she, 'sure, it slipped out with the laughin' …' or 'Tear away,' said she, 'me mother's a dressmaker …'

I do not know where these little gems originated, but there has to be a story to them all. Like my friend Tom's mother, walking home with friends one night, after a rubber of bridge. Without warning, as so often happens, she broke wind. Embarrassed, she apologized profusely. 'Ah, don't bother ma'am,' said one of her companions, 'sure, the gun's your own ...'

## BALLS OF FIRE

My friend David Hatch returned from BBC Manchester to be Head of Radio Light Entertainment, and bought a windmill in Hertfordshire. Ball of fire that he was – and always will be – he started several successful new series, broke new ground with *Week-Ending*, and nurtured talents like Griff Rhys Jones, Mel Smith, Jimmy Mulville. Even the BBC cannot ignore talent that bites your legs, and David was made Controller of Programmes, Radio 2.

He dropped in most mornings while I was on the air, for a chat and a coffee, and we became the close friends we have ever remained. He charged up the rungs of the BBC ladder: Controller Radio 4, Deputy Managing Director, Managing Director, and, finally, Special Advisor to the Director-General.

Call me partial, but he was the finest senior BBC executive I ever worked for. The BBC's attitude to its staff and its contracted artistes has always been cavalier – no, remote – even pre-Birt. Nobody bothers to tell you whether you are doing a good, bad or indifferent job. The attitude, obviously Reithian in its origins, seems to be: be grateful that you are working for the BBC, and get on with it.

David Hatch never subscribed to that philosophy. When someone did a good job, he dropped them a note of congratulation. When they cocked up, he told them so. He was inspirational, motivational, and he loved rugby. What's more, he invited me as his guest to all the Twickenham internationals. What larks! To sit around a table with Peter Cook, Richard Briers, Alan Coren, Clement Freud, and, over the years, virtually every distinguished broadcaster in the land, and follow it with a rugby international, was very heaven for a Limerick lad.

Peter Cook usually turned up in a sports coat and T-shirt, whatever the weather. Pretty well 'inoculated' by the time he arrived, I don't think he felt much. I would occasionally invite the merry band back for dinner at Wogan Towers, and Peter would arrive in the same outfit in which he had attended the game. He had simply driven around the hostelries of Bucks and Berks, until it was time to knock on our door. He dazzled for two courses as only he could, then fell asleep into the pudding.

Alan Coren talks every bit as brilliantly as he writes; Richard Briers is an hysterical mixture of the theatrical and the bawdy; and Clement Freud is the most congenial of men, while preserving an outer carapace that would repel a tank. If you do not know him he will frighten you to death.

I watched at the Twickenham bar, as a man came up and asked him for his autograph:

'No,' said Clement, with the nasality that is all his own.

'Oh, sorry,' apologized the man, as if he needed to.

'No,' said Clement. 'You see, I never sign autographs, for a very good reason.'

He then went on to explain, very fully, his philosophy. It took about ten minutes, as I watched and listened. Eventually, Clement released his prey, who wandered back to his table bemused and autographless. Freud could have signed a hundred autographs while he was explaining why he did not sign any.

David Hatch, his 'Mouse' Ann, Helen and I shared many a table and drink together, as we watched our children grow. Although she had a will of iron and a backbone of steel, Ann always seemed fragile, and after a couple of years of failing health, and heartbreak, for David and her family, she slipped away.

David had retired from the BBC without a word of reproach or rancour. Whatever his beef with the Birtians, and I am sure he hated the direction his beloved BBC was being driven, he said nary a word. He was right. Who cares, except yourself? Ranting and fulminating about what was, or might have been, is pathetic. The pointing of fingers, the settling of old scores in articles or biographies is saddening. If you are going, go – and take your baggage with you ...

David threw himself into his work for the National Consumer Council, and as a magistrate. His children and grandchildren were a comfort, and he never moaned. But Helen Wogan was not happy. David needed love and care; a woman's tender touch. And she had the very woman.

Mary Clancy is the eldest of the Clancy clan, bright, attractive, vivacious, but she had never married. Helen put David and Mary together at a dinner party, and, within a year, they had tied the knot. The Taplow Dating Agency wins again! It was a wonderful wedding at Farm Street, followed by a spectacular reception at the Savoy.

I was the proud best man, and, earlier in the day, was standing in all my finery in the hotel's foyer, when an American came up to me. I was all ready with a smile, pen poised for an autograph, when she said: 'Can you show me the way to the restaurant, please? ...'

David and Mary have hardly left each other's arms since that great day, and it is wonderful to see two of our greatest friends so happy together. We still go to the rugby internationals, David and I – still eat, drink, sing and shout. He never brags too much when England win, I never boast when Ireland do. I wish I had the chance ... I remember one England/Ireland game, which, as per usual, was not going the way of the boys in green. To put it mildly, the boys had gone walkabout. After one particularly painful passage of fumbles, dithers and knock-ons, a sorrowful Irish voice behind me roared: 'Ah, come on Ireland! Be serious!'

## UP AND RUNNING WITH WOGAN

*Song for Europe, Eurovision, Children in Need, Variety Club Awards*, various Saturday early-evening turkeys, all were marching on for me ... But Parkinson had left for the morning TV débâcle, and a chat-show in the Antipodes, and Bill Cotton had a hole in his late Saturday evening schedule.

It is hard to believe now, after the contumely and abuse of the latter days of *Wogan* in the nineties, but the press were all for me then: 'Give him his own chat-show with all the old Parkinson trimmings, and just watch the redoubtable Terry take off!'

They did and I did ...

Marcus Plantin, with whom I had worked happily on *Blankety Blank* came in as producer/director, and Doctor Death himself, Chris Greenwood, was chief researcher. Among his minions was Jeremy Beadle, a creative and energetic researcher. I would love to know what became of him.

We recorded at Television Centre on Friday evening, and, after Marcus had sweated blood in the editing suite all Saturday, *Wogan* went out on BBC 1 on Saturday evenings, in Parky's old slot.

It was a success from the start, with unprecedented viewing figures that often topped ten million. Even in those days of less competition from terrestrial networks, cable and satellite, it was a lot of people for a load of old talk. Marcus Plantin put a new spin on the thing: instead of the guests coming down a staircase like Ginger Rogers to meet me, they were already seated, and I went to meet them. It seemed to work, in most cases.

I remember Neil Kinnock being testy, for reasons that have since escaped me, and Sir Robin Day being curmudgeonly for the usual reasons.

I am not a believer in taped, meticulously edited talk-shows. A talk-show is a piece of cheap light entertainment. Compared to a sit-com, a drama, variety, comedy or pop music, it costs next to nothing. The whole point, it seems to me, of doing a talk-show, is for the spontaneous, unexpected moment. And, yes, even for the embarrassed pause and the trance-like stare. It is the live element that gives the talk-show its edge, its point. Otherwise it is just another sanitized production, in which no one, and certainly not the host, ever stumbles, falls or makes a prat of themselves.

However, exceptions can prove to be the rule. No one in their right mind would ever have attempted to interview the late Oliver Reed live, and Freddie Starr is another who could only be saved by the tape-editor's razor blade. The world's most frightening interviewee, Freddie came on to Saturday night *Wogan* and proceeded to reduce it to rubble. His talented interpretation of 'Penis Rising' unfortunately never made it to the final edit ...

Jerry Lee Lewis, mercurial piano-trasher, was another whose interview benefited from a bit of spit-and-polish from Marcus Plantin. Good ol' Jerry Lee had a look in his eye as I approached him that told me we were not sharing the same planet – and so the interview was to prove. I could see that there was a lot going on in Jerry Lee's head, but very little of it was seeing the light of day through his mouth. A cryptic smile, a sage nod, a word or two, and then the eyes would glaze over again as the brain took off once more for Mars.

The great thing about an edited talk-show is, of course, that you can talk to a stumer of a guest for an age, and eventually you are bound to get a few minutes that you can use. Live, you are trying to make bricks without straw. This is tough, but it is also what imparts the *frisson*. Even the editing suite could not save Chevy Chase. There was just nobody at home ... I was probably ringing the wrong bell.

Cilla Black had been in the shadows for a few years when she came on *Wogan* and awoke the nation anew to her talents with a hilarious routine about a Liverpool radio phone-in show. On the other side of the Thames, Alan Boyd spotted her and knew immediately who he wanted to front a new people-show he was planning – *Blind Date*.

Rock Hudson came on, looking a shadow of the handsome Hollywood beef-cake that he had once been. Publicists created some cock-and-bull story to excuse his appearance, but later we learned it was AIDS – and that, sadly, took him a short time later.

A picture of bouncy, bonny good health was the unsinkable Dolly Parton. She dropped in on my radio show on the Friday morning, and we came together again at Television Centre for the talk-show. She is the perfect guest: bright, glamorous, sharp as a tack – and can she talk? Sings a bit, as well. She had planned to sing a jolly knock-about number, but I persuaded her to wring the nation's withers with her song from the movie she had just made with Burt Reynolds, *The Best Little Whorehouse in Texas*.

The title of the song was 'I Will Always Love You', and it became a big British hit for Dolly. Whitney Houston did it again, a couple of years ago, but Dolly's the only girl for me. I have chatted her up on television on at least three occasions, and at the last Country Music Awards in Nashville they used great chunks of one of my interviews to illustrate their Hall of Fame tribute to Dolly. I was the face on the cutting-room floor. What was I saying about edited talk-shows?

Lovely ladies abounded on Saturday-night *Wogan* – Victoria Principal, newly-wed to her plastic surgeon, and at the height of her glamour and fame as Pam, Bobby Ewing's wife, in *Dallas*, pulled in a huge audience of 12 million seekers after high-sounding intellectual chat. I note a passing press cutting:

> *Wogan's send-up of Victoria Principal was a joy to all those who like to watch a painless execution ...*

I don't remember it being any more than gentle joshing on the goings-on at Southfork.

I remember Raquel Welch, though: a smile like a razor blade, and a personality to match. Raquel and I just did not hit it off. I mistook her for a glamour girl, when she was, according to herself, a serious artiste, something of a brain-box, who had just married for the third – or was it the fourth? – time.

This time she had married someone closer to her own cerebral level, a 'Renaissance man', as she described him, a veritable Michelangelo *de nos jours*. The less seriously I took her, the more terse she became. It did not end in tears, but let's just say she didn't hang around 'hostility' afterwards to renew our acquaintance.

Lee Marvin did, and we went out to dinner together afterwards. Forbidding of appearance – and with a reputation for biting the arse of anyone or thing that looked crossways at him – Marvin proved to be the very antithesis of the rumours. He was terrific: preserving the image of threatening gruffness, but letting the smile and good nature break through. An urbane and witty man, with a terrible smoker's cough, that, sadly, was to be his nemesis.

Mel Brooks was a joy, living up to everything I had expected of him, after his film triumphs of *The Producers* and *Blazing Saddles*. Perhaps the only American I have ever met who understood irony, he was sarcastic, iconoclastic, anarchic and anything else that ends in -ic, with the possible exception of chic.

I like to think that I stayed the course with Mel Brooks, and regard our confrontation as one of my most successful television interviews, but I am probably wrong – you are never the best judge of your own performance. Which is why I cannot bear to watch myself on television, or listen to myself on the radio. It is not false modesty – I am as immodest as the next megalomaniac.

Alan Bennett always says that he watches his television plays from behind the settee. I go further: I leave the room before I come on. My family have learned not to watch me either, which is as it should be. It is not me on the screen or on the air. It is some eejit that has temporarily taken over my body.

Just as Mel Brooks was everything I could have wished for, so his wife, the actress Anne Bancroft, was exactly the opposite, when I interviewed her, some years later, on the thrice-weekly live *Wogan*. I had been looking forward to our meeting with great anticipation, but a cold hand of fear clutched my vitals when we first met, in make-up.

Anne Bancroft was weeping – and shaking. I moved to comfort her, as she stammered through her tears: 'I don't wanna be here! It's live. I don't do live! I don't do interviews! Whaddam I doing here?'

After ten minutes which might have been better spent attending to my mascara, I felt pretty confident that I had assuaged the great actress's tears, and that it would be a different, calmer Bancroft who would present herself to me and the viewing public when she walked on the stage of the Shepherd's Bush TV Theatre. And so it was to prove.

Gone were the tears and the convulsive sobs. Anne Bancroft was calm, thank goodness. No, hang on, she was not so much calm as catatonic. As I watched, she walked slowly across the stage, counting. Counting her steps? Or maybe she was chanting a mantra. She parked herself in between me and my first guest, Ben Elton.

To his eternal credit, Ben has never held the show against me, although I do catch him giving me the odd remorseful glance every so often.

The Bancroft interview was all that was best on live television chat: hesitant, embarrassing to the point of pain, and riveting. It was my worst-ever television interview, and the one for which I will always be remembered. As her answers became more monosyllabic, my questions became longer:

'Anne, you're married to the great scriptwriter/producer Mel Brooks. A very happy marriage it's been, too, by all accounts. You, a great actress, and he a legendary producer. You both must be an enormous artistic inspiration to each other?'

'No.'

So, the long evening wore on. Merciful time has once more drawn a veil over my memory of the interview, but I remember thinking with some justification: 'What the hell are you doing here, if you don't want to talk?'

I muttered *that* several times, *sotto voce*, during the years of the thrice-weekly *Wogan* shows. Certainly, I muttered it at Christopher Lloyd, who had made his name on the television shows *Taxi*, and then as 'Doc' in the *Back to the Future* movies. This time, the questions were longer than the answers because Christopher did not speak at all. He smiled in a not unkindly way, but not a syllable escaped his lips. His co-star in *Back to the Future*, Mary Steenburgen, said, helpfully, 'He's not very good at this.'

I didn't feel that Christopher Lloyd was being bloody-minded, or deliberately uncooperative. He just could not work without a script – an affliction that seemed to cast its shadow over John Malkovich as well, and Jennifer Beals, the star of *Flashdance*. David Bowie would not speak, or at least not sensibly, and would not allow his backing group to talk, either. He will never know how close he came to a slap on live television.

## WINE-TASTINGS

The Saturday *Wogan* finished in April, and started again in the autumn. I was still doing my daily radio show, the Los Angeles Olympic Games, the Royal Variety show, and a documentary on wine, for a film company I had formed with a good friend, John Howson. Down the Gironde we sashayed, and up the

Loire. Vouvray one weekend, Château Lafite the next.

After dinner in another Château, Loudenne, we crept in through the gates of Lafite, and through the open baronial door, in the half-light, we could see a green salon, and beside, it a red one. Then, from the top of a great granite staircase, a diffident voice hailed us:

'Hello, welcome! I'm Baron Rothschild.'

He was charm incarnate, speaking in slightly hesitant, public school English: 'Would you like a cognac?'

'No, thank you, Baron. I think we'll head straight for bed; it's been a hard night and we've a long day ahead ...'

'Very well,' said the Baron Rothschild, 'let me show you to your rooms. What would you like for breakfast?'

And the good Baron, clad in a dressing-gown and shod in furry ski-boots, took a pen shaped like a banana and wrote down our orders. Next morning, sure enough, it was delivered on a silver tray by a flunkey in full fig.

The Baron showed us around the Château Lafite with its portraits of the great family Rothschild – founders of banks in all the capitals of Europe, financiers to kings and governments. On the day we visited, the French Government had lifted a punitive restriction imposed for some years on the Rothschilds and other private banks. The Baron smiled: 'It's very hard to stamp out a weed ...'


## NEAR MISSES

We flew back from France that weekend in a little private plane, and it was nearly the death of us. Storm clouds ringed London, but the pilot obviously had a pressing engagement in the vicinity of Elstree, from where we had taken off. He persisted in trying to slip by the storm unnoticed, while the little plane was thrown hither and yon about the black sky.

Flung up and down the little plane's cabin, I really did think my end had come, but eventually, by dint of gentle persuasion and a threat that even if he *did* land safely in Elstree the pilot would never leave the airport alive, the madman put it down in Biggin Hill and we waited out the storm.

I missed my dinner, but I managed to live with it.

Now that I think of it, I have had my fair share of hairy moments in little aeroplanes – mainly when flying in and out of Dublin to see rugby matches. No matter how desensitized you may be by copious ingestion of a hundred per cent proof alcohol, it can still cause a mild *frisson* when looking out of the pilot's window, to see the runway approaching at an angle of sixty degrees. My brother Brian, who works in operations for Aer Lingus at Dublin Airport, would not take a king's ransom to board a small plane.

Then there was the helicopter …

For several years, my Dublin friend Tom's brother, Mick, organized the Terry Wogan Golf Classic. Thanks mainly to Mick, with help from Jo Gurnett, we raised a lot of money for Irish charities, in the six years of the Classic. Stars of the stage, screen, labour exchange, running track, football, rugby and hurling field swarmed to help and play, from the UK and Ireland.

They were marvellous days, and a great dinner was always held afterwards, with the stars providing the cabaret for the delight of sponsors and paying guests. The evenings were like Royal Command Performances, with the cream of Irish talent thrown in.

For the first four years, we played golf courses in Dublin, and the last two were in Limerick and Waterford. Naturally, it rained in Limerick, but the evening was such a success that the Mayor left the table, drove home to his house, dragged his wife and children out of bed, and brought them back to enjoy the show.

Yet it is the Waterford trip that looms large in my memory: we flew back by helicopter, because I had an appointment to see Charles Haughey TD, Taoiseach, at his house in north Co. Dublin. A heavy mist had closed in, and any sensible pilot would have advised the train, but our man was not going to be the one to let the Prime Minister down.

Up we went, but not very high. Our pilot's plan was to follow the railway line, from Waterford to Dublin, and the railway line was only visible from a height of a hundred feet. On we went, making our peace with Our Maker, fully aware that if we bumped into a haystack, or a tall cow, we were finished.

As it was, we lost sight of the railway line, and hit a tree. I was for getting out there and then, putting the thing down in a field, and walking, but wiser counsel prevailed: 'How could we let Charlie down?' Back to Waterford we went, re-established contact with the railway line, and eventually your man, the pilot, put her down on a sixpence in the Taoiseach's backyard.

Charles Haughey, Prime Minister of Ireland, welcomed me into his home, and led me into his inner sanctum, a room that he had designed as an Irish pub bar. Long Power and Jameson mirrors, wooden chairs and tables, and a real pub bar with draught beers and stouts.

The Prime Minister went behind the bar, and pulled a couple of pints for himself and myself. This was where he entertained friends, captains of industry, prelates, ministers, ambassadors and visiting Heads of State. A man of immense style and charm, Charlie showed me round his bar-room, replete with memorabilia: photographs taken with the Pope, with Reagan, with Kennedy, with Thatcher. There were silver and crystal, carvings – and there in the middle of the display, a finely chased and honed wooden harp, bearing the proud legend: 'To Charlie – From all the boys at Long Kesh.'

In case you were up the Hindu Kush at the time, Long Kesh was where IRA prisoners were incarcerated. I only hope he put it out of sight when he was entertaining Unionist politicians, the British Ambassador or Margaret Thatcher, but, somehow, I doubt it. Charlie Haughey was a reckless man, a rascal, and the Irish loved him for it ... For a while, anyway. But isn't that the way? How does the song go? 'Next day on your dressing room they hang a star ... The day after that, no one knows who you are ...'

But I digress from *Wogan* ...


## A HELL OF A RISK

Bill Cotton took me to lunch. His idea was a three-nights-a-week talk-show, starting, say, at about 10 to 10.30 p.m., and repeated as soon as it was finished, just to catch the night-owls. It was a revolutionary idea – at least for British television. He had suggested it before, almost ten years earlier, with Michael Parkinson, but, heaven knows why, the BBC Governors had thrown the idea out.

This time, Bill had got the green light. A thrice-weekly show would mean my giving up the daily radio show, and, of course, the Saturday night chat-show. It was a big decision. I could sit tight on the success of both these shows, and go on forever, or as long as anybody goes in this strange game. I did not have to take the risk, I was sitting pretty on top of the ratings and the popularity polls.

Now, as I look back, it *was* a hell of a risk, but I have never played safe, taken the soft option, in my career. Careful in everything else, cautious, conservative – but in my career, if not exactly careless, certainly reckless. Remember, I walked away from my permanent, pensionable bank; left a career in Ireland for a six-week contract in Britain; elbowed *Come Dancing* and Beauty Contests; said goodbye to *Blankety Blank*, the most popular quiz on TV; and now? Now, I was being asked to fold the most successful programme on British radio, and take on a live television talk-show, three times a week.

Of course I said 'yes'. It's a risk-taking business; only a fool plays it safe, settles for predictable mediocrity. Would I still be doing the Saturday night talk-show if I had said 'No' ? Would I still be doing the *Wake up to Wogan* radio? I doubt it.

As Eamonn Andrews said, a long time ago, what gets you the push is not the public, but the people at the top. The great BBC maxim is: 'If it ain't broke – break it …' I am only still doing the radio show because I took a seven-and-a-half-year break from it, to do *Wogan*.

I told Derek Mills the bad news and he passed it on to Geoff Owen. The TWITS were distraught. Jo Gurnett and I entertained their leaders to a slap-up breakfast, and they were sweetness itself. But they were not happy. They resented me going. Some never forgave me, and did not return to the fold when I did, in 1993. It took a good year before some grudgingly returned.

Indeed, Frances Line, the Controller of Radio 2, who, under David Hatch's promptings, had brought me back to the early-morning radio show, had serious doubts about the wisdom of her action. Not unkindly, I pointed out that, while she was fully aware that I was back in action on the Radio 2 breakfast show, and I knew about it, we were probably in the minority. The BBC, as usual, was expecting the public to be aware by a process of osmosis.

Frances was persuaded to sanction a series of ads in the newspapers. They were quirky, along the lines of 'Wogan's other listener spotted by Elvis –' but they did the trick. My listening figures rose spectacularly, and they have been going upwards ever since, taking the network's audience with them. As I write, my peak-time audience has just reached 7 million, the largest radio audience, not only in Britain, but in Europe – and Radio 2 now commands Britain's biggest audience nationally.

## FULL CIRCLE

Meanwhile, back at the Concrete Doughnut (that was then – it is more like the Deserted Doughnut, these days), Michael Grade, newly repatriated from Hollywood, was gung-ho. He was going to nail his former employers, commercial television, in the crossfire of a new soap – *EastEnders* – and *Wogan*.

He elbowed Bill Cotton's idea of the late-night chat, and insisted instead that the thrice-weekly *Wogan* go out at seven o'clock every Monday, Wednesday and Friday evening, to catch the early-evening trade and set the tone for the rest of the evening on BBC 1. He was right: *Wogan* averaged 8 million viewers for the next seven and a half years, before being sacrificed on the altar of Blessed Julia Smith, who, having – successfully – got *EastEnders* underway, was about to work the oracle again with *Eldorado*. Oops!

Michael Grade did not last very long at the BBC, bridling at the idea that he had to defer to John Birt, who had been junior to him at London Weekend, and leaving in a marked manner for Channel 4. It blew all Bill Cotton's best-laid schemes out of the water, leading to the appointment of Jonathan Powell as Controller BBC 1 and Alan Yentob as Controller BBC 2 – positions for which Bill had never intended them.

All of this happened in 1985, fifteen years ago, but it feels more like five. But then I can't get away from the idea that it was only a few years ago that I arrived over here, fresh-faced, from Ireland.

There is lots more to tell, of the last fifteen years, but this labour of love is already taking on the appearance of a tome. Another fifteen years' worth of reminiscence, and it will be *War and Peace*. This is a good place to let it lie. Fifteen years on, I am in exactly the same groove as I was in 1985: presenting the most popular radio show, and some of the most popular on television – *Auntie's Bloomers* (not so much of a programme, more of a pension), *Points of View*, *Children in Need*, *The Eurovision Song Contest*.

It feels like I have come full circle. Which is not to say that I would be averse to throwing it all up in the air again, and chancing my arm, if something came along …

In the meantime, I will just go on, if it is all the same to you, enjoying every moment, and counting my blessings. That'll do …

# INDEX